Becoming a Team Coach

Jonathan Passmore • Paul J. Barbour •
Lucy Widdowson • Katerina Kanelidou

Becoming a Team Coach

The Essential ICF Guide

 Springer

Jonathan Passmore (iD)
Henley Business School
University of Reading
Henley-on-Thames, Oxfordshire, UK

EZRA
London, UK

Lucy Widdowson
Performance Edge Partners Ltd
Horsham, UK

Paul J. Barbour
Performance Edge Partners Ltd
Horsham, UK

Katerina Kanelidou
Team Coaching Global Alliance
Kifisia, Greece

ISBN 978-3-031-63545-8   ISBN 978-3-031-63546-5   (eBook)
https://doi.org/10.1007/978-3-031-63546-5

This Springer imprint is published by the registered company Springer Nature Switzerland AG
The registered company address is: Gewerbestrasse 11, 6330 Cham, Switzerland

If disposing of this product, please recycle the paper.

Foreword

Welcome to this new book *"Becoming a Team Coach: The Essential ICF Guide,"* by Jonathan Passmore, Paul Barbour, Lucy Widdowson, and Katerina Kanelidou, an important new addition to the growing literature on the expanding field of team coaching. They have kindly asked me to write a foreword to set this book in the wider history and context of team coaching and how it is unfolding, including the many challenges and developments that lie ahead.

Team Coaching is a discipline, practice, and profession in its own right. Many in the coaching profession see it as a more recent and the fastest growing branch of coaching. However, team coaching has many roots (Hawkins 2021, chapter 4). It is a core facet of organizational development as it developed through the 1940s and 1950s by pioneers such as Kurt Lewin and the National Training Laboratories in North America and by the Tavistock in the UK. This stream came into a greater flowering in the 1960s and 1970s with the publication of the Addison Wesley series of books and the teaching of these authors such as Schein (1985, 1988) on process consultation and Dyer (1977) on team building as well as the development of master's trainings in organizational development.

In parallel came the development of understanding the centrality of learning in organizations and communities, from Bateson (1972), Argyris and Schon (1978), Senge (1990), Pedler, Boydell and Burgoyne (1991) and Hawkins (1986, 1991, 1994, 2019).

In the late 1990s and early 2000s came greater research on effective teams (Katzenbach & Smith, 1992; Hackman, 2002, 2011; Wageman et al., 2005; Michael West, 1996, 2012; Clutterbuck, 2007/2022; Hawkins, 2011/2021). This created a developmental leap in the field, as previously the focus had been on improving the interpersonal relationships between the team members. Now it became clear that what was much more important was the team having a clear purpose, that could only be achieved through collaboration and which everyone understood and were aligned behind. "It is the purpose that creates the team and not the team members who create the purpose." Hawkins (2021).

But a purpose without a plan is just a pipe-dream, so it became clear that the purpose needed to be translated into team priority objectives, clear roles and processes, and other elements that made up the team charter. Only then could we look at how the team needed to relate, in order to achieve what was collectively necessary to fulfill its purpose.

This in turn can still leave the team inward-focused, and only recently has there been the realization that the team does not exist as an end in itself, or to be a well-tuned high performing system, but to co-create beneficial value with and for all its stakeholders. In our formulation of "Systemic Team Coaching" we stress how the work needs to start "future-back and outside-in" (Hawkins, 2021, 2022; Leary-Joyce & Lines, 2024). To focus, not on what the team members want from the team, but on what the stakeholders and the future, require from the collective team. Then at the heart of these different disciplines is the learning team—a team that are continuously growing their collective capacity to co-create greater beneficial value. A discipline that draws on the many years of research into Organizational Learning.

These areas of research suggest a number of key models that are outlined in section three of this book, including Hackman and Wageman "Six Conditions" (Chap. 19), my own model of the "Five Disciplines of High Value Creating Teams," (Chap. 17) and Clutterbuck's PERILL model (Chap. 18). The final model they outline on coaching the "Team of Teams" has far less research, but currently Dr Catherine Carr and myself supported by global research partners are finalizing our research on this area (Hawkins and Carr, forthcoming 2025).

So to become a systemic team coach requires a variety of competencies, capabilities, and capacities. We need to unlearn the modern, atomistic, mechanistic thinking, and perceiving dominated by the left-hemisphere neo-cortex, that has dominated western education, and learn to experience the world through whole brain and whole body systemic awareness. Alongside systemic awareness, we need to develop the capability of systemic doing and the capacity of systemic being, both of which take many years of learning from our failures, reflection, and supervision.

The coaching profession only recently has developed basic competencies for team coaches, with parallel competencies being developed by a number of the main coaching bodies. This book does a great service by unpacking the competencies of one of these bodies, the ICF, and showing trainees a step-by-step approach to develop these. This is an important beginning, but much remains to be done, by integrating the different competencies of coaching bodies around the world, as a prerequisite to working with the other "roots" of team coaching, such as: Organizational Development, Organizational Learning, Systemic thinking and awareness, Team research, etc. to develop competencies that bring together all these important approaches. Then the even more difficult work begins of developing not just competencies, but also the capacities and capabilities and ways of assessing them. Competencies tend to measure learnt skills, whereas capabilities look at the ability to apply the right skill, at the right time in the right way. Capacity moves beyond the realm of skill and involves vertical rather than horizontal development, wisdom learnt through experience and maturation, rather than knowledge and skill learnt from training.

But it is important that we remember that beyond developing competencies, in order to become accredited, in order to do work as a team coach, lies being in service of the purpose of our work. So what is that purpose? After nearly 50 years of doing this work, and in the light of the polycrisis of our times, in my heart I believe the purpose of all our team coaching work is to be in service, of the collaboration that is needed between all eight billion humans that live on this earth, in order to heal the split between us and the "more-than-human" world. We are not there to serve team members, or even team performance, but to partner with the team, in service of what is needed.

Renewal Associates, Rush Hill   Peter Hawkins,
Bath, UK

Bibliography

Argyris, C., & Schön, D. (1978). *Organizational learning. A theory of action perspective.* Addison Wesley.

Bateson, G. (1972). *Steps to an ecology of mind.* Ballantine Books.

Clutterbuck, D. (2007). *Coaching the team at work.* Nicholas Brealey.

Dyer, W. G. (1977). *Team building: Issues and alternatives.* Addison-Wesley.

Hackman, J. R. (2002). *Leading teams: Setting the stage for great performances.* Harvard Business School Press.

Hackman, J. R. (2011a). *Collaborative intelligence: Using teams to solve hard problems.* Berrett-Koehler.

Hawkins, P. (1986). *Living the learning*, PhD thesis, University of Bath Management School.

Hawkins, P. (1994). The changing view of learning. In J. Burgoyne (Ed.), *Towards the learning company.* McGraw-Hill.

Hawkins, P. (2011, 2014a, 2017, 2021). *Leadership team coaching: Developing collective transformational leadership.* Kogan Page

Hawkins, P. (Ed.). (2014b, 2018, 2022). *Leadership team coaching in practice: Developing high-performing teams.* Kogan Page.

Hawkins, P. (2019). Systemic organizational learning and the coevolution of organizational culture. In A. R. Örtenblad (Ed.), *The handbook on the learning organization* (Chap. 10). Oxford University Press.

Hawkins, P., & Carr, C. (2025). *Coaching the team of teams.* Kogan Page.

Katzenbach, J., & Smith, D. (1993, 1999). *The wisdom of teams: Creating the high-performance organization.* Harvard Business School Press.

Leary-Joyce, J., & Lines, H. (2017, second edition 2024). *Systemic team coaching.* Academy of Executive Coaching

Pedler, M., Burgoyne, J. G., & Boydell, T. (1991). *The learning company: A strategy for sustainable development.* McGraw Hill.

Senge, P. (1990). *The fifth discipline: The art and practice of the learning organization.* Doubleday.

Schein, E. H. (1969). *Process consultation: Its role in organizational development.* Wesley.

Schein, E. H. (1985). *Organizational culture and leadership.* Jossey-Bass.

Schlein, E. H. (1988). *Process consultation: Its role in organisational development* (2nd ed.). Wesley.

Wageman, R., Nunes, D., Burruss, J., & Hackman, R. (2008). *Senior leadership teams.* Harvard Business School Press.

Contents

About the Authors

Jonathan Passmore is a professor of coaching and behavioral change at Henley Business School and a senior leader in the digital coaching industry. He is a chartered psychologist, holds five degrees and two coaching accreditations with the ICF and EMCC. He has published widely with over 40 books and 250 scientific papers and book chapters. His work includes *The Coaches' Handbook* (Routledge, 2021), *Third Wave Cognitive Behavioural Coaching* (Pavilion, 2022) and the sister book to this title *"Becoming a Coach: The Essential ICF Guide"* (2nd ed.) (Springer 2024), three volumes of *Coaching Tools* (Libri, 2021, 2022, 2023) and *The Digital & AI Coaches Handbook* (Routledge, 2024). He was the Inaugural Chair of the British Psychological Society Division of Coaching Psychology. He has worked for PricewaterHouseCoopers, IBM, OPM, CoachHub, and the Adecco Group during a 40-year career. Jonathan continues to coach and supervise coaches and leaders through his private practice.

Paul J. Barbour is an accredited executive coach (PCC), team coach (ACTC), and Certified Business Psychologist (CBP) and was one of the first team coaches globally to achieve the ICF ACTC team coaching credential. Paul's main areas of research interest include human collaboration, conflict resolution, and team coaching. He is a co-author of Building Top-Performing Teams (Kogan Page, 2021). Paul has also published peer-reviewed papers on team coaching and conflict resolution and is a popular speaker in his areas of interest.

An award-winning student on both his Master's degrees, Paul was also awarded "Best Newcomer" to Personal Construct Psychology at the 14th Biennial European Personal Construct Association Conference (2018). Paul's interest in the psychology of teams began during a successful 20-year career as a senior leader at Kerry Group PLC. Paul is a lead tutor on the Henley Professional Certificate in Team and Systemic Coaching and is also on the UK ICF Team Coaching Working Party.

Lucy Widdowson is a Master Certified Coach (MCC), team coach (ACTC), coach supervisor, lead tutor on team coaching at Henley Business School and Director of Performance Edge, a coaching and team coaching consultancy. Her passion is to help individuals, teams, and organizations collaborate better to achieve sustainable change. Lucy's corporate background was as an HR Director in retail and airlines where she led award-winning teams. She is a Fellow of the CIPD, has an MSc in Coaching and Behavioral Change and was one of the first team coaches globally to achieve the new ICF ACTC team coaching credential. In 2023, she was also a finalist for the ICF Global Circle of Distinction Award for her contribution to team coaching.

On behalf of ICF Global Lucy co-led in-depth research into team coaching competencies which was summarized in an academic journal article published in 2020. She also represented the UK ICF as a subject matter expert in developing the Global ICF team coach competencies and has contributed to the development of the team coaching speciality designation. Along with this work, Lucy has co-authored a book on team coaching with Paul J Barbour "Building Top Performing Teams: A practical guide to team coaching to improve collaboration and drive organizational success" (Kogan Page 2021).

Katerina Kanelidou is a Master Certified Coach (MCC), certified trainer, educator, and mentor, passionate about coaching, leadership, and citizenship. Her mission is to empower humanity one team at a time. She was one of the Subject-Matter Experts who worked on the development of the ICF Team Coaching Competencies and served as co-leader of the ICF's Team & Group Coaching Community of Practice. She currently runs her own coaching business, as well as being the co-founder and trainer of Team Coaching Global Alliance. Furthermore, she is often a guest speaker at international conferences and events on coaching, her surveys on coaching are published on the research portal of the ICF and she has authored articles for several professional publications (online and printed). Additionally, she holds the Advanced Certification in Team Coaching by the ICF and a master's degree in Dramatherapy and Psychodrama from the University of Barcelona.

Part I

Chapter 1
What Is a Team

Introduction

Over the past 150 years, the nature of work has changed, moving from home to a working space—known as "the office" or "the factory" and the nature of production has changed moving from being primarily an individual pursuit to being a collaborative one. Teams are now the most common way of organizing production. In this chapter, we will explore briefly the nature of this transition and the development of the idea of a "team." We summarize how practitioners, writers, and professional bodies tried to conceptualize the idea of the team as a starting point to explore team coaching as a developing practice.

The Changing Nature of Work

Until the start of industrialization most work was undertaken in the family—from the worker on the land or caring for livestock, to the production of clothing and goods. These processes were usually undertaken in or adjacent to the home in the blacksmith's foundry next to the cottage, or collecting and sorting eggs from hen house in the "back-yard."

Industrialization brought a change in these processes: a movement of production from the home to the factory and the office, and a movement from production being contained largely in the extended family group to working with individuals who were biologically unrelated, producing goods in exchange for a daily or hourly wage. This change also brought the introduction of "machines," firstly to supplement humans, and latterly to replace humans in these production processes. Alongside these "technological" innovations also came a greater specialization, as individuals changed from a crafts person, making the whole object, towards a

© The Author(s), under exclusive license to Springer Nature
Switzerland AG 2024
J. Passmore et al., *Becoming a Team Coach*,
https://doi.org/10.1007/978-3-031-63546-5_1

collective process, where individuals collaborated as a group, sharing a common purpose in producing the object or item, with each individual each focusing on one part of the production task. The "team" was born.

In the twenty-first century workplace, teamwork is now at the heart of work. Few individuals have the privilege, opportunity, or skill to complete tasks wholly by themselves. Instead groups of workers are engaged in physical manufacturing or knowledge creation, working as a team to produce products or create knowledge. Each bringing their unique contribution to the process, each coordinating their efforts with other team members, and each being supervised by a "team leader."

But the division of labor brings opportunities, for example of specialization in an increasingly complex production environment, it also brings the challenge of coordination and collaboration. It is here that teams either excel or flounder.

What Is a Team?

Before considering how we define team coaching, it is important to consider what constitutes a team and how a team compares to a group.

There are a number of definitions of a team including: "a small number of people with complementary skills who are committed to a common purpose, performance goals, and approach for which they hold themselves mutually accountable" (Katzenbach & Smith, 1993, p. 45).

> A team can be defined as (a) two or more individuals who (b) socially interact (face-to-face or, increasingly, virtually); (c) possess one or more common goals; (d) are brought together to perform organisationally relevant tasks; (e) exhibit interdependencies with respect to workflow, goals and outcomes; (f) have different roles and responsibilities; and (g) are together embedded in an encompassing organizational system, with boundaries and linkages to the broader system context and task environment (Kozlowski & Ilgen, 2006, p. 79).

How Does a Team Compare to a Group?

What is a team versus a group? Many groups incorrectly refer to themselves as a team. Forsyth (2014) suggested that while some definitions of a group highlight the need for a shared purpose or goal, this is not normally the case. The same author has noted that most agree that a group is two or more individuals who are connected by and within social relationships (Forsyth, 2014, p. 4). Thornton (2016) has highlighted that learning groups are focused on the learning needs of the group members and has stated that the "learning group" is a group brought together for the purpose of learning (Thornton, 2016, p. 12)

What Is a High Performing Team?

The debate of teams has moved from simply understanding the nature of a team to considering how teams can be designed, crafted and coordinated towards being a high performing team. This is a team which consistently produces high-quality outcomes.

Writers like Katzenbach and Smith (1993) have suggested high performance is not the natural state of a team, but needs careful curation and a journey of development. This process may start with an informal group of individuals coming together in the form of a working or task group. The group is charged with the delivery of a short-term outcome. As a result, team members may feel focusing on team processes is less relevant than "doing the job."

A second type of team are pseudo teams. These may have the name of a team but lack a shared purpose or goal. The focus instead is on the relationship not the outcome. There is much joy but little productivity in such groups and in that sense these are the lowest on the performance team curve.

The third type are potential teams. These have a shared purpose but processes such as accountability have yet to be baked in and thus the team still has potential for productivity improvement.

The fourth are real teams, here the ingredients are present: group size, clarity of purpose, mechanisms of accountability, but these elements have yet to be fully coordinated to achieve the outcomes desired.

The final type of team according to Katzenbach and Smith are high performance teams. These are teams where all of the ingredients are present; and there is a strong commitment to the team and its success over personal achievement.

The five types of groups, proposed by Katzenbach and Smith are summarized in Table 1.1.

Why Does Creating a High Performing Team Matter?

If teams are the most common, and one might say "normal" organizational structure for delivering value in modern organizations, organizations need to consider not just individual development, but also team development.

Organizational leaders need to have processes in place to facilitate both their team and individual development, enabling teams to create a shared and maintain a shared purpose, which is aligned with the wider organizational purpose. They need to enable teams throughout their organization to identify individual team member strengths, arrange activities which recognize these strengths to optimize the production process. They need to be able to communicate and coordinate throughout these processes, and fundamentally, in a dynamic environment to be agile in flexing and adapting both individual tasks, processes and ways of interacting to maintain both effective team relationships and efficient team outcomes.

Table 1.1 Team performance curve

Working group	The members of this group interact primarily to share information, best practices, or perspectives, and to make decisions to help each individual perform within his or her area of responsibility. There really is no reason for either a team approach or common/mutual accountability. To members of this group, team building activities are pointless and take time that could be spent "doing real work."
Pseudo team	This group is trying to be a team. There often is no common shared goal, or the goal is not seen as a valuable contribution for the organization. Comments from team members may include, "We love this team stuff but there's not time to get the work done." Pseudo teams are the weakest of all groups in terms of performance impact. They almost always contribute less than working groups because their interactions detract from each member's individual performance without delivering any joint benefits. For a pseudo team to become a potential team, the group must define goals so it has something concrete to do as a team that is a valuable contribution to the company.
Potential team	Potential teams may share a common, significant performance goal and may be trying to address teaming obstacles. Typically the potential team requires more clarity about purpose, goals, or work products, and more discipline in hammering out a common working approach. It often has not yet established collective accountability. Or perhaps team members have not been relieved of other responsibilities, forcing them to prioritize their time and effort.
Real team	This is a small number of people with complementary skills who are equally committed to a common purpose, goals, and working approach for which they hold themselves mutually accountable. The possible performance impact for the real team is significantly higher than the working group in that the contribution of the whole is greater than the possible sum contribution of individuals on the team.
High performance team	This is a group that meets all the conditions of real teams and has members who are deeply committed to one another's personal growth and success. That commitment usually transcends the team. The high performance team significantly outperforms all other like teams and outperforms all reasonable expectations given its membership.

(Adapted from Katzenbach & Smith, 1993)

Katzenbach and Smith (1993) expressed these ideas in a three-sided model: skills, accountability, and commitment (Fig. 1.1).

We might consider such teams to be high performers, but constantly achieving these outcomes requires constant development, feedback, and support. In our view, this is how coaching can play a part, helping teams move along the development curve from pseudo team to high performing team by resolving key questions and constantly correcting their course as they move forward.

Fig. 1.1 High performing
team (adapted from
Katzenbach & Smith,
1993)

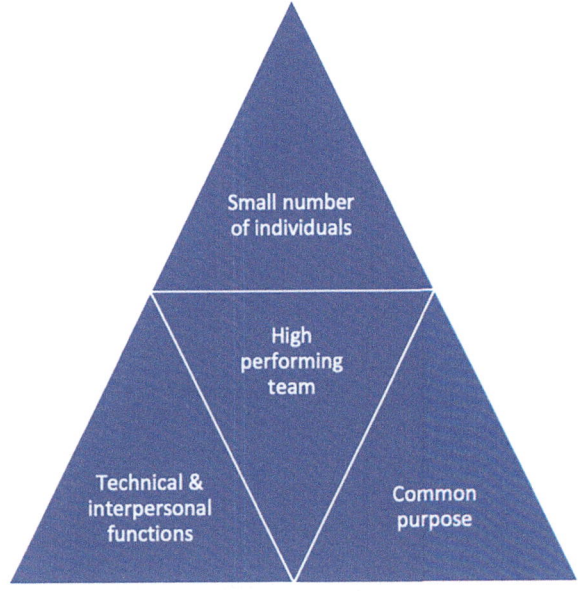

Conclusion

In this chapter, we have looked at the development of team working as a result of the
changing nature of work. We have sought to define a team and explored what makes
for a high performance team and why high performance is a desirable aspiration in
modern organizations. In the next section, we will explore what we mean by team
coaching.

Chapter 2
What Is Team Coaching?

Introduction

Team coaching has developed significantly over the past decade, and is now one of the most rapidly growing forms of coaching. Like coaching during the late 1990s and early 2000s, the theory and research in team coaching is lagging behind the practice. In coaching this led some to label the new sector of coaching as the "Wild West," where there were few agreed rules of engagement and coaches did what they wanted, how they wanted, with little or no accountability (Sherman & Freas, 2004) and with little reference to research or evidence (Grant et al., 2010b). At this time Sherman and Freas estimated the value of the coaching industry to be $1bn. Today the value of the industry is in excess of $10bn worldwide, and the frontier has moved to "team coaching." In this chapter, we aim to review definitions of coaching, explore the definitions of team coaching, how team coaching compares with other group interventions and contribute to the establishment of standards or practice for the frontier of team coaching.

Definitions

One might question in a book about practice why theory and definitions matter. One might argue "coaching" is what we do. But definitions matter for three reasons (Passmore & Lai, 2019). Firstly, definitions are essential for practice. By creating a shared and commonly understood definition of an intervention, coaches and their clients can better understand what they are doing together. A lack of a shared understanding is the equivalent of a shop which purports to sell "yard brooms," but is in fact selling "toothbrushes." Cleaning the backyard may be a very different experience with a toothbrush than with a yard broom. While it is possible to use a

© The Author(s), under exclusive license to Springer Nature
Switzerland AG 2024
J. Passmore et al., *Becoming a Team Coach*,
https://doi.org/10.1007/978-3-031-63546-5_2

toothbrush for that task, I would be very disappointed in the shop which offered it for sale! The importance of agreeing on a shared perspective is advocated by many professional bodies, including the ICF, who encourage coaches to include an exploration of the nature of coaching during the contracting phase with their clients (Passmore & Sinclair, 2024).

A second reason for definitions relates to research. Researchers need to clearly delineate the domain before they can test the phenomena. As Jones and her colleagues note "The absence of a clearly defined construct is hindering the development of a rigorous theory of Team Coaching" (Jones et al., 2019, p. 62). Shared definitions matter for the same reasons in research as they do in practice. A yard broom may be highly effective as a tool to sweep the yard of leaves. If we call a "toothbrush" a "yard brush," our time on a task is likely to rise significantly, and we would rightly question if "yard brushes" are worth the investment for clearing leaves.

Thirdly, a consistent definition is vital for coaching education and qualification; with a scientific-based framework to support its pedagogy. The work undertaken by practitioners with professional bodies has helped establish competency frameworks for team coaching. This is the first step, but this, and other books, can help delineate the domain and the practices within them which can contribute to effective outcomes, and contribute to coach education programs in team coaching.

What Is Coaching

The period 1985–2010 was a period of significant debate about what is, and is not, coaching. However as this period developed, while precise terminology continues to vary, a broad consensus has been reached about the nature of coaching.

As a starting point for considering the nature of team coaching, we thought it was important to set out what we mean by "coaching." In the partner book to this title, "Becoming a Coach: The Essential ICF Guide" (Passmore & Sinclair, 2021) we set out a number of different definitions. We have included three key definitions in Table 2.1.

What's clear is there were differences in terminology and language. These differences often reflect the background of the writer, as well as the audiences they were writing for. As an example, John Whitmore, a pioneer of coaching, focused on the visionary nature of coaching, inspiring and encouraging others to explore the potential of coaching. Passmore and Fillery Travis's definition tries to avoid any ambiguity through a process definition, describing those involved, what they do, and the outcomes they seek to attain, and thus provide a definition suitable for research purposes.

Even now coaching is sometimes confused with other one-to-one or organization interventions such as mentoring, counseling, psychotherapy, performance management, and training. What is clear is that at its heart, coaching is a facilitative process, led by the client, with a future focus.

Table 2.1: Definitions of coaching

Practical definition
"Coaching is unlocking a person's potential to maximize their own performance. It is helping them to learn rather than teaching them" (Whitmore, 2009, p. 10)

Academic definition
"A Socratic based future-focused dialogue between a facilitator (coach) and a participant (coachee/client), where the facilitator uses open questions, active listening, summaries and reflections, which are aimed at stimulating the self-awareness and personal responsibility of the participant" (Passmore & Fillery-Travis, 2011, p. 74)

Professional Body definition
"ICF defines coaching as partnering with clients in a thought-provoking and creative process that inspires them to maximize their personal and professional potential. The process of coaching often unlocks previously untapped sources of imagination, productivity and leadership" (ICF, 2023a)

The history of coaching shows that it has multiple roots, most notably its use in debating societies in the 1900–1920s (Huston, 1924), sports in the 1920–30s (Griffiths, 1926) into workplace learning (Gordy, 1937). While its growth was slow during the postwar period, 1950–1980, the 1980s brought renewed interest in personal development and coaching is now commonplace practice in most organizations, widely used for supporting people's performance and wellbeing.

What Is Team Coaching

When thinking about team coaching we might just assume the difference is the size of the group. Instead of coaching one to one, the coach is working one to many. This would be wrong. While coaching is a key element of team coaching, there are some significant differences which are important to consider as they have implications for the team, the coach, and the process.

It might be helpful to start by recognizing that team coaching is a team-based learning and development intervention that considers the team to be a system and is applied collectively to the team as a whole. The focus of team coaching is on team performance and the achievement of a common or shared team goal. Team learning takes place via specific team coaching activities for self and team reflection, which are facilitated by the team coach(es) through the application of coaching techniques such as open questioning which raises awareness, builds trusting relationships, and improves communication, feedback and exercises which can encourage exploration of assumptions, values and interpersonal working styles.

While Sherman and Freas (2004) highlighted the unregulated nature of coaching, as well as its potential, they also drew attention to team coaching, stating, "worthy as it is to help one person or team, the most valuable executive coaching comes from developing an organization's entire senior executive rank."

Others have shared that view and over this period, a range of definitions have been discussed, as practitioners have tried to capture the essence of their practice.

Thought leaders in the field, Richard Hackman and Ruth Wageman, defined the team coaching process as "direct interaction with a team intended to help members make coordinated and task-appropriate use of their collective resources in accomplishing the team's work" (Hackman & Wageman, 2005b, p. 269). David Clutterbuck described the process as "helping the team improve performance and the processes by which performance is achieved, through reflection and dialogue" (Clutterbuck, 2007, p. 77). While Peter Hawkins defines team coaching as a systemic process by which "a team coach works with the whole team, both when they are together and when they are apart, in order to help them improve both their collective performance and how they work together, and also how they develop their collective leadership to more effectively engage with all their stakeholder groups to jointly transform the wider business" (Hawkins, 2014, p. 80).

As we did in Table 2.1 for coaching, we have set out various definitions of team coaching in Table 2.2. These can help us to contrast a practitioner perspective with academic definitions and definitions offered by the main professional bodies.

What we can conclude from this developing debate is that team coaching is a team-based learning and development intervention. As with one to one coaching within an organization, team coaching is best seen as systemic, and thus applied collectively to the team. Its focus, like one to one coaching, is on performance, but this time performance of the team, and the achievement of the team's common or shared team goal.

As with coaching, the debate as to what is and is not team coaching is not finished. This does not reflect the immaturity of team coaching, but reflects the fact that incremental and sometimes revolutionary change continues to happen because coaching and team coaching are live disciplines, where the modes of delivery, for example the emergence of digital coaching (see Passmore & Evans-Krimme, 2021) continue to evolve and develop.

How Does Team Coaching Differ from Other Interventions?

As with one to one coaching there is often discussion or confusion between team coaching and other forms of development and group coaching. In an effort to try and minimize this confusion and discuss the boundaries between these, we have briefly compared team coaching with other popular team interventions.

Team Training

While team coaching is primarily based on facilitation with no predetermined agenda or syllabus, training typically involves a more directive approach and usually contains specific learning outcomes which were agreed in advance. We believe both interventions have value. Team training can help teams to master new

Table 2.2 Definitions of Team Coaching

Author/s	Type	Definition
Hackman & Wageman (2005)	Academic	A direct interaction with a team intended to help members make coordinated and task appropriate use of their collective resources in accomplishing the team's work.
Thornton (2010)	Practitioner	The coaching of a team towards the achievement of collective goals, as a vehicle for delivering additional value through the creation of high performing teams.
Clutterbuck (2007)	Practitioner	A learning intervention designed to increase collective capability and performance of the group or team through application of the coaching principles of assisted reflection, analysis and motivation for change.
Hawkins (2011)	Practitioner	A process, by which a team coach works with a whole team… in order to help them improve the collective performance, and how they work together, and also how they develop their collective leadership to more effectively engage with all of their key stakeholder groups to jointly transform the wider business.
Jones, Napiersky, & Lyubovnikova (2019)	Academic	A process which involves a common goal, team performance, team learning and reflection, team coaching activities, focus on the team as a system, advanced coaching skills, coaching techniques, and the long term.
EMCC (2020)	Professional body	Team coaching focuses on helping the team collectively achieve the team's work in terms of both task work and team work through sustained professional dialogue that raises the individual and collective level of reflection and self-awareness, and challenges the team's thinking and behaviors as they develop their own sustainable solutions and practices.
ICF (2023a)	Professional body	Team Coaching is partnering in a co-creative and reflective process with a team on its dynamics and relationships in a way that inspires them to maximize their abilities and potential in order to reach their common purpose and shared goals.

knowledge or skills, while team coaching is focused on the team's alignment and development and delivery of a shared goal.

Hawkins (2011) has differentiated group coaching, with its similarity to action-learning sets, as: the coaching of individuals within a group context compared with team coaching, where: the primary client is the whole team, rather than the individual team members (p. 71). The key difference from team coaching is "the coaching of individuals within a group context," therefore individuals will have their own objectives rather than be working on the collective objectives of a team.

Team Building

Team building tends to focus on improving interpersonal relationships, productivity, and improved alignment with an organization's goals, and typically consists of short, often one day, interventions (Kriek & Venter, 2009). In contrast, team coaching is considered to typically take place over a series of sessions (Jones et al., 2019). The key difference from team coaching is the one-off nature of an intervention, compared to a series of interventions when team coaching.

Team Facilitation

While a coach may at times use facilitation skills, facilitation can be considered as a way of helping a team manage their interrelationships, in our view team coaching is broader than this. Relationships are only part of this process, and the focus on team coaching is about empowering the team to take ownership of their own processes, while also creating and managing the delivery of the shared vision.

Hawkins (2011) proposes a continuum of team development (Table 2.3) ranging from team facilitation through to transformational leadership team coaching. For Hawkins, the key difference between team facilitation and team coaching is the ownership of the change. While the facilitator supports the team as they engage in dialogue, the team coach aims to enable the team to become self-sufficient.

Group Coaching

This is often where the greatest confusion exists. While teams are a group, they differ from a group in that they are a special form of a group, one which shares a common purpose and works together to achieve this. A group can be more than one person waiting at a bus stop. The people share a common purpose, but they are not working together to achieve an outcome. In the same way "new managers" may be a group, but the fact they come from disparate parts of the organization means that

Table 2.3 Team development continuum

Team facilitation	Team performance coaching	Leadership team coaching	Transformational leadership team coaching
The focus is on helping the team manage their team processes	The focus is on both team processes and performance	The focus is on how the team focus their collective leadership	The focus is on working with the team to help them transform the business

(Adapted from Hawkins, 2011)

they are likely to have different goals: one may be focused on paying creditors, another on achieving sales and a third on employee experience.

In our view, group coaching can be delivered by any experienced coach. What makes team coaching more complex and specialized is the interrelationships between the team members making for a dynamic process.

Thornton (2010) suggests that group coaching consists of two broad areas: team coaching and coaching learning groups, which have come together for the shared purpose of learning. While this definition acknowledges that teams are a special type of group, the definition is less helpful and has resulted in many writers, particularly practitioners, in conflating these two, separate interventions.

For this reason we prefer to restrict group coaching to a distinct learning focused intervention delivered around a shared set of learning objectives supported by a facilitative style. In many ways group coaching is similar to action-learning sets, developed by Revans (1971), and often includes the provision of content, followed by a non-directive facilitated discussion to develop personal insights and application.

We have summarized the common features of action-learning sets in Table 2.4.

One potential difference in how some are using group coaching is that group coaching often contains a period of content sharing. This may take place before the session through an invitation to engage with an article, book, or video, or during the session, with the facilitator providing content, which becomes the focus for the group process.

As with team coaching, group coaching is growing in popularity, but is not the focus for this book, readers instead might turn to other texts such as Christian Thornton's excellent book on group coaching (2010), which although now more than a decade old, is one of the few texts which specifically discusses group coaching.

Table 2.4 Common features of action learning/group coaching

Real-world problems	Participants are invited to explore real-world problems
Learning by doing	Participants learn through the process of taking action and reflecting on the results
Small groups	Groups are usually composed of 4–8 members to ensure active participation by all members
Diversity	Groups may come with diverse backgrounds and perspectives
Questions and reflection	The facilitator asks open questions and encourages reflection on actions and outcomes
Shared responsibility	All members share responsibility for contributing to the problem-solving process through asking open questions
Facilitator (coach)	A facilitator guides the group, not by providing solutions, but by asking open questions, and ensuring the group remains focused on learning
Commitment to action	Groups commit to taking action
Feedback	Feedback is a key part of the process
Reflection on the learning process	Participants regularly reflect not only on the problem-solving process but also on their learning process to develop personal insights.

Table 2.5 The myths and realities of team coaching

Limiting mindsets	Responses
Team Coaching only needs to happen when the team first forms	The best teams engage in lifelong learning and development
Team Coaching only needs to happen when things are getting difficult	If the first time you address relationship issues is in the divorce court you have left it too late!
The performance of the team is the sum total of the team members' performance	A team can perform at more than the sum of its parts or less than the sum of its parts. It is important to focus on the team added value
Team Coaching is about relating better to each other	Team Coaching is also about how the team relates to all its stakeholders and is aligned to the wider organization's mission
Team Coaching is about the team having better meetings	Team performance happens when the team, or sub-parts of it, engage with the team's stakeholders. The team meeting by itself is the training ground, not the match
Team Coaching only happens off-site in away-days	Team Coaching can be assisted by off-site away-days but the core development happens in the heat of working together
We are not a team unless we work on the same things together	A team is defined by having a shared enterprise that cannot be done by the members working out of connection with each other
Team Coaching is about the team trusting each other	Absolute trust between human beings is an unrealizable goal, particularly in work teams. A more useful goal is the team trusting each other enough to disclose their mistrust
Conflict in teams is a bad thing	Too much or too little conflict are unhelpful in a team. Great teams can creatively work through the conflicting needs in their wider system
Team Coaching is an end in itself	Team Coaching is only valuable when it is linked to improving the team's business performance

While team coaching continues to grow, multiple myths still exist and thus we close this chapter with a Table (Table 2.5) which helps the reader bust some of the most popular myths and misunderstandings about team coaching.

Conclusions

In this chapter, we have reviewed the definitions of team coaching with the aim of establishing greater clarity about the intervention. We concluded by noting that there is a growing consensus on a definition for "team coaching" which has been helped by the work of professional bodies to set standards in this area of practice, along with definitions on how it differs from other similar team interventions, both of which provide a platform for the development of team coaching competencies.

Chapter 3
Exploring the Practice of Team Coaching

Introduction

In this chapter, we will explore the world of team coaching in practice. We will consider when the team coach should coach and when they may move to consulting or other modes of team development. We will also briefly discuss referrals for individuals who may be members of the team, but where a referral to another helping professional is required.

When to Coach, When to Consult, and When to Train?

Like many areas of practice the boundaries between one intervention and another can be blurred. This can make it tricky to identify when any intervention is the right one to be used. In this section, we explore some of the boundaries between team coaching and group coaching, team coaching and consulting, team coaching and training, and team and one-to-one coaching.

Group Coaching

Group coaching and team coaching, though similar in their collaborative nature, serve distinct purposes. Understanding these differences is essential for both the team and the group coach.

Group coaching typically involves guiding a group of individuals who, while they may share common challenges, do not work as a cohesive team in their day to day roles. They are more typically individuals who are coming together primarily

© The Author(s), under exclusive license to Springer Nature
Switzerland AG 2024
J. Passmore et al., *Becoming a Team Coach*,
https://doi.org/10.1007/978-3-031-63546-5_3

for personal growth, skill development, or to look for solutions to common challenges. The magic of group coaching lies in the diversity of perspectives and experiences that each participant brings to the table and the ability of the coach to help facilitate the sharing process as well as personal insights. This diversity enriches the learning process, as participants not only gain insights from the coach, but also learn from each other's experiences, feedback, and viewpoints.

In contrast, team coaching is focused on a specific team, a group of individuals who regularly work together and share a common objective or purpose. Team coaching, as we have discussed earlier, is designed to enhance the team's collective performance, improve their working relationships, and align their efforts towards achieving these shared goals. Team coaching explores the dynamics of the team, addressing issues such as communication, collaboration, role clarity, and conflict resolution and through this process, helps deepen understanding, collaboration and ultimately the collective strength of the team.

In reflecting on the skills required for each, there is a clear overlap, as there is with one-to-one coaching. Group coaching requires the coach to focus more on facilitating discussions among the group, ensuring that the group session is inclusive and that each participant's voice is heard. In contrast the team coach faces a more demanding role, which is why a separate accreditation has been developed, reflecting these additional skills. The team coach needs to have the skills to assess the team's current state, identify areas for improvement, and manage discussions among team members which explore these issues and themes but which ultimately promote team cohesion and performance.

As a result we might choose to select group coaching for a number of reasons. Firstly, if the group is not a team, that is they do not share a common purpose. Secondly, where the collective process may add to the participants' insights, for example as a result of norming or observing how others tackle similar challenges and problems. Finally, group coaching can be a low cost way to introduce coaching, where funds for one-to-one coaching are not available. Each person may experience some personal coaching and benefit from observing the coaching process, which they can apply to their own team when back at work.

Consulting with Teams

Another common intervention is consulting. This can occur at an organizational as well as a sub-organizational level, such as a department or a team. Consulting is a process where an external expert provides specific solutions, strategies, or problem-solving expertise to the organization or a team. The approach is typically directive; the consultant analyzes the team's challenges or objectives and then offers recommendations, action plans, or solutions based on their expertise. The focus is on addressing specific business needs or objectives, such as improving efficiency, implementing a new system, or developing a strategic plan.

Team coaching, on the other hand, is more about facilitating the team's own growth and development. Rather than offering direct solutions, a team coach helps the team reflect on the dynamics within the team, its processes, values, assumptions and ultimately its performance through discovery, discussion, and reflection. Reflecting the ICF definition of coaching, the process is highly collaborative and exploratory. Ultimately the team coach seeks to empower the team to find its own solutions as opposed to disempowering them by solving their problems.

The skills required in these two roles are distinct, reflecting the difference between co-creation and facilitation used in team coaching and analysis and expert advice used in consulting. While the coach will be an expert in the coaching process, they may possess very limited knowledge about the technical problems the team or organization faces. In contrast, the consultant is a subject matter expert, who is prepared to provide answers.

Training with Teams and Groups

Team or group training and team coaching, while seemingly similar, serve distinct purposes in the realm of organizational development and by their nature require different skills. Team training requiring more subject matter knowledge than team coaching.

Team training is best viewed as an educational process. It is where a group of individuals come together to learn new skills or knowledge. This training is often structured, with a set curriculum designed to enhance the team's knowledge or capabilities in specific areas such as project management, or media skills. The essence of team training lies in its collective approach; it is not just about individual growth, but about elevating the entire team's proficiency in the specific knowledge area. This method is thus particularly effective when introducing a new process or to manage a change in the working practices of members of the group.

As we have discussed above, team coaching is less structured, with no syllabus to cover and more personalized; where the team coaching focus is on improving the team's dynamics, interactions, and collective performance through the collaborative, non-directive coaching style.

In terms of skills, both practitioners need to be highly skilled, While the team coach is an expert in the coaching process, the trainer needs to have both facilitation and possibly coaching skills, but also must be a presenter as well as being knowledgeable in the syllabus to be covered, and able to deal with questions and challenges from the group. Many trainers also have learning design skills, understanding how adults learn, and designing the process to optimize the acquisition of the new knowledge or skill.

Personal Coaching

We have talked extensively about personal coaching in "Becoming a Coach: The Essential ICF Guide" (Passmore & Sinclair, 2024). The difference is that in one-to-one coaching the focus is solely on the needs of the individual client. This contrasts in team coaching where the focus of the engagement is on the team, even if one-to-one coaching forms part of the wider team coaching assignment (Table 3.1).

Methods in Team Coaching

Coach the Team

Team coaching as we have discussed is an approach that seeks to enhance the performance and dynamics of a team. This method of coaching is not just about improving output; it is about fostering the team dynamic, enhancing communication, and aligning goals to create a more cohesive and effective team.

In this book, we will be examining the ICF competencies which complement personal coaching competencies for ICF credentialed coaches. Before moving to examine these in detail in Chaps. 6–13, we wanted to share some general themes to prepare you for what is to come.

As a starting point it is important to note that in team coaching, the team itself is viewed as the primary client, a singular entity composed of diverse individuals. Each team member plays a pivotal role in the coaching process, bringing their unique perspectives to the table.

This goal is achieved through the actions of a team coach maintaining objectivity. This ensures that all interactions with team members, sponsors, and stakeholders are free from bias, with no individual or sub-group perceived as being favored above others, this includes the chief executive or sponsor.

Table 3.1 Comparing team, group, and one-to-one coaching

Intervention	Who	What	By who
Team coaching	A group who share a common purpose	A process focused on improving team processes, creating greater alignment and enhancing team performance	By an accredited team coach
Group coaching	A group of relative strangers	A process to enhance individual member performance through exploration and understanding of a shared topic	By an accredited coach, with skills in group learning or facilitation
Personal coaching	One individual	A process to enhance insight and promote personal behavioral change.	By an accredited coach

The team coach also needs to work openly, allowing the dynamic process to evolve with the team, and in so doing recognize undercurrents of each session, and be ready to adapt and respond to the emerging needs of the team.

Finally in working across the group the team coach needs to respect confidentiality, particularly in individual conversations. Breaches of confidentiality can derail the process and result in the team taking a step back as opposed to moving forward.

Managing the Boundaries

Team development is a multifaceted process that encompasses various modalities including team coaching, team building, team training, team consulting, team mentoring, and team facilitation. Each of these approaches contributes uniquely to the growth and effectiveness of a team.

A team coach is a central player to a team's developmental journey. They may need to collaborate with others involved in consulting, training, or other team processes. This collaboration is particularly helpful when the situation demands specialized knowledge or skills beyond the coach's expertise.

In this chapter, we have already delineated the differences between these various development modalities, but we recognize that the boundaries are not fixed but fluid, not black and white but gray. Team coaches need to navigate these boundaries collaboratively with the team, helping them identify when different skills may be required.

This referential approach can ensure that the team receives comprehensive support tailored to their unique challenges and goals. It allows for a holistic development approach, leveraging the strengths and specialties of various professionals, with the team coach, often acting as the conductor, inviting in additional support when needed.

Multimodal Practice

In practice, this means that a team coach must be well-versed not only in the fundamental principles of coaching, but also in the specific nuances and techniques of each development modality they employ. Whether it is team building, training, consulting, mentoring, or facilitation, the coach should have a deep understanding and competency in these areas. This diverse skill set allows the coach to seamlessly integrate various strategies and interventions, enhancing the team's overall growth and performance.

It is also worth noting here that this role is demanding and the use of a supervisor, also skilled in team coaching, can provide the reflective space and support to help the team coach navigate this complexity and protect their own wellbeing.

Directive, When Required

In the landscape of team coaching, the role of a coach often demands a more directive approach compared to one-to-one coaching scenarios. This directive style, however, is not a blanket strategy but is reserved for specific situations where it can significantly contribute to the team's development. The aim of adopting a directive stance in team coaching is to illuminate growth areas within the team, facilitate an understanding of the team coaching process and to navigate critical junctures in the coaching sessions.

These directive moments are pivotal. They are used to highlight both positive and negative dynamics within the team, serving as a catalyst for recognizing areas of strength and those needing improvement. The coach's directive interventions are crucial in guiding the team through these discovery phases, providing insights and suggesting paths forward.

However, it is essential that these instances of directive coaching serve to broaden, rather than constrict, the team's perspective on their situation. The goal is to expand the team's understanding and outlook, fostering a more comprehensive view of their dynamics, challenges, and potential solutions. This approach enables teams to develop a deeper insight into their functioning, encouraging a more cohesive and productive journey towards their collective goals. In summary, while directive coaching plays a critical role in team development, its application is nuanced, aiming to enrich the team's collective understanding and growth.

Fulfilling Multiple Roles

Finally, in their multimodal approach, the team coach must remain clear about their different roles, how these affect one another and how stepping between them requires sensitivity in order to maintain the trust, transparency and clarify what clients should rightly expect from professional practitioners.

Conclusion

In this brief chapter, we have explored the boundaries of team coaching as an intervention with other commonly used team interventions. We also looked briefly at the methods used by team coaches. We will be unpacking these methods and how they have been translated into coach competencies and frameworks in the following chapters.

Chapter 4
The Science of Team Coaching

Introduction

Evidence should sit at the heart of any professional. Research creates the evidence to establish our understanding of an intervention: what it is, how to apply it best, and what effects it has on users. Coaching, in this sense, is no different from medicine or other sciences. How coaches then apply the evidence, reflecting the individual client, the situation, and their own style, may then be considered the art of coaching. In this chapter, we will look briefly at coaching research: What this evidence tells us about the effectiveness of coaching as an intervention to help individuals learn, change, and grow. We will start by briefly looking at the research on one-to-one coaching. We will then move to consider team coaching, examining the literature of process and effect.

Coaching Research Reviewed

Coaching as a workplace intervention has grown dramatically over the past three decades. In the 1990s, there were fewer than 5000 people describing themselves, or their practice, as coaching. By the mid-2020s, this number had grown to in excess of 100,000 coaches. This growth in numbers is also reflected in the growth of the market, which was estimated to be $4.56 billion (ICF, 2023a). As AI, digital team, and group coaching grow in popularity we estimate the market potential could exceed $20 billion by the early 2030s.

Over the same period coaching research has also developed, both in the quantity and in the depth of the research. In this sense, coaching has seen a gradual movement up the hierarchy of research from best practice reports and case studies, which were common in the 1990s, through respected qualitative and quantitative research methods to meta-analysis studies appearing in the 2020s (Fig. 4.1).

Literature Reviews & Meta Research

Over this period several authors have sought to summarize the literature to provide researchers with a platform upon which to build. The first comprehensive review noted the quickening pace of coaching research (Grant et al., 2010a, 2010b). Since then there have been a growing number of quantitative studies (for example, Passmore & Rehman, 2012), systematic literature (for example, Athanasopoulou & Dopson, 2018) and meta-analysis studies (for example, Wang et al., 2022).

We believe there are now over 30 quasi-experimental, Randomized Control Trial (RCT) and similar design studies demonstrating the efficacy of coaching. Some

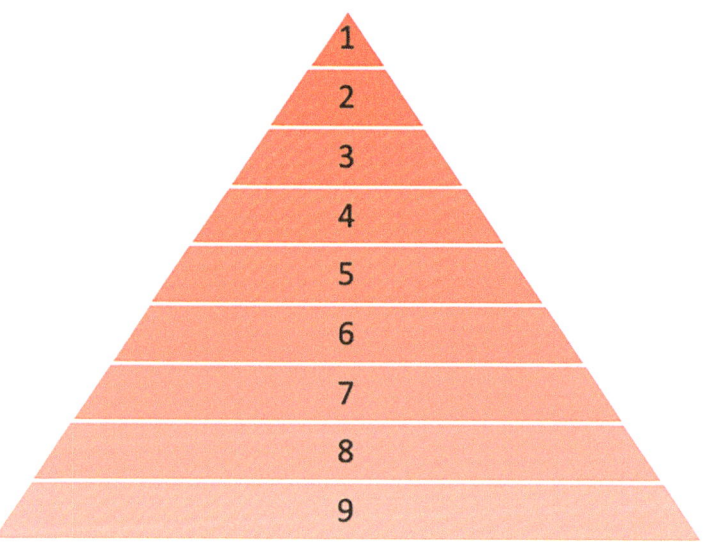

Level 1: MAA
Level 2: Meta analysis
Level 3: Systematic Review
Level 4: Cohort study Case control
Level 5: RCT
Level 6: Case control
Level 7: Survey
Level 8: Case study
Level 9: Expert best practice

Fig. 4.1 Hierarchy of research

have claimed there are more than 50 coaching RCTs, but in review these studies cited in detail, the evidence reveals a number use a more directive (mentoring) approach than would be captured by the ICF's definition, some studies are delivered by individuals without any coach training or were based in clinical settings and suggest a more advisory-educational style.

Due to the complexity of delivering true randomization of participants or including comparable interventions for the control group (one group receives coaching and one group receives a similar intervention like training for the same period of time), or double blinded groups (participants and facilitators who are unaware of the full nature of the study) in practice few RCTs have actually been conducted. In fact many of the studies described as "randomized controlled trials" fail to meet the criteria for a true RCT and are better described as experimental or quasi-experimental design.

The RCT studies within coaching that have been completed have typically been undertaken in controlled environments, such as the armed forces, police or similar environments (Passmore & Rehman, 2012: Passmore & Velez, 2012).

We have summarized a sample of these studies with their outcomes in Table 4.1.

In addition to a growing number of quantitative studies, using quasi-experimental design methods, there has also been a growth in meta-analysis research (Table 4.2), which has sought to bring together these quantitative studies to provide effect size measures for the efficacy of workplace coaching.

These have shown that workplace coaching has a small to moderate effect size (measured by Hedges g at between 0.2 and 0.5 depending on the aspects being measured–cognitive change, behavioral change, etc.), and thus is broadly comparable with other well used organizational interventions from leadership development to skills training.

Table 4.1 Examples of RCT, experimental, and quasi-experimental design studies in coaching

Authors	Findings
Duijts et al. (2008):	Coaching reduced levels of sickness absence
Passmore and Rehman (2012)	Coaching more efficient and effective than instructional training
William and Lowman (2018):	Coaching increases leadership competencies
Trom and Burke (2022):	Coaching increases employee wellbeing and sense of gratitude
Fontes and Dello Russo (2021):	Coaching increases job satisfaction and organizational commitment
de Haan et al. (2020)	Coaching increases goal attainment and resilience
Rafferty et al. (2023)	Leadership development combined with coaching produces superior outcomes than leadership development alone.

Table 4.2 Meta-analysis
studies in coaching

De Meuse et al. (2009)
Theeboom et al. (2014)
Jones et al. (2015)
Sonesh et al. (2015)
Burt and Talati (2017)
Graßmann et al. (2020)
Wang et al. (2022)
de Haan and Nilsson (2023)
Cannon-Bowers et al. (2023)
Tomoiagă and David (2023)

Team Coaching Research Reviewed

While one-to-one coaching has made positive steps in building an evidence base over the past three decades, team coaching is relatively early on its journey. Following a similar path to one-to-one coaching, team coaching's early research has focused on discussions about definitions, boundaries, competencies, and the development of training.

The research work which followed in the second phase was largely qualitative in nature, dominated by case study, reports of practice, and small-scale studies, while lacking in quantitative research (Hastings & Pennington, 2019; Widdowson et al., 2020). A detailed review of this literature suggests there is little evidence of the impact of team coaching on aspects of team life such as team relationships, member wellbeing, team performance, or psychological safety.

As a relatively new area of practice, research is developing all the time, with new studies appearing, we expect to see team coaching entering a third phase during the mid and late 2020s with more quantitative research studies providing evidence of team coaching's impact, alongside a continuation of qualitative studies.

In the following sections, we will review the research published to date. We have divided this section into three parts: literature reviews, models and processes, and impact.

Literature Reviews

The first area of literature which we will consider are the reviews of the literature. In 2010, Hicks' review identified two case studies. This may be an understatement as Grant (2009) in a review of all coaching research identified six studies which referred to team coaching. By 2013, Carr and Peters identified 16 studies (four models, four empirical studies, and eight case studies). This had grown to 17 empirical studies by their 2019 review (Peters & Carr, 2019). Most studies related to coaching as a leadership style within a team leadership context, as opposed to an external, independent accredited team coach working with a team. These studies which focused on external coaches were most frequently case studies, undertaken by the consultants delivering the program and often more descriptive than analytical in nature.

Widdowson et al. (2020) conducted, as part of the development process of the ICF team coaching competencies, a team coaching literature review. The team noted the growing pace of team coaching, a point also highlighted by Lanz (2016).

Our analysis suggests there remains a gap in team coaching research with more work needed to fill the void in our understanding about its efficacy and its application: for example, when should team coaching be used and when other forms of team development?

Models and Process Research

As we noted above, early writing in team coaching was dominated by discussions of definitions and processes, questions of: *What is this?* and *How do we do it?* Coaching models (for example, Clutterbuck, 2007; Hackman & Wageman, 2005a; Hawkins, 2021; Moral & Angel, 2009) have offered alternative ways to think about and engage in the team coaching process. We will explore many of these models in later chapters.

These models and frameworks mostly draw on the practitioners' past experience, sharing what they have learned from previous assignments and have been drawn together in a recipe for others to apply.

Impact Research

A further strand of team coaching research has explored the impact achieved from team coaching assignments. Measuring the impact of personal development can be difficult. Multiple models have been published. One favored model is Kirkpatrick's four levels of evaluation: Reaction, Learning, Behavior, and Results (1959). The framework was originally developed for training evaluation, but the framework can equally be applied to team coaching.

Some work has been done to evaluate the impact of team coaching. Heimbecker (2006) claimed significant benefits from team coaching in his unpublished university thesis, based on interviews with team participants. Similarly, Anderson et al. (2008) claimed benefits from a consulting engagement their firm delivered at Caterpillar, with "90% of senior teams" who claimed to have benefitted from the process.

However, such studies have been compromised as a result of the researchers (authors) acting as both facilitators and evaluators of their own practices. Further, in these and other studies, the methods sometimes use one-to-one coaching, in addition to or instead of team coaching, while failing to clearly describe the exact methods used. The impact metrics are often ill-defined, or based on reactions (Level 1—Kirkpatrick), as opposed to learning (Level 2) or behavioral change (Level 3). In combinations these aspects make such studies difficult to repeat or be certain of which aspects led to the claimed positive effects.

Passmore and colleagues (Passmore et al., 2024) in a small-scale double-blind randomized control trial examined individual team member changes on psychological safety and perceived team cohesion. They found that team coaching outperformed the control group teams who received a team development session. The effects of the changes also appeared to be sustained in the team coaching group in a follow-up assessment two months later.

While this is the first team study, and has limitations, not least around the number of participants, teams, and measurement, we expect to see a growing number of studies exploring the effects using similar methods during the 2020s and beyond as the number of team coaches grows.

Overview of Research

In summary, as with examples from early coaching practice (see Sauer, 1999; Tobias, 1996; Winum, 2005) the focus of published work in team coaching has largely been on the personal experience examined through qualitative methodologies and case studies. While these provide a useful starting point for further exploration of a phenomenon, the effectiveness of an intervention requires more robust research designs, such as an RCT (Passmore et al., 2024).

Given the sparsity of the literature, the objective for this study was to examine the effectiveness of team coaching as an organization intervention, and its impact on individual team members.

Conclusions

In this chapter, we aimed to briefly review the literature on team coaching research and share insights to date from the limited number of studies undertaken. These studies confirm at an experiential level that team coaching is well received, but the evidence from quantitative research is more limited, confirming the need for more research in this area to help practitioners understand where team coaching can best support team development.

Part II

Chapter 5
Introduction to Team Coaching

Background

The International Coaching Federation (ICF) is the largest professional coaching organization in the world. The ICF was founded in 1995 as a non-profit organization for coaches to support each other and grow the coaching profession. By 2024, it had grown to more than 58,000 members and over 50,000 credential-holders in 146 countries and territories worldwide.

During its existence, the ICF has developed and revised a competency framework to support coach development and assessment. The ICF Coaching Core Competency model (Table 5.1) includes eight core competencies within four domains.

In response to the growing discipline of team coaching and its increasing importance in organizations, including private companies, government agencies, and not-for-profit organizations, in 2020 ICF Credentials and Standards developed the ICF Team Coaching Competency model.

The model sets the much-needed requirements and standards for team coaches globally, designed to build upon and integrate with the ICF Core Competencies. The core coaching competencies provide the foundation for the team coaching competencies; additional team coaching competencies are detailed for each core competency. This will be explored further in this chapter and Chaps. 6–13.

For each chapter, we set out the core competency and show the supplementary team competencies as shown in Boxes 5.1 and 5.2 below. In each chapter, we then explore each of the supplementary team competencies. For a description of the ICF Core Competencies, you should read "Becoming a Coach: The Essential ICF Guide" (Passmore & Sinclair, 2024).

J. Passmore et al., *Becoming a Team Coach*, https://doi.org/10.1007/978-3-031-63546-5_5

Table 5.1 ICF Core Competencies

ICF Core Competency Model
A. Foundation
1. Demonstrates Ethical Practice
2. Embodies a Coaching Mindset
B. Co-creating the Relationship
3. Establishes and Maintains Agreements
4. Cultivates Trust and Safety
5. Maintains Presence
C. Communicating Effectively
6. Listens Actively
7. Evokes Awareness
D. Cultivating Learning and Growth
8. Facilitates Client Growth

The competency is defined and described in Box 5.1.

> **Box 5.1 Demonstrates Ethical Practice**
> Definition: Understands and consistently applies coaching ethics and standards of coaching.
>
> 1. Demonstrates personal integrity and honesty in interactions with clients, sponsors, and relevant stakeholders
> 2. Is sensitive to clients' identity, environment, experiences, values, and beliefs
> 3. Uses language appropriate and respectful to clients, sponsors, and relevant stakeholders
> 4. Abides by the ICF Code of Ethics and upholds the Core Values
> 5. Maintains confidentiality with client information per stakeholder agreements and pertinent laws
> 6. Maintains the distinctions between coaching, consulting, psychotherapy and other support professions
> 7. Refers clients to other support professionals, as appropriate

In addition to these, the team coach practitioner must demonstrate the supplementary competencies described in Box 5.2.

> **Box 5.2 Team Coach Supplementary Competencies—Demonstrates Ethical Practice**
> (a) Coaches the client team as a single entity
> (b) Maintains the distinction between team coaching, team building, team training, team consulting, team mentoring, team facilitation, and other team development modalities
> (c) Demonstrates the knowledge and skill needed to practice the specific blend of team development modalities that are being offered
> (d) Adopts more directive team development modalities only when needed to help the team achieve their goals
> (e) Maintains trust, transparency, and clarity when fulfilling multiple roles related to team coaching

How Were the ICF Team Coaching Competencies Developed?

A research project was conducted to develop team coaching competencies and set global standards for team coaching. This aimed to establish the knowledge, skills, abilities, and other characteristics (KSAOs) required to perform the role of a team coach. These are in addition to the ICF Core Coaching Competencies (Table 5.1).

The development process involved:

- A literature review of more than 100 pieces of team coaching literature culminating with the publication of a peer-reviewed article in the International Journal of Evidence-Based Coaching and Mentoring (Widdowson et al., 2020).
- Workshops with subject matter experts from across the globe to understand the knowledge, skills, abilities, and other characteristics of team coaches and how they differ from one-to-one coaching.
- Qualitative interviews to understand how team coaches approach team coaching engagements and what team coaching means to them as a profession.
- A global survey to understand the KSAOs, their relationship to other team modalities and the importance of specific team coaching tasks.
- Development of team coaching critical incidents, exploring how team coaches manage and react to opportunities and challenges when working with teams.
- Competency model workshops to review job analysis information.

As a result, in November 2020, the ICF launched their Team Coaching Competencies, giving guidance on what was needed to be an effective team coach practitioner.

ICF Team Coaching Definition

The Team Coaching Competency model (Table 5.2) also defines what team coaching is:

> Partnering in a co-creative and reflective process with a team and its dynamics and relationships in a way that inspires them to maximize their abilities and potential to reach their common purpose and shared goals.

Team Development Modalities

The project explored how team coaching differed from other forms of team intervention. Team training, consulting, and mentoring were viewed as more directive. As a result, team coaches should avoid using these modalities as this could cause confusion within the team and reduce the chances of the team coach taking a more generative coaching approach.

How does team coaching differ from facilitation?

There was agreement that team coaching and team facilitation were closer, but had some naked differences.

Firstly, the level of depth of exploration: While team coaching often delves deeper into the dynamics and patterns of behavior within the team, facilitation generally stays at more of a surface level.

Table 5.2 ICF Team Coaching Competency Model

Element of the definition	What does this mean in practice?
Partnering and co-creating	The team coach will work in partnership with the team as a single entity, the team leader, and stakeholders to design and develop the team coaching journey; enabling them to meet the needs and objectives of the team, its stakeholders and the wider system.
Reflective process	During the team coaching journey, the team will reflect on how effectively they are working together, explore their learning about how they work as a collective both when together and apart.
Dynamics and relationships	Team coaching aims to help a team build psychological safety and connection, which in turn builds trust and the ability for the team to have open and honest conversations. Team dynamics will also be illuminated both by the team coach and the team itself.
Maximize their abilities and potential	Team coaching involves a series of interventions rather than a one-off event, giving the opportunity for the team to embed and sustain their learning. This in turn helps the team to learn and grow together, leverage their strengths, and maximize their potential.
Common purpose and goals	Team coaching helps a team work collectively on achieving their common purpose and collective goals.

ICF (2020a)

Secondly, the ownership of the dialogue: Facilitation tends to manage the dialogue with the team, pulling the dialogue out from individuals within the team, whereas, in comparison, team coaching shifts the dialogue to the team itself. One might use an analogy of juggling to illustrate this difference. In facilitation, the facilitator juggles each ball in turn, asking questions of team members. In team coaching, the juggling balls are passed to the team for them to juggle themselves. As a result, the ownership of the dialogue in team coaching sits within the team.

The following table, Table 5.3, aims to clarify the key differences for each of the team modalities. The various modalities are explored further in Chap. 2.

ICF Code of Ethics

The ICF Code of Ethics (ICF, 2020b) describes the standards, values, and conduct for all members and credentialed coaches. This includes coaches, team coaches, mentors, coach supervisors, coach trainers, and those studying to become coaches. Chapter 6 explores how ethics apply to team coaches.

ICF Advanced Certification in Team Coaching (ACTC)

To recognize the knowledge, skill, and competence of advanced team coach practitioners, the ICF Credentials and Standards team developed the Advanced Certificate in Team Coaching (ACTC) and launched this credential in 2021.

In achieving ACTC team coaches demonstrate competence in the following:

- Ability to understand and explain the difference between the different team development modalities.
- Enable teams to take ownership of their own development.
- Manage and help teams illuminate complex dynamics and patterns of behavior and resolve conflict.
- Partner and co-create a team coaching approach with key stakeholders.
- Work with a team to help them make long-term sustainable change.
- Support teams to communicate and collaborate more effectively.
- Partner with the team to establish a common purpose, identity, and goals.

The exact requirements to earn the ACTC are presented in detail in Chap. 9.

Table 5.3 Team development modalities

	Team building	Team training	Team consulting	Team mentoring	Team facilitation	Team coaching
Time frame	Short—1–5 days	Short—1–5 days	Variable	Staccato—Hours over a sustained period	Short—1–5 days	Longer term—Months
Process	Exercises	Work with the team through a curriculum	Consultant shares expertise	Mentor shares experience	Facilitate dialogue	Team and coach partner
Growth area	Enhanced relationships	New knowledge or skills	Additional insights	New knowledge	Clarity	Achieved goals—Team sustainability
Team dynamics/ conflict resolution	Minimal	Minimal	Minimal advisory	Minimal	Minimal	Integral
Expert; ownership	Instructor	Trainer	Consultant	Mentor	Facilitator and team	Team

International Coaching Federation (2020b)

Conclusion

In this chapter, we have briefly discussed the ICF's core coach and additional team coaching competencies. The following chapters in this section explore each of the team coach competencies, skills, and knowledge in more depth and explore what this means in practice when working with teams.

Chapter 6
Demonstrates Ethical Practice (Competency 1)

Introduction

Within the Foundation Domain there are two core competencies:

1. Demonstrates Ethical Practice
2. Embodies a Coaching Mindset

These competencies relate to applying coaching ethics and standards, along with developing a mindset that is open, curious, flexible, and client-centered. They are, generally, less observable but underpin the essence of a competent coach: their ethical behavior and their professional identity.

Demonstrates Ethical Practice is the first ICF Core Competency and the first in the Foundation Domain.

The competency is defined and described in Box 6.1 and has been reviewed in detail by Passmore and Sinclair (2024).

In addition to these, the team coach practitioner must demonstrate the supplementary competencies described in Box 6.2.

Team Supplementary Competencies

Coaches the Client Team as a Single Entity

The ICF Team Coaching Supplementary Competency Background Explanation

The client for a team coach is the team as a single entity. A team is made up of individual team members and each one must be heard and play an integral role in team discussions.

Box 6.1 Demonstrates Ethical Practice
Definition: Understands and consistently applies coaching ethics and standards of coaching.

1. Demonstrates personal integrity and honesty in interactions with clients, sponsors, and relevant stakeholders
2. Is sensitive to clients' identity, environment, experiences, values, and beliefs
3. Uses language appropriate and respectful to clients, sponsors, and relevant stakeholders
4. Abides by the ICF Code of Ethics and upholds the Core Values
5. Maintains confidentiality with client information per stakeholder agreements and pertinent laws
6. Maintains the distinctions between coaching, consulting, psychotherapy, and other support professions
7. Refers clients to other support professionals, as appropriate

Box 6.2 Team Coach Supplementary Competencies—Demonstrates Ethical Practice
(a) Coaches the client team as a single entity
(b) Maintains the distinction between team coaching, team building, team training, team consulting, team mentoring, team facilitation, and other team development modalities
(c) Demonstrates the knowledge and skill needed to practice the specific blend of team development modalities that are being offered
(d) Adopts more directive team development modalities only when needed to help the team achieve their goals
(e) Maintains trust, transparency, and clarity when fulfilling multiple roles related to team coaching

Further, the team coach must remain objective in all interactions with team members, sponsors, and relevant stakeholders. The team coach should not be perceived as taking sides with any subgroups or individual members of the team, should remain open to what is emerging in the sessions, and should be completely honest in all dealings with the team. Discussions with individual team members will need to remain confidential to the team coach and team member unless the team member allows disclosure of information to others and as per the team coaching agreement.

The first challenge for the team coach can emerge while simultaneously one-to-one coaching is provided to members of the team. Questions that need to be addressed in this case are:

- What information can be and what cannot be shared?
- Is there disclosure regarding who is doing one-to-one?

Due to multiple challenges, there are many team coaching practitioners who resolve to exclusively focus on coaching the team. While other team coaching practitioners hold the view that coaching individuals one-to-one in the team and the team as a whole is possible. They seek to overcome these challenges through the structure of their program and by addressing the challenges in advance through open and transparent agreements.

Some factors to consider when making the decision to provide both services concurrently are:

- Cultural factor. Some cultures might feel very uncomfortable having individual and team coaching sessions at the same time.
- Biases management. Does the team coach feel confident to remain unbiased and unaffected by those one-to-one sessions so that no biased context is brought into team coaching?
- Confidentiality issues. How will they manage confidentiality between multiple one-to-one sessions and the team session?
- Suitability. If one-to-one coaching is part of the program, is the team coach the best choice for the one-to-one sessions?

The team coach needs to consider each team and the unique factors before making a decision. The decision should always be that which is in the best interests of the team.

Yet another challenge may occur when an individual team member desires to share "confidential" information regarding the team with the team coach off-session, e.g. during a coffee break, with the request not to share this information with the team. Van Hoey (2023) suggests a way that the team coach can deal with such a request appropriately and ethically, is by asking the following questions:

- How could we turn this conversation into something that helps the team?
- What is underneath your wish, real motive, for confidentiality?

It is worth mentioning that a clear and thorough agreement with the team always frames what you can talk about outside the actual coaching sessions and how to deal with the exceptional situation when information in respect of the team is shared with the coach off session.

The presence of the team leader who is synchronically the boss of team members may cast complications for team members. For some teams or individuals it can reduce both the psychological safety or the perception of equality in the conversations.

In these situations, it is the team coach's responsibility to cultivate equality and support the team members and team leader to securely assume they are one single entity and to contract to create a psychologically safe environment for open and honest conversations.

Maintains the Distinction between Team Coaching, Team Building, Team Training, Team Consulting, Team Mentoring, Team Facilitation, and Other Team Development Modalities

The ICF Team Coaching Supplementary Competency Background Explanation

> Team development can involve many modalities, including team coaching, team building, team training, team consulting, team mentoring, and team facilitation. The team coach should partner with other experts when the demands of a specific team coaching engagement warrant or when specific knowledge and skill levels are required. While the distinction between these modalities may not always need to be highlighted, caution should be applied if interventions beyond coaching are undertaken. Team coaches may need to refer clients to many types of professionals and also receive assistance from a co-coach, a supervisor, or other team development professionals.

In Chap. 5 (*Introduction to Team Coaching Competencies*), the team development modalities table presents the different modalities that fall under the umbrella of Team Development:

team building, team training, team consulting, team mentoring, team facilitation, and team coaching.

Team coaches need to be very clear about the distinctions of these and other modalities that may be required for a specific engagement, understand their differences, and know when and if they should undertake them. As we have outlined in the previous chapter, some team coaches feel that these three modalities should not be undertaken by the team coach, apart from team facilitation, as team coaches frequently wander into facilitation mode to promote dialogue amongst the team members.

This supplementary competency conveys that team coaches should partner with other experts either due to the demands of the engagement or because of the knowledge and skill required.

Among tangible issues the team coaches need to reflect on to make build decisions are:

- When is it appropriate to move into different modalities?
- Who are the experts in these modalities, and if they are a good fit for the client, aside from their expertise?
- If the team coaches themselves plan to do these modalities, are they the best option, and why does the coach believe they are the best placed coach to undertake the work?

An additional challenge here can be when the sponsor requests a modality that is not the best approach for this specific engagement. Either due to their characteristics and culture, or due to goals, another modality or blend of modalities would serve the team better, but the team coach is apprehensively unconfident or not knowledgeable enough to express an opinion.

Demonstrates the Knowledge and Skill Needed to Practice the Specific Blend of Team Development Modalities that Are Being Offered

The ICF Team Coaching Supplementary Background Explanation

> A team coach is sufficiently skilled to competently practice all of the team development modalities that the team coach is offering as part of a team coaching engagement.

In the case that team coaches undertake engagements that include multiple team development modalities, they should be able to competently practice those. Hence, the consecutive need of the team coaches for ongoing professional development to acquire knowledge and skills in the modalities they include in their offering.

One question team coaches can ask themselves at this point is if they are choosing the right modalities for this team, or if their choice is influenced by their level of knowledge. In case of the latter, they have the responsibility to request support for the modalities the engagement might require.

Adopts More Directive Team Development Modalities Only when Needed to Help the Team Achieve their Goals

The ICF Team Coaching Supplementary Background Explanation

> In general, there are more times when a team coach will need to be directive than when working with a client on a one-to-one basis. These instances, however, should remain limited to those opportunities that require a directive approach to bring awareness to growth areas for the team and to help them understand the team coaching process. They may be critical moments in team coaching sessions, pointing out positive and negative team dynamics, and introducing ways to move forward. These moments of being directive should broaden, rather than narrow, the team's perspective on their current situation.

Team coaches have the opportunity to be more direct. The challenges here are:

1. When to distinguish that a directive modality is appropriate.
2. How to adopt this modality without guiding the team or narrowing its perspective.

    Examples when directive modality maybe appropriate:

- The team considers diversity as an obstacle and source of conflict
- The communication pattern/culture of the team reinforces negative team dynamics
- Toxic behaviors are noticed
- The team misses the systemic perspective and the needs of the wider system(s)
- There is a gap in knowledge or understanding that could help the team expand their perspective and ways forward

Maintains Trust, Transparency, and Clarity when Fulfilling Multiple Roles Related to Team Coaching

The ICF Team Coaching Supplementary Competency Background Explanation

> In the event that a team coach offers multiple team development modalities, the coach must be clear about these different roles and how one role may affect another.

In our work as team coaches we find much confusion for both clients and coaches about what team coaching is and its clear distinction from other team development modalities. In Chap. 5, we defined the key differences between the various types of team intervention. Contracting becomes once again important for the team coach, the team, and the sponsor to establish transparency and clarity of what is being offered, the modalities that could or would be used, the expectations of each party, and if and how each role could affect the other. That means that as team coaches we are also very clear about what each team's modality really is about and entails and how their role as a consultant, for example, could affect their role as a coach.

One question that arises is, if the team coach must inform the team every time they "switch" roles. There are team coaches who have a certain set path in their offering and process of working with teams. But on the other hand, there are other team coaches who move in a more subtle way among the necessary modalities as seen appropriate from what is emerging as the work with the team progresses.

Conclusion

Team coaches still abide to the same ICF Code of Ethics with the principles that guide ethical behavior being more complex and unique in Team Coaching than in individual coaching. These supplementary competencies highlight the team as an entity is the client, the opportunity to use different modalities and a using more directive approach when required.

Chapter 7
Embodies a Coaching Mindset (Competency 2)

Within the Foundations Domain there are two competencies:

1. Demonstrates Ethical Practice
2. Embodies a Coaching Mindset

Embodies a Coaching Mindset is the second ICF Core Competency. The competency is defined and described in Box 7.1 and has been reviewed in detail by Passmore and Sinclair (2024).

In addition to these, the team coach practitioner must demonstrate the supplementary described in Box 7.2.

Box 7.1 Embodies a Coaching Mindset
Definition: Develops and maintains a mindset that is open, curious, flexible, and client-centered.

1. Acknowledges that clients are responsible for their own choices
2. Engages in ongoing learning and development as a coach
3. Develops an ongoing reflective practice to enhance one's coaching
4. Remains aware of and open to the influence of context and culture on self and others
5. Uses awareness of self and one's intuition to benefit clients
6. Develops and maintains the ability to regulate one's emotions
7. Mentally and emotionally prepares for sessions
8. Seeks help from outside sources when necessary

© The Author(s), under exclusive license to Springer Nature
Switzerland AG 2024
J. Passmore et al., *Becoming a Team Coach*,
https://doi.org/10.1007/978-3-031-63546-5_7

> **Box 7.2 Team Coach Supplementary Competencies—Embodies a Coaching Mindset**
> (a) Engages in coaching supervision for support, development, and accountability when needed
> (b) Remains objective and aware of team dynamics and patterns

Team Coach Supplementary Competencies

Engages in Coaching Supervision for Support, Development, and Accountability When Needed

The ICF Team Coaching Supplementary Background Explanation

> It could be easy for a team coach to become entangled in the team dynamics and become unaware of issues that should be addressed. Because of this, team coaches should be working with a coaching supervisor. Team coaching can be much more intense than one-to-one coaching given the input from many team members at once. Supervision uses reflection on past events, awareness of the coach's part in those past moments or the present moment, and the effect it has on the coach's behavior. A supervisor is an excellent resource for a team coach as an impartial observer and aid to the reflective practice and its part in the team coaching process.

The first key element in this supplementary is Coaching Supervision. The ICF defines Coaching Supervision as *a collaborative learning practice to continually build the capacity of the coach through reflective dialogue for the benefit of both coaches and clients.*

At this point we consider it essential to clarify the difference between coaching supervision and mentor coaching. Mentor coaching provides the opportunity for the development of the coach's skills; it is focused on how the coach applies the competencies.

Mentor coaching is a collaborative process in which a qualified mentor coach observes a live or recorded coaching session and provides feedback to the coach practitioner about the ICF Core Competencies. Mentor coaching thus acts as a route to continuous professional development focused on the ICF competency framework and supports the journey of coach progression through associate certified coach (ACC), to professional certified coach (PCC) and on to master certified coach (MCC).

Coaching supervision, on the other hand, is a reflective practice that according to Hawkins and Smith (2013), has three elements:

1. Qualitative—adding an external perspective to their work with clients to ensure quality of practice.
2. Developmental—with elements of mentoring to develop their practice.
3. Resourcing—including gaps in the coaching training, or blind spots.

Hirsch Pontes (2024) has described supervision as "*a restorative space where we can reflect about our work in an extremely meaningful relationship.*"

Hullinger and DiGirolamo (2020) have argued that supervision is one way that coaches can maintain and develop their skills. It provides space for robust reflective practice, offers a broader opportunity for support ensuring the work of the coach practitioner is professional and ethical, and offers developmental insights in the way the coach works with clients.

Supervision is critical for team coaches due to the complexity of the work and ease with which a team coach can get entangled in the dynamics of the team or the broader system(s) in which the team operates and exists.

Examples of topics a team coach may bring in supervision include:

– To handle the complexity of multiple contracts: the sponsor, the team, the team members, the team leader, the co-coach.
– Ethical dilemmas that arise.
– Toxic dynamics or dysfunctional patterns observed within the team.
– Own confidence of the team coach.
– Feeling or being stuck.

When we read this supplementary, one key phrase we notice is *"when needed"* and not "if"; hence the ability of the team coach to recognize these moments—cases or topics—and work on them with the supervisor.

Gillian Walter (2023) gave the following idea of practice to help the team coach practitioner decide when such moment are worth bringing to supervision:

• Before a team coaching session, check in with yourself. Actually observe what is already there, in your mind, in your physical body, and in your thoughts.
• After the team coaching session, check in again and notice if anything new is there, or if something has changed.
• Take notes of your observations. For instance, there might be a new emotion, a tightness or shift in body sensation, a new thought or looping narrative. This is neither good, nor bad; it is simply data for reflection and exploration.

Reflecting back to the words *"support, development, and accountability,"* we can recognize them in the six common themes that Turner and Palmer (2019) have identified in the many definitions of supervision:

Support by:

• Providing fresh perspectives
• Being a place to resource the team coach
• Interconnecting relationships, involving systemic work

Development by:

• Attending to how team coaches develop personally and professionally
• Growing high levels of self-awareness

Accountability by:

• Attending to quality and safe practice

Taking under consideration the complexities of team coaching, we would say that coaching supervision is a practice that the team coach should consider adding to their ongoing support and development structures, which is also reflected in the requirements for the ICF Advanced Certification in Team Coaching.

Chapter 28 explores further what supervision is, how it works in practice, how to find a suitable supervisor, and how to get the best out of supervision.

Remains Objective and Aware of Team Dynamics and Patterns

The ICF Team Coaching Supplementary Background Explanation

Teams are made up of individuals who have unique personalities, knowledge, skills, and motivations. The combination of these individuals working together will bring about many dynamics of power, control, expertise, and disparate goals. The team coach must be aware of and alert to how these dynamics might play out in team interactions, the team's agenda, internal disputes, beliefs, alliances, and must remain objective at all times.

Kanelidou (2023) names three main challenges of this supplementary:

1. To have knowledge and understand team dynamics
2. To be able to recognize these dynamics and their patterns
3. To remain objective at all times

One of the key themes in Team Coaching is its complexity. An example that can reflect this complexity has to do with the multiple relationships that bring their own dynamics.

Relationships inside the team include:

– coach–team
– coach–team leader
– coach–team member
– coach–co-coach
– team leader–team
– team leader–team member
– team leader–co-coach
– team member–team
– team member–team member
– team member–co-coach
– co-coach–team

In addition to the above stated dynamics, are the relationships that the team has with others outside of the immediate team across the wider systems inside and outside the organization. This will include other teams, departments, sites, and extends to shareholders, customers and service users, the media, government, regulators and stakeholders. These systemic relationships can consciously, and unconsciously, impact the dynamics of the team inside the sessions.

But what exactly is "team dynamics" in the context of team coaching? Team dynamics refers to the behavioral relationships between the members of a team: How a team interacts, communicates, and works together. How the members make decisions, manage conflict, their alignment and other interactions. Understanding a team's dynamics can alert the team coach as to how the team can progress towards their goals.

Douglas (1995) refers to three factors on how a group progresses to achieve their goals, which can apply to teams:

1. The nature of the ways in which team members interact with each other: It includes participation, cohesiveness, value system, leadership, and the team's internal structure.
2. The relationship of the team to larger teams of which it is part of: The organization in which the team belongs, another team of the organization, or society at large. How the larger team influences and pressures the team, and the impact on a team's behavior and performance.
3. The psychological structure of the team: How much the team members like each other, their commitment, sense of belonging, of rewarding, team members' roles, and the team's rules.

Team dynamics can be positive. The members will work together more effectively, and the team coach will observe behaviors such as:

• Respectful debates even when they disagree
• Contribution by all
• Increased self-awareness
• Appreciation of their diversity and inclusion
• Taking initiatives and admitting mistakes
• Generously and transparently sharing ideas, resources, and knowledge
• Asking for help

Overall, the team coach will observe behaviors and ways of interaction that support the progress of the team.

Team dynamics can also be negative. Some patterns that can be observed in such case are:

• Not speaking openly
• Scapegoating
• Transferring blame
• Cliques and favoritism
• Subgroups, in and out groups, alliances
• Exclusion of subgroups or team members
• Social loathing
• Mirroring, show us what we want to see
• Projections
• Unresolved conflict
• Emotional closure

- Power struggles
- Anxieties (for performance, acceptance, etc.)
- Defensive forms
- Competition for status, and more

A significant reference here is that when we have a team of coaches—in the case of co-coaching—this team comes with its own dynamics, which can impact the dynamics of the entire team, for example, by modeling effective communication.

How a team coach can improve the ability to observe and remain objective to team dynamics
- Prepare; check your own intentions
- Practice mindfulness; observe the self in the moment
- Not to entangle; stay responsive to observed behaviors instead of reactive
- Observe how decisions are achieved. Have all members contributed ideas?
- Suspend judgement and consider all behaviors and patterns observed as data for team awareness
- Take unresolved issues to supervision
- Manage your own energy and engage in self-care
- Choose the co-coach wisely to balance dynamics and/or to help observe the room

Some questions for the team coach to reflect on, as they develop their skills on this supplementary:

- What dynamics have you met in a team that were the most challenging for you?
- What is your biggest challenge as a team coach to remain objective and aware of team dynamics and patterns?
- Can you as the coach of a team compromise their dynamics? How?

Chapter 26 delves deeper into some of the dynamics experienced in teams and between teams, examples of how they can manifest and ideas on how a team coach can best remain objective.

Conclusion

Team coaches need to embody a coaching mindset. In doing so they also need to recognize how the mindset for team coaching differs from one-to-one coaching. It is more complex, dynamic, and more systemic, requiring both greater flexibility and greater support during the coaching assignment.

Chapter 8
Establishes and Maintains Agreements (Competency 3)

Introduction

Within the Co-Creating the Relationship Domain, there are three competencies:

1. Establishes and Maintains Agreements
2. Cultivates Trust and Safety
3. Maintains Presence

These competencies relate to creating clear agreements for the coaching relationship, process, plan, and goals, along with how to create a safe and supportive environment to enable client growth and development.

Establishes and Maintains Agreements is the third ICF competency and the first in the Co-Creating the Relationship Domain. The competency is defined and described in Box 8.1 and has been reviewed in detail by Passmore and Sinclair (2024).

The ICF Core Competencies form the foundation of the team coaching competencies. In addition, to be an effective team coach practitioner further supplementary have been developed. The three additional supplementary are shown in Box 8.2 and explained further below:

© The Author(s), under exclusive license to Springer Nature
Switzerland AG 2024
J. Passmore et al., *Becoming a Team Coach*,
https://doi.org/10.1007/978-3-031-63546-5_8

Box 8.1 Establishes and Maintains Agreements
Definition: Partners with the client and relevant stakeholders to create clear agreements about the coaching relationship, process, plans, and goals. Establishes agreements for the overall coaching engagement as well as those for each coaching session.

1. Explains what coaching is and is not and describes the process to the client and relevant stakeholders
2. Reaches agreement about what is and is not appropriate in the relationship, what is and is not being offered, and the responsibilities of the client and relevant stakeholders
3. Reaches agreement about the guidelines and specific parameters of the coaching relationship such as logistics, fees, scheduling, duration, termination, confidentiality, and inclusion of others
4. Partners with the client and relevant stakeholders to establish an overall coaching plan and goals
5. Partners with the client to determine client–coach compatibility
6. Partners with the client to identify or reconfirm what they want to accomplish in the session
7. Partners with the client to define what the client believes they need to address or resolve to achieve what they want to accomplish in the session
8. Partners with the client to define or reconfirm measures of success for what the client wants to accomplish in the coaching engagement or individual session
9. Partners with the client to manage the time and focus of the session
10. Continues coaching in the direction of the client's desired outcome unless the client indicates otherwise
11. Partners with the client to end the coaching relationship in a way that honors the experience

Box 8.2 Team Coach Supplementary Competencies—Establishes and Maintains Agreements
(a) Explains what team coaching is and is not, including how it differs from other team development modalities
(b) Partners with all relevant parties, including the team leader, team members, stakeholders, and any co-coaches to collaboratively create clear agreements about the coaching relationship, processes, plans, development modalities, and goals
(c) Partners with the team leader to determine how ownership of the coaching process will be shared among the coach, leader, and team

Team Coach Supplementary Competencies

Explains What Team Coaching Is and Is Not, Including How It Differs from Other Team Development Modalities

The ICF Team Coaching Supplementary Competencies Background Explanation for the Competency

It is important for the team coach to highlight the difference between team coaching and other team development modalities. Given the unique nature of individuals' personalities, teams may need to be very intentional about the process to determine team and team coach compatibility.

What Does this Mean in Practice?

In our work as team coaches and team coach educators, we find time and time again, much confusion for both clients and coaches about what team coaching is. In Table 5.3, we outlined the key differences between the different types of team intervention. Some valuable points to explain to clients can be:

- What is team coaching?
- How does team coaching differ from team building, team facilitation, group coaching, team training, etc.?
- What is the benefit of a team coaching approach?
- What is the role of the team coach?

What Is Team Coaching?

Definitions of team coaching express the importance of teams having a common goal, group collaboration and performance (Thornton, 2010), increasing collective capability (Clutterbuck, 2014; Jones et al., 2019) and discuss the need for teams to think about the wider system in which they operate (Hawkins, 2011). Team coaching is defined by Widdowson and Barbour (2021) as follows:

Team coaching helps teams work together, with others and within their wider environment, to create lasting change by developing safe and trusting relationships, better ways of working and new thinking so that they maximise their collective potential, purpose and performance goals. (Widdowson & Barbour, 2021, p. 8)

Key areas to emphasize within this definition are:

- Team coaching—a coaching approach is at the heart of team coaching, with the ownership for change and action being in the hands of the client.

- Team working together, with others and the wider system—this recognizes that teams do not operate in isolation; they are part of the internal and external system in which they exist.
- Create lasting change—team coaching usually involves a series of interventions (Jones et al., 2019) rather than one-off events.
- Safe and trusting relationships—building psychological safety and connection in teams will enable team members to feel comfortable to contribute and challenge.
- Better ways of working—the team coach will help the team become aware of how the team works both together and within the wider organization and may, for example, look to improve this through better decision-making, improving processes and meetings.
- New thinking—through creating a safe space, team members can feel free to explore new ideas, share diversity of thought and differences, pay attention to their well-being, and learn and grow together.
- Maximize their collective potential purpose and performance goals—helping the team to explore what is the work that only the team can do together that they cannot do apart and what is the output needed from them.

How Does Team Coaching Differ from Team Building, Team Facilitation, Group Coaching, Team Training, Etc.?

As a relatively new specialism within coaching, it is hardly surprising that debate continues to exist about the nature and focus of team coaching, its boundaries and its practice. One might argue that such debate reflects the live, creative, and current nature of an emerging profession.

How Do You Decide Whether to Work with a Client?

Many factors may be considered when deciding as a team coach if you should work with a client. These may include:

- Is the sector of interest to you or one where you feel comfortable to add value?
- How aligned is the cultural fit to your ethics as a team coach?
- Are the values of the team and organization aligned with your own?
- How was the chemistry between you and the client?
- Is the team ready and open to making a change?

Researching and exploring these before and during the client meeting is essential to establish if the work is the right fit for you as a team coach.

Partners with All Relevant Parties, Including the Team Leader, Team Members, Stakeholders, and Any Co-Coaches to Collaboratively Create Clear Agreements About the Coaching Relationship, Processes, Plans, Development Modalities, and Goals

The ICF Team Coaching Supplementary Competencies Background Explanation for the Competency

> The team coaching agreement must be agreeable to all parties, including the individual team members and the co-coach, when working with one, as well as sponsors, as appropriate. Confidentiality regarding what takes place in team coaching sessions should be addressed, as well as private discussions between the team coach and individual team members. It is also important to consider the role and extent to which the organization's culture, mission, and overall context influences the team coaching engagement.

How Do You Contract?

Team coaching is multi-dimensional and can be complex as it involves dealing with many different stakeholders, including:

- Team members
- Team leader
- Stakeholders
- Team commissioner or sponsor
- Team coach partner

We get asked by team coaches, "How do I know who are the key stakeholders for the team and who is the team commissioner?" Invariably, stakeholders will be the internal and external stakeholders that the team interfaces with; for example, customers, companies they partner with, and other organizational functions. The team commissioner or sponsor commissions the team's work; this could be the budget holder and often the team leader's line manager. It is important to discover who are all the key stakeholders in the first contracting conversations with the team leader.

Contracting, as in one-to-one coaching, is an essential aspect of team coaching at the start of a team coaching intervention and throughout the whole journey. Our experience as team coach practitioners and trainers is that failing to contract thoroughly and recontract can be a recipe for disaster in team coaching. Team coaching is complex, often involving many team members with unique personality preferences, styles, and objectives. Our perception therefore, of how a session is going may not always be the reality for the team. Asking questions to explore the teams' perceptions is therefore critical, for example:

- How useful/valuable is this work?
- What are the most important areas for you to explore as a team?

- What questions do you need to explore that have not yet been discussed?
- What is working/not working right now?
- What would you like more of or less of?

You have the added dimension of working with a team coach partner in team coaching. We will look at this key relationship in more depth in Chap. 24. However, it is crucial to mention the need to discuss and agree on how you will work together before, during, and after the team coaching intervention. Areas you may want to discuss with your team coach partner will include:

- How will you work together in an equitable way as partners?
- How do you swap the roles of lead and observer during the intervention?
- How will you recontract together if a change of direction is needed for the team?
- How will you allocate roles and responsibilities, e.g. design of the interventions, meetings, and pre- and post-calls with the team leader?
- What behaviors will help you work most effectively together?
- How will you manage different styles, approaches, or opinions?
- How will you have open and honest conversations?

You will be role modeling being a team together, providing rich data for the team about how effective teams work together in practice.

Understanding How to Contract: A Few Areas to Consider When Contracting for Team Coaching

Establishing Clear Agreements at the Beginning of the Team Coaching Journey

Contracting will take many forms in team coaching, as discussed with multiple stakeholders. Before beginning a team coaching journey, there may be a number of ways to contract with the team, including:

- One-to-one meetings to agree on objectives, discuss the approach and roles during the journey.
- One-to-one diagnostic interviews—to find out from the team, team leader, and any other key stakeholders what is working well in the team and what could be improved.
- Team 360 diagnostic questionnaire—to discover how effective the team is against key characteristics of high-performing teams.

One-to-One Meetings

One-to-one meetings aim to understand the objectives for the session, discuss the approach, and agree on roles within the team coaching session. The one-to-one meetings provide an opportunity to contract with the team leader, the team, and other stakeholders about confidentiality, how you will work together, the team coaching approach, how this differs from other types of team intervention, and what you will expect from each other. Exploring the organizational culture and context during these meetings will enable the team coach to understand how these may influence the team coaching engagement. For example, if the culture is very reactive, then the team coach may want to consider how they will contract with the team leader and team to ensure that team coaching sessions are committed to and upheld.

One-to-One Diagnostic Interviews

In most cases, before any team coaching intervention, the team coach will likely have a phase of diagnosis where they will hold one-to-one interviews with the team leader, team members, and other stakeholders. It is essential to contract at the start of one-to-one interviews regarding confidentiality. To create a feeling of psychological safety, the team coach will need to stress that the discussions are confidential. Where the agreement is for verbatim comments to be used, the team coach will need to be clear that comments are included anonymously, and where a comment could be attributed to the interviewee that they agree on how that will be captured. Alternatively, interview themes may be summarized instead of verbatim comments. With key themes, the team coach will contract that comments will only be shown as a theme if they appear across multiple interviews.

Team 360 Diagnostic

A team diagnostic can provide valuable data about what works well within the team and areas they want to improve. A team 360 has the added benefit of giving feedback from different stakeholder groups, including the team commissioner, stakeholders, and direct reports of the team members and the team itself. Contracting with the team leader and team about when and how you will use a team 360 is critical in your meetings with the team leader.

Partners with the Team Leader to Determine How Ownership of the Coaching Process Will Be Shared Among the Coach, Leader, and Team

The ICF Team Coaching Supplementary Competencies Background Explanation for the Competency

One of the purposes of team coaching is to help build a sustainable team that does not require the presence of the coach to maintain forward momentum. While the team coaching process may initially be directed by the coach, agreement should be reached as to how the ownership is gradually turned over to the team leader and the team as a collective.

How to Contract Around Ownership of the Team Coaching Process?

There are a number of opportunities during the team coaching engagement to contract around ownership of the team coaching process, including:

- At the start of the program, during one-to-one meetings
- When working with the team and contracting and re-contracting during the sessions
- At pre- and post-meetings with the team leader

Start of the Program

The one-to-one meetings conducted before a team coaching engagement are an important time to explain what team coaching is and what it is not. This provides the ideal opportunity to discuss the role of the team leader and team during the team coaching engagement and how the ownership of the process and dialogue within the team will shift to the team leader and team as the team coaching engagement progresses.

It is helpful to discuss with the team leader how they will show up during the team coaching sessions. To work with the team as a single entity, it is key that the team leader is present in the sessions as one of the team rather than their usual role as the leader, where the team may look to or defer to them for the decision-making. This will help to develop the concept of distributed leadership among the team, with all team members taking ownership and accountability for the progress and actions of the team.

During Team Coaching Sessions

The start of a team coaching session will usually include a session to discuss how the team wants to work together and what the team coach and team want from each other. A team coach will also want to agree on what is in and out of scope for the team coaching session. For example, often we find teams request that the team coach challenge them by highlighting unhelpful behaviors, asking challenging questions, etc. This provides the opportunity for the team coach to say that they can challenge; however, their role is to help create a safe space so the team can have those open, honest, and challenging conversations for themselves. If the ownership of these conversations shifts more to the team, then their work will be more sustainable than the team coach taking ownership.

Clutterbuck (2007) suggests that the difference between team facilitation and team coaching is that team facilitation is about the team coach pulling the dialogue out from the team, in contrast to team coaching where the team owns the dialogue.

At Pre- and Post-Meetings with the Team Leader

Meetings held with the team leader before and after a team coaching session are ideal for reviewing ownership of the team coaching process. The conversation may include what role the team leader adopts during the session, progress against personal and team commitments for the team members, and explore any obstacles to the team taking ownership of actions and next steps.

Conclusion

Contracting and re contracting in coaching are essential. However, it can be argued that it is even more important for team coaching. With the complexity of multiple stakeholders and, at times, with different objectives, it is critical to agree on roles and responsibilities, objectives, outcomes, and the approach to the team coaching engagement.

Chapter 9
Cultivates Trust and Safety (Competency 4)

Introduction

Within the Co-Creating the Relationship Domain there are three competencies:

1. Establishes and Maintains Agreements
2. Cultivates Trust and Safety
3. Maintains Presence

Cultivates Trust and Safety is the fourth ICF Core Competency, and the second of the Co-Creating the Relationship Domain. The competency is defined and described in Box 9.1 and has been reviewed in detail by Passmore and Sinclair (2024).

> **Box 9.1 Cultivates Trust and Safety**
> Definition: Partners with the client to create a safe, supportive environment that allows the client to share freely. Maintains a relationship of mutual respect and trust.
>
> 1. Seeks to understand the client within their context which may include their identity, environment, experiences, values, and beliefs
> 2. Demonstrates respect for the client's identity, perceptions, style, and language and adapts one's coaching to the client
> 3. Acknowledges and respects the client's unique talents, insights, and work in the coaching process
> 4. Shows support, empathy, and concern for the client
> 5. Acknowledges and supports the client's expression of feelings, perceptions, concerns, beliefs, and suggestions
> 6. Demonstrates openness and transparency as a way to display vulnerability and build trust with the client

© The Author(s), under exclusive license to Springer Nature
Switzerland AG 2024
J. Passmore et al., *Becoming a Team Coach*,
https://doi.org/10.1007/978-3-031-63546-5_9

In addition to these, the team coach practitioner must demonstrate the supplementary competencies described in Box 9.2.

> **Box 9.2 Team Coach Supplementary Competencies—Cultivates Trust and Safety**
> (a) Creates and maintains a safe space for open and honest team member interaction
> (b) Promotes the team viewing itself as a single entity with a common identity
> (c) Fosters expression of individual team members' and the collective team's feelings, perceptions, concerns, beliefs, hopes, and suggestions
> (d) Encourages participation and contribution by all team members
> (e) Partners with the team to develop, maintain, and reflect on team rules and norms
> (f) Promotes effective communication within the team
> (g) Partners with the team to identify and resolve internal conflict

Team Coach Supplementary Competencies

Creates and Maintains a Safe Space for Open and Honest Team Member Interaction

The ICF Team Coaching Supplementary Competency Background Explanation

> In order for each team member to participate freely and meaningfully, the team coach must build a safe space within which each team member feels free to disagree with teammates or raise sensitive topics. When working with an individual client, the coach is aware and respectful of the client's cultural context. In team coaching the team may have its own culture, which is a variant of the organization's culture and may add an additional layer of complexity to the engagement.

One key element of this competency is the ability of the coach to create psychological safety.

Psychological safety is the foundation of healthy relationships; it is about establishing trust and feeling safe to be vulnerable. In the case of Team Coaching psychological safety means that team members feel secure enough to share thoughts and ideas without worrying about negative consequences or how they are perceived.

According to Edmonson (2020), the most common misconception is that psychological safety is about being nice, whereas it is about being and helping others be vulnerable. It is about being respectful and confident in being open.

Clark (2020) defines four stages of psychological safety:

1. Inclusion safety
2. Learners safety

3. Contributor safety
4. Challenger safety

Although the first stage allows team members to feel connected and included, it is at the fourth level that teams start to openly explore the difficult questions, provide ideas, dare to raise sensitive topics, and manage disagreements constructively.

What does that mean for the team coach, and how do they create this environment?

The first step is to have a strong sense of how the team coach shows up (McCann, 2021). Is the team coach themself open and vulnerable? How do they demonstrate a "commitment to openness" (Solomon & Flores, 2001)?

Promotes the Team Viewing Itself as a Single Entity with a Common Identity

The ICF Team Coaching Supplementary Competency Background Explanation

> An element of team sustainability is the perspective of each member that the team is a single, high-performing unit. The team coach should consistently promote team identity and self-sufficiency.

One of the first things the team coach will do when starting sessions with a team is contracting and that is exactly where the team coach starts promoting the team as a single entity: while the team, team members and coach(es) co-create the contract.

One model that can be used is the contracting model of Transactional Analysis. Berne (1966) describes three levels of contracting:

- Administrative contract—In team coaching, this is the agreement on any administrative aspects of the coaching assignment, e.g. where the sessions will take place, and it is usually addressed before the sessions begin.
- Professional contract—This refers to the purpose of the team coaching, what are the roles in this process.
- Psychological contract—This is where the team coach opens the conversation about expectations and hopes, but also concerns and fears.

The level that is of utmost interest in this supplementary competency is the second, where the team co-creates its purpose. When team members start co-creating this level, the sense of a common identity begins to form and team members start seeing themselves as members of an entity, sharing an agreed upon purpose, vision, beliefs, and values. The identity of the team is not its purpose. For McLeod (2000), it includes a set of manifestations, values, and beliefs. It involves adjusting to the needs of the team, creating a shared purpose across the organization, and alignment of what the team exists to deliver. The task of the team coach to promote the team perceiving itself as a single entity does not end with a single contracting activity, it is ongoing throughout the entire work of the coach with the team.

Fosters Expression of Individual Team Members' and the Collective Team's Feelings, Perceptions, Concerns, Beliefs, Hopes, and Suggestions

The ICF Team Coaching Supplementary Competency Background Explanation

> The team coach may need to encourage team members to speak freely in team meetings to share their individual feelings, perceptions, concerns, beliefs, hopes, and suggestions. It is also important for the coach to understand and clarify the collective feelings, perceptions, concerns, beliefs, and hopes of the team.

During the third level of contracting—the psychological contract—team members are already invited to share their personal feelings, concerns, hopes, and more. The team coach gives space for both the individual and the collective: expectations and fears that collectively the team has. During this critical part, team members will start to experience sharing and being heard with acceptance, acknowledgement, even curiosity and care, and no judgment. This is a door that the team coach needs to open and give the opportunity, while simultaneously, explore with the team which ones are only individual and which ones are similarly collective—or the opposite. Same as the previous supplementary, this does not end with contracting, but rather is ongoing throughout the entire team coaching.

Encourages Participation and Contribution by All Team Members

The ICF Team Coaching Supplementary Background Explanation

> It is important to get the full benefit from the knowledge and skill of each team member.

The invitation to participate and contribute starts with the contract, as the team coach invites all the team members to co-create it. This is done respectfully, acknowledging the preference of each team member, without forcing participation, hence the word "invitation." An easy way to introduce participation is by quick one-word check in and check out rounds at the beginning and at the end of each session. During sessions, techniques like conversational turn-taking, questions, and games can facilitate participation. Team coaches need also to remember that modeling their own vulnerability will contribute to the team's willingness to share. This may include acknowledging their own mistakes, expressing uncertainty and anxiety and demonstrating a willingness to experiment.

This supplementary competency is also connected with Competency 3 and more specifically team dynamics, as the team coach needs to stay alert of any dynamics that could prevent or indicate lack of participation and contribution by all members.

Partners with the Team to Develop, Maintain, and Reflect on Team Rules and Norms

The ICF Team Coaching Supplementary Competency Background Explanation

> Rules and norms can help teams to be more productive and perform at a higher level. Clarification and codification of these rules and norms can also help a team to be more self-sustainable.

Once again, the third level of contracting: The second part of this level is about the ground rules and norms. Simple questions, such as "what do we need from ourselves and others to feel safe?" or "What are the rules we would like to maintain throughout the coaching process to make it a positive experience?" can be utilized by the team coach to allow the team to co-create these rules and norms which will be present throughout the entire process. Furthermore, the team could use these rules and norms as a reference point when, for example, the team needs to hold difficult conversations, deal with difficult situations, or act as reminders for what is important. These agreed upon "rules of engagement" reflect what a safe space looks like for this specific team in a very concrete manner.

One common mistake is to abridge this last part rapidly because, for example, of fear of insufficient time, or because of the assumption that these rules are a given. Sometimes, some team members could react as if this is a waste of time. The fact is, if this level is not carefully completed, it could jeopardize the entire process. Additionally, these rules should be defined, agreed, and explained into specific behaviors, and when need be, the team can revert to them. These also shape the culture of the team.

Promotes Effective Communication Within the Team

The ICF Team Coaching Supplementary Competency Background Explanation

> Good communication amongst team members can often be challenging, however, a good flow of information is vital to team success. The team coach should ensure that communication from individual members of the team is directed to the team and consistently redirects communication within the team when it is directed to the coach.

With the team coaches modeling confident and effective communication, and the rules and norms of their interactions, communication included and agreed, the team coach can meaningfully redirect the flow of information from the members to the team. It has been observed in some teams that the team members may see the coach initially as an "authority" figure and direct their comments to the coach instead of the team. Simple techniques like returning the information to the team or creating a circle where eye contact is equally shared can help with a sense of equality through those participating in the session.

Partners with the Team to Identify and Resolve Internal Conflict

The ICF Team Coaching Supplementary Competency
Background Explanation

> It is inevitable that there will be some conflict within every team. It is important to bring conflict to the surface and deal with it in a constructive manner that promotes learning and growth.

One of the myths of psychological safety is that it is about the absence of conflict. But in fact, the best teams are not conflict free; they do not even have more conflicts. What they have is that they address conflict differently with respectful debates, candor, and transparency.

One obstacle here could be the need for control. Control can be considered actually as the opposite of trust in the context. Control of emotions, of reactions, of what might happen, etc.

Question for the team coach to ask oneself are:

– What as a team coach you might tend or be tempted to control?
– Where does this impulse or need for control come from?
– How do you overcome this need?

When the team coach feels more comfortable letting go of control, trusting oneself and the team to resolve a conflict, the team coach would be more confident to bring such conflict to the surface. In a safe space, team coaches understand that key skills to positively manage conflict include many factors, these include:

• Consider conflict resolution as an opportunity to learn from a difficult or challenging situation
• Communication and the ability to really listen
• Manage expectations and check assumptions
• Acknowledge, understand, and manage emotions
• Accept the inevitability of conflict and welcome the challenge to resolve it
• Help team members to better understand differences

Conclusion

Trust is a pragmatic actionable asset that we can create. It is a multidimensional construct and by starting to see, speak, and behave differently we will have an enormous impact on establishing and growing trust. The first challenge in building trust is the recognition that this needs to be built and make it a priority. Even having the best intentions is not enough. We consciously and intentionally develop and sustain trust and a safe environment for our team to develop and flourish.

Chapter 10
Maintains Presence (Competency 5)

Within the Co-Creating the Relationship Domain, there are three competencies:

1. Establishes and Maintains Agreements
2. Cultivates Trust and Safety
3. Maintains Presence

Maintains Presence is the fifth Core Competency and the third competency in the Co-Creating the Relationship Domain.

The competency is defined and described in Box 10.1 and has been reviewed in detail by Passmore and Sinclair (2024).

In addition to these, the team coach practitioner must demonstrate the supplementary competencies described in Box 10.2.

Box 10.1 Maintains Presence
Definition: Is fully conscious and present with the client, employing a style that is open, flexible, grounded, and confident.

1. Remains focused, observant, empathetic, and responsive to the client
2. Demonstrates curiosity during the coaching process
3. Manages one's emotions to stay present with the client
4. Demonstrates confidence in working with strong client emotions during the coaching process
5. Is comfortable working in a space of not knowing
6. Creates or allows space for silence, pause, or reflection

© The Author(s), under exclusive license to Springer Nature
Switzerland AG 2024
J. Passmore et al., *Becoming a Team Coach*,
https://doi.org/10.1007/978-3-031-63546-5_10

> **Box 10.2 Team Coach Supplementary Competencies—Maintains Presence**
> (a) Uses one's full range of sensory and perceptual abilities to focus on what is important to the coaching process
> (b) Uses a co-coach when agreed to by the team and sponsors and when doing so will allow the team coach to be more present in the team coaching session
> (c) Encourages team members to pause and reflect how they are interacting in team coaching sessions
> (d) Moves in and out of the team dialogue as appropriate

Team Coach Supplementary Competencies

Uses One's Full Range of Sensory and Perceptual Abilities to Focus on What Is Important to the Coaching Process

The ICF Team Coaching Competencies Background Explanation for the Supplementary Team Competency

> The team coach will often be overloaded with information, necessitating full sensory awareness and perception of what is happening in the room throughout the coaching engagement.

These pieces of information will come from various sources, including:

- The team members
- Interactions between the team members and team coaches
- The co-coaches
- The team and their connection to the wider environment and system

It is unsurprising then that team coaching is seen to be complex and challenging. Hawkins noted when talking about systemic team coaching that the coach is required to "focus on the multiple relationships of the team, both the internal relationship among team members and the external relationship between the team as a whole and their commissionaires, stakeholders and their future" (Hawkins, 2021, p. 107).

As team coaches, we need to be aware of what is happening in ourselves, our reactions, triggers, senses, and behaviors, as well as what we are sensing from the team and other sources. Paying attention to all of this information as a developing team coach can be overwhelming and exhausting at times.

A team coach's competencies are made up of three elements: knowing, doing, and being. Knowing relates to the team coach's knowledge of team coach models, frameworks, and group dynamics. Doing is about how the team coach applies their skills and knowledge (Widdowson & Barbour, 2021). Being derives from the seminal work of Rogers (1975) and refers to the team coach's ability to build empathy and relationships with others. To do this, Rogers proposed that the person has to be comfortable in their own self and can therefore focus on others and put their agenda aside. When working with a team, this can range from picking up signals regarding disagreements, difficult conversations the team needs to have, exploring what's not being said, when team members are experiencing anxiety, and when they attempt to scapegoat, turn their attack or challenge you as the team coach (Hawkins, 2021).

To explore this concept further, Widdowson and Barbour (2021) proposed the 4 C's of a team coach's way of being, including:

- Connection—the ability of the coach to connect at a deeper level with the team to build relationships and trust with the team and create a psychologically safe space.
- Courage—how the team coach raises difficult topics to challenge and support the team and help them have open and honest conversations.
- Confidence—is about the team coach being comfortable to be themselves, own their own story, and be willing to display their vulnerability, creating a container for the team to respond and share their vulnerability.
- Continuing—is the team coach's ability to be willing to learn, grow, develop, and appreciate that they will never be the finished article.

What does this mean for the team coach in practice? Through the team coach connecting with the team, showing their vulnerability, creating a safe space and role modeling challenge and support, the team will feel more able to be themselves and reciprocate among their team. This in turn, will provide more sensory information for the team coach.

What Senses Does the Team Coach Employ?

When team coaching, we are using our senses in a wider capacity. Hawkins (2021) referred to systemic team coaching as working not only with the whole brain, including the neo-cortex, the limbic and the amygdala "but also the sensing and knowing of the heart, the gut and the wider body" (Hawkins, 2021, p. 309).

Blake (2018) refers to listening deeply with all your senses to what others are saying and not saying and being attuned to your own sensations. As a result, sensory skills may include:

- Sight (vision)
- Hearing (auditory)
- Touch (tactile)
- Smell (olfactory)
- Taste (gustatory)
- Vestibular (movement—for balance and head position in space)
- Proprioception (body position—information from the muscles and joints)

The team coach can receive information from any of these senses. In practice, this means that the team coach will need to be conscious of the following:

- Noticing body language
- Non-verbal "vibes" in a team
- Be aware of their physiology and others—noticing breathing, heart rate, and physical signals such as twitches, fidgeting, facial expressions, eye contact or avoidance, any tension and sensations in their own body
- Feelings and emotions
- Tuning in to everyone in the team and the environment around you

Team coaches must listen attentively when working with a team and be fully present with every aspect of their antenna, fully alert to pick up as many signals as possible. Once again, this is where having a co-coach can help enormously.

Uses a Co-Coach When Agreed to by the Team and Sponsors and When Doing So Will Allow the Team Coach to Be More Present in the Team Coaching Session

The ICF Team Coaching Competencies Background Explanation for the Competency

> Working with a co-coach can take pressure off the singular team coach, given the significant amount of information emerging during team coaching sessions. A co-coach can help to observe team dynamics, team and individual behavior patterns, provide alternative perspectives, and model team behavior.

Working with a co-coach can add a valuable additional dimension to the work of the team coach, including:

- Enabling the team coach partners to be more observant of team dynamics and individual and team behavior patterns. This provides the opportunity for one team coach to hold the room while their team coach partner pays attention to observing the dynamics and behaviors
- Provide an additional perspective and view on the design of a team coaching program and how to flex the design in the moment when working with the team
- Allow more space for the team coaches to reflect and notice what is happening within the team
- Role modeling, being, and working as a team. As a team of two, the team coaches will model to the team how to collaborate, support, and challenge each other and leverage differences and diversity
- Share the workload and challenge of team coaching. As mentioned earlier in this chapter, team coaching can be exhausting therefore having two team coaches can help the team coaches manage their energy and ensure sufficient time for reflection and observation

Encourages Team Members to Pause and Reflect How They Are Interacting in Team Coaching Sessions

The ICF Team Coaching Competencies Background Explanation for the Competency

Encouraging team members to pause and reflect begins the reflective practice work for a team. The team coach can then follow through with raising awareness of their own actions, subsequent behaviors, and potential improvements in the moment or in future team interactions.

How Can the Team Coach Help Teams to Pause and Reflect?

When contracting with teams, we always ask, "What would you like from us as team coaches?" Invariably, teams ask us to "hold up the mirror" to share what we see happening in the team. This could be about helpful or unhelpful dynamics; patterns of behavior and helpful or unhelpful language used; and the impact on others in the team or their wider system. While we see this can be the role of the team coach initially, it is vital for the team coach to help the team become their own mirror. Techniques to help the team hold up the mirror and raise awareness of their own actions:

Pause and reflect—take opportunities to pause the team and ask them to reflect on their behaviors. Helpful questions could include:

- What is working well?
- What can you improve as a team?
- What specifically has helped the team to progress?
- What has got in the way?
- What behaviors have been helpful?
- What behaviors have been less helpful?

Share a metaphor to help the team become their own observers, for example, balcony and dance:

- Dancefloor to the balcony—explain that when the team are "doing their work," it is like them being on the dance floor. The team can move up to the balcony, look down on their work and observe what is happening (Innegraeve, 2023).

Moves In and Out of the Team Dialogue as Appropriate

The ICF Team Coaching Competencies Background Explanation for the Competency

Since one of the objectives of team coaching is for the team to become self-sufficient, the team coach should enter into the dialogue only as necessary to enhance the team process and performance. The team coach should be present for the team as a whole and simultaneously for each individual. This can be a challenge at moments of high intensity and when many team members are involved.

A key difference in team coaching compared to facilitation is enabling the team to take ownership of their own dialogue. Clutterbuck (2007) clearly stated that team coaching empowers the team to manage their own dialogue, whereas facilitation elicits the dialogue from the team. However, the ownership often stays with the facilitator.

How does the team coach know when to move into the dialogue?

Knowing when and how to move into the team dialogue can be challenging for a team coach. The team coach needs to be able to allow the team to control their own dialogue. While they are still responsible for holding the team, their role is to guide the team rather than control or push it to solve complex problems before they have ample time to discuss the issues (Hawkins, 2021). We discuss staying out of the dialogue further in Chap. 11, Listening Actively, so we will explore when to move in within this section.

What situations might the team coach move in:

- When the team are getting distracted from the question they want to answer or the decision to make
- If the team dialogue is circling for an extended period with team members stating different views however unable to come to any consensus
- To bring in the systemic perspective and enable the team to consider the needs of the wider system, e.g. their customers, stakeholders, the wider community, their own long-term needs, etc. (Hawkins, 2021).

How would the team coach move in?
Some interventions the team coach might use can include:

- Getting the team to hold up their own mirror, i.e. asking the team to become their own observers and reflect on the effectiveness of their conversation. Questions you might ask include: What are they noticing about the conversation?
- How is the dialogue helping you to answer the question or decision? What is getting in your way of answering question x?
- The team coach can also share their observations of what they are noticing in the team, e.g. what is helping them to come to a decision or answer the question and what is getting in the way?

- Bring the system into the room—ask team members to become the customers, stakeholders, etc., and ask them what they need from this team. What conversation do they need the team to have?
- Recontract with the team—where do they want to go now?

Conclusion

Knowing when to pause or move into the dialogue can sometimes be extremely hard for the team coach to read. The team coach must use all their sensory information to pick up the signals emitted from the team and the wider system to view the right time. They may not always get it right, but they will need to have the courage and willingness to be wrong. The support of the co-coach and supervisor here can help the team coach decide when to intervene, learn, and reflect on their experiences.

Chapter 11
Listens Actively (Competency 6)

Within the Communicating Effectively Domain there are two competencies:

1. Listens Actively
2. Evokes Awareness

Listens Actively is the sixth ICF Core Competency, and the first of the Communicating Effectively Domain. The competency is defined and described in Box 11.1 and has been reviewed in detail by Passmore and Sinclair (2024).

In addition to these, the team coach practitioner must demonstrate the supplementary competencies described in Box 11.2.

Box 11.1 Listens Actively
Definition: Focuses on what the client is and is not saying to fully understand what is being communicated in the context of the client systems and to support client self-expression.

1. Considers the client's context, identity, environment, experiences, values, and beliefs to enhance understanding of what the client is communicating
2. Reflects or summarizes what the client communicated to ensure clarity and understanding
3. Recognizes and inquires when there is more to what the client is communicating
4. Notices, acknowledges, and explores the client's emotions, energy shifts, non-verbal cues, or other behaviors
5. Integrates the client's words, tone of voice, and body language to determine the full meaning of what is being communicated
6. Notices trends in the client's behaviors and emotions across sessions to discern themes and patterns

---

© The Author(s), under exclusive license to Springer Nature
Switzerland AG 2024
J. Passmore et al., *Becoming a Team Coach*,
https://doi.org/10.1007/978-3-031-63546-5_11

> **Box 11.2 Team Coach Supplementary Competencies—Cultivates Trust and Safety**
>
> (a) Notices how the perspectives shared by each team member relate to other team members' views and the team dialogue.
> (b) Notices how each team member impacts the collective team energy, engagement, and focus.
> (c) Notices verbal and non-verbal communication patterns among team members to identify potential alliances, conflicts, and growth opportunities.
> (d) Models confident, effective communication and collaboration when working with a co-coach or other experts.
> (e) Encourages the team to own the dialogue.

Team Coach Supplementary Competencies

Notices How the Perspectives Shared by Each Team Member Relate to Other Team Members' Views and the Team Dialogue

The ICF Team Coaching Competencies Background Explanation for the Competency

> It is important for team members to listen and communicate well for shared understanding and subsequent high performance. Exploring below the surface of what is being said often allows a deeper meaning and understanding to emerge. This can help to resolve conflict and enhance innovation and problem-solving sessions.

We discussed the importance of a team coach listening within Chap. 10, Maintains Presence. From our experience working with teams, we find that this is a behavior and skill most teams need to develop.

How Can Teams Listen more Effectively?

One helpful framework to share with teams is the "Levels of Listening." There are many different versions. One example is Covey's five levels of listening (Covey, 2004):

1. Ignoring
2. Pretend listening
3. Selective listening
4. Attentive listening
5. Empathetic listening

1. Ignoring

The first of the five levels of listening is ignoring. At this level, team members are trying to avoid the conversation. This is also reflected in their body language as they look away or show disinterest.

2. Pretend listening

Pretend listening is when team members give the impression that they are listening by using their body language or cues while thinking about other matters. Needing to ask multiple follow-up questions or an inability to carry out a task can indicate that they have not been listening.

3. Selective listening

Team members' body language will look like they are actively listening. However, they may only absorb the parts of the conversation they are interested in and disregard the rest.

4. Attentive listening

Attentive listening involves team members concentrating and paying attention to what is being said. This is where their body language shows they are actively engaged and their responses are appropriate. Practicing attentive listening involves maintaining consistent eye contact, pondering the content, and paraphrasing the other's comments to ensure mutual understanding.

5. Empathetic listening

Listening with empathy involves being fully present when listening. At this level, we listen to understand the intent behind the message and respond appropriately. It requires the most mental and emotional energy because it requires us to focus entirely on the other team members using our ears, heart, and brain.

Sharing this with a team and then asking them to self-assess their level of listening can help create awareness for team members about what they need to do to fully listen in an empathetic style, with all their senses tuned to the speaker.

Encouraging the team to pause and reflect on their listening levels and creating a safe space to practice empathetic listening without interrupting, can help significantly improve the quality of their dialogue.

Notices How Each Team Member Impacts the Collective Team Energy, Engagement, and Focus

The ICF Team Coaching Competencies Background Explanation for the Competency

A team coach can greatly enhance team performance by bringing to light individual team member behaviors that add to and take away from team momentum, engagement, creativity, and focus.

This section will explore signals the team coach may want to pay attention to, indicating shifts in individual team members that can impact the team.

What Might the Team Coach Notice?

Signals in the Team

The team coach will use all their senses to pick up individual behaviors from the team members, as discussed in Chap. 10. The team coach will be tuned to the energy level of team members, including:

- Increases in positive energy and enthusiasm, e.g. more uplifted body language, voice tone, and intonation.
- Decreases in energy, e.g. lower body posture, lowering voice tone, less intonation in their voice, feeling of heaviness.
- Use of positive language, e.g. "This is exciting," "I am looking forward to x," "I feel we can achieve this," etc.
- Use of negative language, e.g. "I am stuck," "Don't know where we are going," "This isn't my thing," "I don't have any ideas," etc.

Signals in the Team Coach

When team coaching, the team coach is connected to the team and is a "resonance chamber for receiving the non-verbal communication, in body language, interpersonal contact and rhythms of voices" (Hawkins, 2021, p. 314). The team coach will therefore need to use all their senses and whole body when listening to notice what is happening in the team, including:

- Listening verbally and non-verbally to what is happening in the team at Level 5—Empathetic Listening
- Be aware of their own feelings and emotions; for example, if they have feelings of sadness or frustration, it is likely it is also present within the team
- Notice their own body, e.g. if they notice tension in their chest or swirliness in their stomach, be curious about where this is coming from

All of this information can provide valuable data for the team. It is helpful for the team coach to share what they notice and explore what this means for the team.

Notices Verbal and Non-verbal Communication Patterns Among Team Members to Identify Potential Alliances, Conflicts, and Growth Opportunities

The ICF Team Coaching Competencies Background Explanation for the Competency

> Observing, understanding, and enhancing team dynamics may be significant factors in improving team performance. Team coaches must be able to observe the subtlety of team dynamics evident from verbal and non-verbal communication.

Chapter 7, Supplementary Competency (b) Remains objective and aware of team dynamics and patterns, explored some of the positive and challenging behaviors a team coach may observe in teams. These range from positive dynamics, such as respectful debates, to negative dynamics, such as transferring blame and defensive behaviors. Chapter 27, Going Deeper on Team Dynamics, delves into more depth on dynamics that may be observed or present within teams and the wider system in which they operate.

Some helpful techniques that the team coach can share with the team to help the team manage dynamics include:

- Conversational turn-taking—each team member has the opportunity to share their view (Woolley et al., 2010).
- Time to Think—applying principles to team interaction, for example, each team member shares their view and is heard, and then the next team member acknowledges what they have said and builds on it. Allow team members to speak without interruption. Give permission to tell the truth. Allow people to share their feelings. End with appreciation for the meeting and each other (Kline, 1999)
- Reflecting individually before discussing as a team
- Team Emotional Intelligence—agree on norms and behaviors within the team, for example, agreed language for recognizing and acknowledging emotions (Druskat & Wolff, 2001)
- Observer position—ask the team to pause and take an observer position looking in on themselves in the team. Ask them to reflect on—what dynamics are helping the team, what dynamics are hindering the team, what they want to continue doing, and what they want to stop doing

As discussed earlier, the team coach needs to use all their senses and physiological reactions when listening to notice the hidden and unhidden dynamics in the team.

Models Confident, Effective Communication and Collaboration When Working with a Co-Coach or Other Experts

The ICF Team Coaching Competencies Background Explanation for the Competency

> Fluid communication amongst team members is essential for high performance. Team coaches can model this behavior when working with a co-coach and other experts.

We discussed working with a co-coach in Chap. 10 and will explore it further in Chap. 26, Best Practices for Co-Coaching a Team. As suggested, working in a team with a co-coach demonstrates how a team works effectively together and the challenges they may face. The co-coaches role model how to:

- Clearly contract together
- Support each other
- Manage disagreements or differences of opinion
- Challenge one another
- Leverage their strengths and build on their areas of development
- Manage different styles and approaches
- Communicate both verbally and non-verbally
- Have open and honest conversations
- Work in partnership with the team, stakeholders, and organization
- Consider the wider system

Encourages the Team to Own the Dialogue

The ICF Team Coaching Competencies Background Explanation for the Competency

> Team members may tend to direct communication to the team coach, especially at the beginning of team coaching engagements. To enhance sustainability, team coaches should consistently turn the dialogue inward, back to the team. Making choices as a team can be complex. Data may need to come from many team members, bringing the elements of trust and expertise into play. The team must decide how to process data and how to make decisions. Although helping a team to work through such issues may be more aligned with team facilitation, getting the team to become self-sufficient is a team coaching function.

How Does the Team Coach Help the Team Take Ownership of their Dialogue?

Several actions from the team coach can help to signal to the team that the ownership of the dialogue is moving to the team. This can include the team coach:

- Physically stepping away—a movement away from the team, even if slight, can consciously or unconsciously signal to the team that you are leaving the dialogue with them.
- Stopping asking questions and getting the team to ask each other questions.
- Staying silent—enabling the team to have a dialogue among themselves.
- Becoming invisible, for example, turning your camera off if working virtually. It is critical to contract for this and explain to the team that you will be present and observing; however, you will not participate in the conversation.
- Encouraging the team to look at each other instead of the coach, or look to other team members to encourage the team to do the same.

Conclusion

Listening is a crucial skill for a coach, and it is not surprising that it is also critical for a team coach. A team coach needs to be fully tuned in with all their senses to fully listen, observe, and pick up the many different dynamics, attitudes, beliefs, assumptions, and reactions in the team. The team coach also has a vital role as a "resonance chamber" for the team (Hawkins, 2021) where they notice their own reactions and explore with the team where they may have come from within the team's system.

Chapter 12
Evokes Awareness (Competency 7)

Within the Communicating Effectively Domain there are two competencies:

1. Listens Actively
2. Evokes Awareness

Evokes Awareness is the seventh ICF Core Competency, and the second of the Communicating Effectively Domain. The competency is defined and described in Box 12.1 and has been reviewed in detail by Passmore and Sinclair (2024).

Box 12.1 Evokes Awareness

Definition: Facilitates client insight and learning by using tools and techniques such as powerful questioning, silence, metaphor, or analogy

1. Considers client experience when deciding what might be most useful
2. Challenges the client as a way to evoke awareness or insight
3. Asks questions about the client, such as their way of thinking, values, needs, wants, and beliefs
4. Asks questions that help the client explore beyond current thinking
5. Invites the client to share more about their experience in the moment
6. Notices what is working to enhance client progress
7. Adjusts the coaching approach in response to the client's needs
8. Helps the client identify factors that influence current and future patterns of behavior, thinking, or emotion
9. Invites the client to generate ideas about how they can move forward and what they are willing or able to do
10. Supports the client in reframing perspectives
11. Shares observations, insights, and feelings, without attachment, that have the potential to create new learning for the client

---

J. Passmore et al., *Becoming a Team Coach*,
https://doi.org/10.1007/978-3-031-63546-5_12

In addition to these, the team coach practitioner must demonstrate the supplementary competencies described in Box 12.2.

> **Box 12.2 Team Coach Supplementary Competencies—Evokes Awareness**
> (a) Challenges the team's assumptions, behaviors, and meaning-making processes to enhance their collective awareness or insight
> (b) Uses questions and other techniques to foster team development and facilitate the team's ownership of their collective dialogue

Team Coach Supplementary Competencies

Challenges the Team's Assumptions, Behaviors, and Meaning-Making Processes to Enhance Their Collective Awareness or Insight

The ICF Team Coaching Supplementary Competency Background Explanation

A team composed of many individuals brings a multitude of assumptions, experiences, behaviors, and meaning-making processes to the collective effort. The diversity in these factors, if left unchecked, can lead to team dysfunction, but if harnessed properly, they can greatly enhance team performance.

Widdowson and Barbour (2021) argue that "for individuals, teams and organizations, awareness is not just a useful thing to do, it's a necessity." They present four key elements of developing team awareness:

– Team coach awareness
– Team awareness of group dynamics
– Team individual and collective awareness
– Team systemic awareness

We explore team (group) dynamics in Chaps. 7 and 26, supervision is one of the most powerful tools for the team coach's own awareness as we discuss in Chaps. 7 and 28, while Chaps. 14 and 27 present approaches for team systemic awareness.

This supplementary competency is more focused on the team and individual awareness and more specifically on the many layers of diversity that exist in any team. The better the team comprehends what's happening due to their diversity, and why, the more able they are to change it to make something new happen.

One of our favorite exercises to help the team become aware of their diversity and harness it properly is the iceberg. There are several ways to use the iceberg in team coaching, and we are going to explore two of these:

1. We ask the team to draw an iceberg taking into consideration that about one-tenth of the volume of an iceberg is above water. This iceberg represents a person. We then ask them to write inside the part of the iceberg above the waterline what is visible and below the waterline what is not visible. Although behaviors are above the waterline, assumptions, beliefs, values, learning and working preferences, experiences, history, invisible disabilities, and more are below the waterline. This simple exercise allows the team members to increase their awareness and understanding of each other and shift their diversity from a point of conflict and dysfunction to an asset for greater performance.

2. The second activity we can do with the team is the systems iceberg: We divide an iceberg into four levels:

   - The events are at the top level and above the waterline. This is regarding the behaviors, what the team can see. It includes their reactions and observable dysfunctions.
   - Right below the waterline is the pattern's level, what is happening over time.
   - Next below the waterline is what is causing these patterns to occur: the level of structures, which can include forces, norms, rules, mechanisms of the team, etc.
   - The mental models are the last level at the bottom of the iceberg. This is about the beliefs, values, thoughts, world views that create the structures.

The team explores their individual and collective mental models, become aware of their assumptions, gain awareness of their many processes, and can innovate and perform towards their desired direction.

Other methods the team coach can use to create awareness include one-to-one interviews with team members, stakeholders and direct reports of the team, Team 360's and psychometric tools and assessments. The team coach can use many assessments, and psychological and psychometric tests to support a team and its members in building awareness. Based on the ethical guidelines and best practices in testing by Allworth and Passmore (2008), some factors the team coach should keep in mind when selecting an assessment/test are:

- They should be evidence-based and ideally scientifically researched.
- The coach should be certified and/or competent in using the assessment with a team.
- Respect confidentiality of the team members and inform them how the information is going to be used/processed.
- Chosen assessment should be relevant to each team/case and the desired awareness that needs to transpire.
- Avoid labels. Assessments are not meant to put team members in a box, attach labels, or characterize; they are meant to facilitate reflection on preferences, needs, traits, capabilities, and understand with that context their behaviors and how to collaborate best.

Lastly, the team coach can change channels of communication from verbal to non-verbal with somatic or art-inspired exercises to evoke awareness. For example, team members can express their values through drawings, or physically place themselves in the space when holding a certain belief and observe the distance of the members from each other, the impact on the team as a whole, and share insights on their relational awareness.

Uses Questions and Other Techniques to Foster Team Development and Facilitate the Team's Ownership of Their Collective Dialogue

The ICF Team Coaching Supplementary Background Explanation

Just as in one-to-one coaching, questions and other techniques should be used to enhance team development, but in team coaching the work should also foster internal team dialogue and processing.

Crafting Coaching Questions

Working in and with teams often offers unique opportunities to consider multiple perspectives and expertise. Yet, it may pose a relational challenge when the team members may lack a coherent shared meaning of their desired directions, preferred possibilities, and a sense of progress.

Moon (2023) has developed a useful tool for teams to encourage safe and appreciative dialogue called Dialogic Orientation Quadrant (DOQ). The quadrant (Fig. 12.1) offers two intersecting continuums of timeline and preference in narratives, leading to four quadrants:

- Quadrant 1 (Upper-right): Preferred Future
- Quadrant 2 (Upper-left): Resourceful Past
- Quadrant 3 (Bottom-left): Troubled Past
- Quadrant 4 (Bottom-right): Dreaded Future

By sharing the framework with the team and encouraging focus on future-oriented and solution-oriented questions greater progress can be made in relationship and issue resolution.

Another tool that highlights future-focused questions is Reitz's (2019) Questioning Strategy Quadrant (Fig. 12.2). The quadrant divides the questions based on whose understanding they are seeking: the coach's or the client's; and if they are focused on the symptom (past) or the cause (future), leading to four quadrants:

- Quadrant 1 (green, upper-right): about the client's understanding and focused on the cause
- Quadrant 2 (yellow, upper-left): about the client's understanding but focused on the symptom

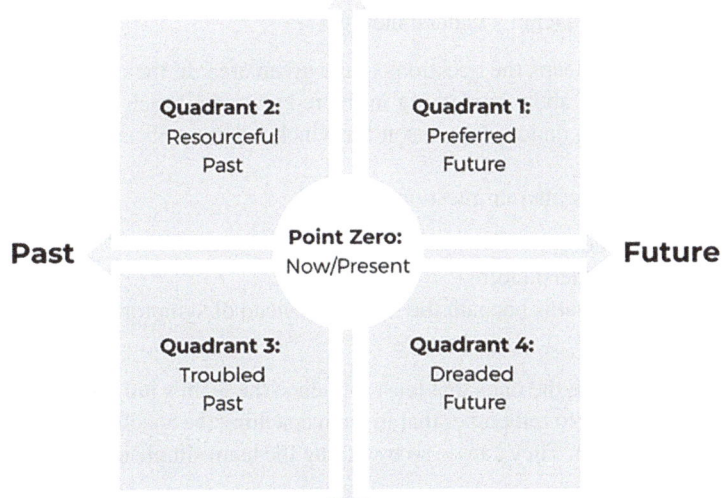

Fig. 12.1 Dialogic Orientation Quadrant (DOQ) (Used with permission of Haesun Moon, 2023)

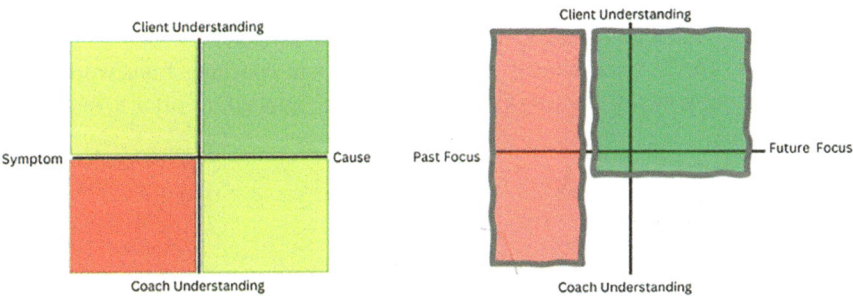

Fig. 12.2 Questioning Strategy Quadrant (Used with permission of Reitz, 2019)

- Quadrant 3 (yellow, bottom-left): focused on the cause but about coach's understanding
- Quadrant 4 (red, bottom-right): about coach's understanding and focused on the symptom

  Reitz (2019) suggests the following criteria for the coach's question:

- Move the team forward.
- Have a future focus. What is in the future that the team can pursue?
- Focus on building a team's understanding.

Ideally the coach keeps the questions in the green area. In the case that the team keeps wanting to talk about something in the red area, the coach can explore with the team if there is an underlying reason for which team members bring this to the conversation.

Summarizing, we want our questions to:

- Be future-oriented
- Strive for team understanding
- Explore causes/what is beneath the surface, instead of symptoms
- Be clean

Clean questions are the ones that least influence the team's judgment.

It is also important to remember that in team coaching the coach wants to pull the dialogue into the team. They can do so by asking the team simple questions such as:

- What questions do you want to ask about x? [the topic at hand]
- What is important to you here?

While in individual coaching, the coach usually holds the mirror to the client, in team coaching the coach wants the team to hold their own mirror, take ownership, and have the dialogue between themselves.

In Chap. 22, we share more coaching tools as useful resources that the team coach can integrate into their practice to support team awareness.

In Chaps. 16–20 we explore five well-known team coaching frameworks and models sharing how the frameworks/models may be applied, to offer a variety of perspectives.

Conclusion

Great questions can evoke awareness within individuals and across the team, deepening personal self-awareness and appreciation of others, and developing the team's understanding and empathy.

Chapter 13
Facilitates Client Growth (Competency 8)

The fourth and final domain, Cultivates Learning and Growth, contains one competency:

1. Facilitates Client Growth

Facilitates Client Growth is the eighth ICF Core Competency. The competency is defined and described in Box 13.1 and has been reviewed in detail by Passmore and Sinclair (2024).

In addition to these, the team coach practitioner must demonstrate the supplementary competencies described in Box 13.2.

> **Box 13.1 Facilitates Client Growth**
> Definition: Partners with the client to transform learning and insight into action. Promotes client autonomy in the coaching process.
>
> 1. Works with the client to integrate new awareness, insight, or learning into their worldview and behaviors
> 2. Partners with the client to design goals, actions, and accountability measures that integrate and expand new learning
> 3. Acknowledges and supports client autonomy in the design of goals, actions, and methods of accountability
> 4. Supports the client in identifying potential results or learning from identified action steps
> 5. Invites the client to consider how to move forward, including resources, support and potential barriers
> 6. Partners with the client to summarize learning and insight within or between sessions
> 7. Celebrates the client's progress and successes
> 8. Partners with the client to close the session

J. Passmore et al., *Becoming a Team Coach*, https://doi.org/10.1007/978-3-031-63546-5_13

> **Box 13.2 Team Coach Supplementary Competencies—Evokes Awareness**
> (a) Encourages dialogue and reflection to help the team identify their goals and the steps to achieve those goals.

Team Coach Supplementary Competencies

Encourages Dialogue and Reflection to Help the Team Identify their Goals and the Steps to Achieve those Goals

The ICF Team Coaching Competencies Background Explanation for the Competency

> Team dialogue and reflection is essential in order to take full advantage of all team members' knowledge and skills. Encouraging full participation helps to identify appropriate goals to maximize team performance.

Gaining the involvement and input of team members during team coaching is crucial to ensure they feel they have ownership of the team coaching journey and the outcomes. There are several ways to ensure team members have the opportunity to share their views and gain buy-in to the process and the work of the team:

- Pre-team coaching during one-to-ones and the team 360 questionnaire
- Contracting and recontracting during the sessions
- During sessions when team members contribute
- At the close of sessions, when agreeing team and personal commitments
- Gaining views of team members during review of progress and evaluation of outcomes

Pre-Team Coaching

One-to-one interviews with team members provide a safe and confidential space for them to share their views regarding what is working well and can be improved in the team. Questions to help team members consider the part they play in the outcomes of the team coaching program will also be important, for example, "How can you help this team be more effective?" and "What can you do in your role to improve the performance of the team?"

Answering the team 360 questionnaire and supplying verbatim comments will also enable the team members to give feedback on the team's work and encourage open dialogue.

During the Team Coaching Sessions

We have discussed the importance of contracting in Chap. 8, both at the start of a team coaching journey, at each session and the need to keep recontracting during the program.

Contracting and recontracting conversations offer team members valuable time to discuss their:

- Role in working with other team members, the team leader, and the team coach
- Goals for the program and session
- Feedback regarding the plan for the session or agreeing to flex and adapt the plan
- Progress against personal and team commitments made

Using the STOKERS framework (Foy, 2021) for one-to-one coaching can also be very helpful in ensuring the team is clear on the outcome they want to achieve in team coaching.

STOKERS refers to:

- Subject
- Timing
- Outcome
- Knowledge
- Energy
- Role
- Start

Helpful questions you may ask as a team coach could be:

Subject—What would you like to focus on in this session?
Timing—Given we have x hours today, what would be a good use of that time?
Outcome—What would you like to have at the end of that time?
Knowledge—How would you know you have that outcome? What will be different at the end of the session?
Energy—What makes this important for you?
Role—How best can we work together to achieve this? What do you need from me as a team coach?
Start—Where would you like to start?

It is also worth recognizing that contracting is not a one-off activity but a nested activity requiring continuous engagement, monitoring, and management (Passmore & Sinclair, 2024).

Acknowledging the contributions of team members, allowing them the space to have a voice during sessions, and the opportunity to share their knowledge and skills, are all important to encourage team members to feel safe and willing to express their views and opinions and share their thinking and ideas. Kline (1999) notes that you have not arrived until you have spoken. The team coach can help create this safe space, for example, by thanking team members when they contribute, asking questions to encourage further sharing, encouraging team members to ask each other questions, and ensuring everyone shares during exercises or discussions.

For example, ask the team, "What questions would you like to ask x member?". Other ideas that can help full participation include:

- Hearing from everyone as they arrive by asking "How are you feeling as you arrive today?"
- Use picture cards and ask team members to select a card that resonates with them about how they are feeling and then share with the team.
- Encourage everyone to share how they want to work together during the contracting conversation.
- Asking reflective questions during sessions and encouraging team members to share responses, a few examples are: "What did you do well as a team in this session?" "What could you have improved?" "What dynamics helped you in this session?" "What dynamics got in the way during this session?"

At the Close of Sessions

Having identified team goals at the start of a session, it is essential to ensure that team members identify appropriate goals and commitments at the end of the session. DOUSE coaching framework can again help the team to hold themselves to account. DOUSE (Foy, 2021) stands for:

- Double check the contract/goal
- Obstacles
- Uncovered
- Support
- Ending

Helpful example questions you may ask as a team coach include:

- Double check the contract/goal—Where are we in relation to the contract/goal for the session? What are your next steps?
- Obstacles—What might get in the way? How will you be accountable?
- Uncovered—What have you uncovered/learnt about yourselves/the team today?
- Support—What resources/support do you need to make it happen?
- Ending—How would you like to close the session?

We find as team coaches that it is also important for team members to verbalize and put in writing the personal commitment they will make to the team. Examples of ways to do this are:

- Ask team members to capture their commitment on a flip chart/whiteboard either one each, or one for the whole team with everyone included, etc. Then share with the team. Encourage the team to take a photo or screenshot of personal commitments.

- Note down commitments on a card and share them with the team which they either keep themselves or pass to a colleague to hold onto for review at an agreed time.

Review and Evaluation Process

Ensuring team members are also included in any evaluation and reviews of team coaching is also important. This could include:

- Involvement in a follow-up Team 360.
- Review session within the team coaching session or after to discuss progress against goals, actions, and commitments.
- Team leader gaining feedback from the team on progress and actions.
- Evaluation surveys/questionnaires to gain their feedback.

What is evident in this chapter is that involving team members throughout the team coaching process is essential to ensure they are fully engaged and able to take ownership of the team coaching process and outcomes.

Conclusion

Coaching is not just about engagement in the moment but is also about longer term personal growth and learning. Great coaches encourage clients to be conscious of themselves, their learning and their future personal growth.

Part III

Chapter 14
An Overview of Approaches in Team Coaching

Introduction

This chapter discusses coaching approaches within team coaching effectiveness. We start by exploring terminology from approaches to models and frameworks to maps. We will consider different approaches and how these may be applied by a team coach.

Understanding Terminology

Before we discuss this, it is essential to acknowledge the confusion in terminology, with terms such as approaches, frameworks, models, and tools often used interchangeably. Lawrence and Whyte (2017) noted, "it became apparent that coaches were using the same words to mean quite different things" (p. 106). Hawkins (2022), agreeing with this confusion, suggested definitions of each in the context of team coaching. These are summarized in Table 14.1, and as far as possible, we have endeavored to use these terms in this way throughout the book.

Like one-to-one coaching team coaches may draw upon a wide range of different approaches, including for example, psychodynamics, appreciative inquiry, structural dynamics, person-centered, solution-focused, and gestalt (see Passmore, 2021). Lawrence and Whyte (2017) categorize these into five broad approaches which reflect different ways of working within team coaching. These include task, relational, developmental, dialogic, and broad systemic. They noted that none of these are mutually exclusive. In discussing these approaches, this chapter has taken a broader perspective on relational, combined task and performance and included dialogic under a coaching approach, thus aligning our thinking closely to James and Corlett (2020) and their "modes of awareness for team coaching practice."

J. Passmore et al., *Becoming a Team Coach*,
https://doi.org/10.1007/978-3-031-63546-5_14

Table 14.1 Definitions and examples of key terms

Term	Definition	Examples
An approach	"a pre-existent perspective that is brought to the field of team coaching from another field."	Psychodynamic approach, relational approach, systemic approach, appreciative inquiry approach.
A framework	"a meta-model, a scaffolding" some of which "draw on other parallel professions" such as family systems, systemic theory, social psychology, etc.	Widdowson and Barbour's (2021) Creating the team edge framework that includes a research-based team effectiveness model, an approach emphasizing a team coach's "way of being," an indicative team coaching process.
A model	"a structure for sorting and separating the different aspects of team functioning or the team coaching activities, as well as, showing the interconnections."	5 Disciplines Model (Hawkins, 2011, 2014, 2017, 2021), PERILL model (Clutterbuck, 2020).
A map (interchangeable with terms such as journey, process, stages, and phases)	"a way of capturing the different stages a team may go through in its evolution and development, or the stages in the journey of a team coaching assignment."	Carr and Peters's (2013) six-team coaching components (phases), CID-CLEAR process (Hawkins, 2021).
A tool or technique	"a method the team coach can utilize to diagnose or orchestrate a team exploration to help … intervene effectively in a team process."	"Check-ins and check-outs." In this book, Sections 3 and 4 include examples of tools and techniques that team coaches can use.

Adapted from Hawkins (2022), pp. 65–66

Task/Team Performance

A focus on team performance and achieving a common team goal are two of the eight defining components of team coaching identified by Jones et al. (2019). Lawrence and Whyte (2017) refer to clarifying roles and responsibilities, team meetings and decision-making when discussing tasks. James and Corlett (2020) describe clarity on purpose, process, and outcomes, shared team language and effective behaviors in their "machine" mode of awareness.

While the team attending to the unique work they can only do by working together is essential, the question is what role can and should team coaching play in supporting? Hastings and Pennington (2019), in their study of the methods used by external team coaches, reported a preference for focusing on relational and systemic aspects, rather than an explicit focus on tasks. Agreeing with this, we would argue that a team coaching dialogue on essential areas, such as team purpose, collective performance goals, behaviors, and the team's real work, is potentially futile if a team is not attending to relational issues and thinking systemically. In our experience, when a team coach maximizes a coaching approach, prioritizes relational matters and the work is deeply systemic, the team will usually feel compelled to improve meetings, decision-making, processes and how they engage with stakeholders, with minimal team coach support.

Helpful questions for a team coach to reflect on:
- How can I best bring awareness to areas of task/team performance that the team might need to consider?
- How can I become more comfortable with the discomfort of letting go, as the team start to coach themselves?
- When I support a team in developing their purpose, behaviors, etc., how can I maximize coaching and minimize facilitation?

Relational

This section will discuss two relational aspects: the relationship between the team and the team coach and the relationship between team members.

The relationship, or alliance, between the team and the team coach, is considered foundational to the success of any team coaching intervention. Alliance is "the quality and strength of the collaborative relationship" (Norcross, 2010, p. 120). Murphy (2023), in their PhD thesis, conceptualized and demonstrated the importance of the "team coaching working alliance." While the importance of the team coaching working alliance is evident, the degree to which it is foundational is yet to be quantified. Notwithstanding this, learning from research in group therapy may be indicative. Writing about group therapy, Hubble et al. (2010) observed that "depending on which study is cited, the amount of change attributable to the alliance is five to seven times greater than that of specific models or techniques" (p. 37).

A strong team coaching working alliance is critical in developing the other essential relational aspect, the relationship between team members. The paramount consideration here is psychological safety, defined as "a shared belief that the team is safe for interpersonal risk-taking" with a "team climate characterized by interpersonal trust and mutual respect in which people are comfortable being themselves" (Edmondson, 1999: 354). Evidence from empirical studies has highlighted the benefits of psychological safety for team performance, individual and team learning, and team member inclusion (Edmondson & Lei, 2014).

Team coach tips on maximizing the working alliance and team psychological safety
- Continually contract with the team, its leader and relevant stakeholders on what the work is (e.g., team owning their dialogue) and where the work goes (e.g., team ownership of journey during and beyond the team coaching).
- Encourage a spirit of partnership from the outset, where both parties explore, learn, grow, laugh (and cry) together.
- Maximize the use of diagnostic one-to-one interviews:
  - before (to seek understanding, build relationships, and ease anxieties)

- during (to check in on team progress or otherwise)
- and after (to evaluate the work and potential next steps).

- Attend to relationships with each team member, being mindful of fairness, team coach bias, and favoritism.
- Support individual and team self-awareness and responses (emotional intelligence—EI—and team emotional intelligence—TEI).
- Be compassionate, humble, show vulnerability, and invite the team to do the same.
- Share concerns, mistakes, and learnings, and invite the team to do the same.
- Create a safe, courageous, reflective space to practice open and honest team dialogue.
- Contract for and earn the right to challenge the team from a position of curiosity (e.g., I'm wondering …), concern (e.g., I've noticed …), and possibility (e.g., What if …).

Developmental

Well-known approaches to a team's developmental journey include forming, norming, storming, and performing (Tuckman, 1965). An alternative perspective is Gersick's (1988, 1989) focus on the importance of beginnings, midpoints, and endings. Gersick's influence is evident in the framework/models/roadmaps in "The 6 Conditions for Team Effectiveness" (Chap. 19) and "The High-Performance Team Coaching" (HPTC) Model (Chap. 20).

Clutterbuck's (2014) emphasis on the importance of team history and Widdowson and Barbour's (2021) assertion that every team will have its own unique development story that deserves exploration, aligns with Lawrence and Whyte's (2017) findings. They discovered only three team coaches out of 36 explicitly referenced developmental frameworks. In contrast, 25 team coaches said their practice was in some way developmental in the broader sense of the term.

Helpful questions and ideas for a team to reflect on how they have developed
- Which aspects of forming, norming, storming, performing, and the idea of team beginnings, midpoints, and endings most resonate and why?
- Pretend you have to write a book about the history of this team. Describe the chapter headings, context, plots, subplots, and characters, including heroes and villains.
- Thinking about the book you have just outlined and what the future requires of the team, what would a second edition entail?
- Ask each team member (or adapt for the team to do together) to draw and then share a timeline history of the team. When drawing, each team member should consider:

  - What they knew or heard before joining.

- Their team highs and lows so far.
- Their hopes for the team in the future.

Coaching

It may be too obvious to highlight a coaching approach as critical for team coaching effectiveness; nevertheless, when discussing this element of team coaching, it is essential to state the obvious. Jones et al. (2019), from their survey of 400 practicing team coaches, identified eight defining components of team coaching, the majority of which are easily attributable to a coaching approach. Similarly, Hastings and Pennington (2019) highlight three purposes for the methods selected by team coaches, all supportive of a coaching approach as critical. At its most pure, a coaching approach is similar to what James and Corlett (2020) describe as the "wonderland" mode of awareness. In this mode, a team coach models openness, shares doubts and confusion, encourages dialogue, and helps the team build self-capacity to reflect and learn.

So, it is clear a coaching approach is at the heart of any team coaching intervention. Despite this, it is not always the reality in practice. When training team coaches, even the most competent and experienced one-to-one coaches often require support to move away from an over-reliance on areas such as facilitation, training, and consultancy. As emphasized throughout this book, while such approaches may play an essential part in the team's development journey, they are not the essence of the work of a team coach.

Helpful questions team coaches can ask themselves include:
- How can I better notice when I start moving away from coaching the team?
- What expertise (e.g., expert trainer, facilitator, or consultant) do I need to let go of, in my role as a team coach?
- When I sense movement away from coaching the team, what question(s) would be helpful to ask myself or the team?

Systemic

Irrespective of what it means to practice systemically, most team coaches claim to. All eight team coaches interviewed for Hauser's (2014) research emphasized the importance of paying attention to "the interrelatedness of the whole system" (p. 59). Hastings and Pennington's (2019) team coaching study reported that "five of the six participants described an underlying, systemic or systems-based focus" (p. 180).

Lawrence (2021b) has proposed five ways of thinking systemically, each with its benefits and limitations. Table 14.2 adapted from Lawrence's paper, describes each area, associated team coaching approaches and corresponding literature. Chapter

Table 14.2 Five ways of thinking systemically

Term	Description	Implications for team coaching	Examples from literature
First order (linear)	An organization is considered a real system that functions logically and can be modeled.	The team coach can objectively diagnose the team. The team coach privileges the team leader role and encourages progress towards achieving the enterprise's objectives as a whole.	Hackman and Wageman (2005a)
First order (non-linear)	An organization is considered a real system; however, some relationships between different parts are less obvious and non-linear.	The team coach does not expect relationships between different components and members to be obvious and predictable. The team is encouraged to slow down and reflect on their functioning.	
Second order	The essence of the system is elusive, with people needing to come together to build a working hypothesis of the system and learn together from the application of that hypothesis.	The team coach is interested in the team's dynamics since the team's ability to understand and integrate the perspectives of others will depend upon the team's ability to engage with itself.	Whittington (2012, 2016, 2020)
Complex adaptive systems	Local agents interact, and aggregate behaviors emerge from these interactions. The interactions continue to evolve as local agents seek to survive in the broader system.	The team coach encourages the team to increase their awareness of the nature of their functioning, especially the impact of things from outside the team. The team is encouraged to understand how things emerge (e.g., goals, objectives, intentions).	Thornton (2010, 2019), O'Connor and Cavanagh (2016), Hawkins (2011, 2014, 2017, 2021), Hawkins & Turner (2020)
Meta-systemic	Organizations are not things at all. They are just processes of communication and joint action. Organizations and teams are social constructs whose boundaries are not real.	The team coach considers the "team" and boundaries as social constructs in a broader dynamic and social network. All practices, processes, and philosophies can be helpful if held lightly.	Lawrence (2021a, 2021b)

Adapted from Lawrence (2021b), p. 60

21, "Team of teams—within and across organization team coaching," will explore some of the ideas behind meta-systemic team coaching.

Helpful questions team coaches can ask themselves include:
- What can I learn from each of the five systemic approaches described?
- From these five systemic approaches, what challenges how I team coach and why?
- Where is my systemic practice today, and what could help develop it further?

Conclusion

It is clear that coaching, relational and systemic approaches are foundational to team coaching. However, attending to the real work of the team (the team task/performance) and the team's development journey are also important.

Chapter 15
Frameworks and Models in Context and Examples of Those Used by Team Coaches

Introduction

In this chapter, we will review a range of different frameworks and models applied by team coaches in their practice, drawing on published sources. Our aim is both to highlight the diversity of approaches and to encourage a team coach to begin to develop their own integrated approach, drawing on a range of different frameworks and adapting to meet the needs of the client teams and organizational problems in the moment.

Frameworks and Models in Context

As with approaches, there are differences of opinion on the use of frameworks and models (and processes, tools, and techniques) when team coaching. We believe frameworks and models can be helpful when used appropriately and that many warnings about their use are overstated for emphasis and, potentially, in some cases, competitive positioning. It is also possible that critiques of frameworks and models place too much emphasis on their constituent parts, rather than the fundamental approach or philosophy their creator(s) espouses.

What do we mean by using frameworks and models appropriately? In summary, frameworks and models (and approaches, processes, tools, and techniques) should never be the essence of the work. They are only ever there to support the work of the team coach. Ideally, they should nearly be invisible to the team, with the team coach flexing and drawing upon whatever is helpful at that moment, rather than being fixated on a particular methodology. Hastings and Pennington (2019) noted that due to the complexity of coaching teams, the coaches in their research "all reported an eclectic and agnostic approach, the key to which is being able to draw from and

J. Passmore et al., *Becoming a Team Coach*, https://doi.org/10.1007/978-3-031-63546-5_15

adapt a wide array of tools, theories and methods" (p. 183). Thornton (2016), when discussing the value of conceptual frameworks and models, commented, "I have yet to find one that is good at all times and in all places" (p. 122). Writing about the idea of a meta-coach, Lawrence (2021a) has stated that the "meta-coach is open to all practices and processes, and to holding lightly underlying philosophies" and that in this context, "all tools are good" (p. 180).

Moving Beyond Frameworks and Models Towards a *Way of Being* as a Team Coach

In the team coaching literature, we welcome the increasing focus on the pre-eminence of a team coach's "*way of being*". Widdowson and Barbour (2021) proposed The "Being, Doing and Knowing" model of team coaching. This framework pre-dated the ICF competencies and set a benchmark for both the ICF and others to consider when reflecting on the behaviors and essence of the team coach.

The model outlined eight doing elements that correlate with the core coaching competencies and nine areas of knowledge. While doing and knowing are each necessary, it is a team coach's "*way of being*" which they highlight as a non-negotiable. They describe "*way of being*" under the 4Cs: "Connection," "Confidence," "Courage," and "Continuing" as "the importance of being able to connect deeply, to display confidence while retaining a sense of vulnerability, to have courage 'in the moment,' and to continue to learn" (2021, p. 8) These aspects are explored in this book in more depth in Chap. 10.

Hawkins (2021) uses the term capacities to describe *being* and proposes ten capacities considered important for team coaches, including (1) self-awareness and listening to the collective team, (2) self-ease and working from source, (3) staying in the partnership zone, (4) taking appropriate leadership, (5) relationship engagement, (6) develops coaching capacity in others, (7) working across difference—transcultural engagement, (8) ecological awareness and engagement, (9) ethical maturity, and (10) a sense of human and humility (pp 314–324).

Can a *Way of Being* Ever Be Enough on Its Own?

Despite its importance, it is clear that a "*way of being*" can never be enough. To help team coaches reflect on this, Widdowson and Barbour (2021) proposed the "Being, Doing and Knowing" model of team coaching development (see Fig. 15.1). They suggested that for a team coach to operate at a transformational level, they must attend to their "*way of being*" and "way of doing and knowing." They also suggest that at any moment, a team coach may find themselves in one or more of the

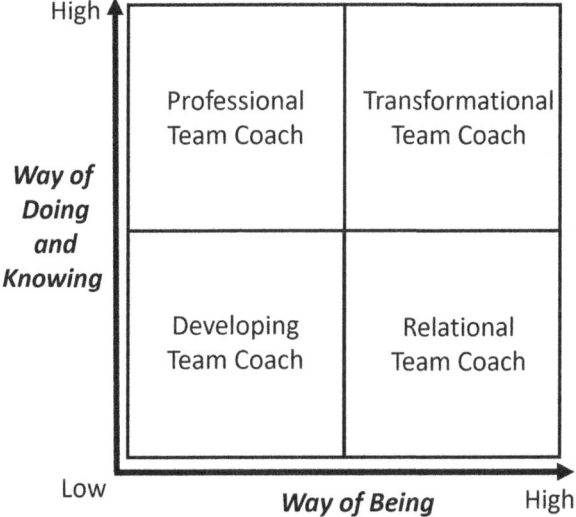

Fig. 15.1 The "Being, Doing and Knowing" model of team coaching development. Adapted from Widdowson and Barbour (2021), p. 39

developing, relational, professional, or transformational quadrants with mastery in team coaching, a non-ending and non-linear journey.

Through our involvement in team coach education, we regularly witness experienced one-to-one coaches rigidly cling to frameworks and models that give them certainty while recognizing the value of applying an integrated or eclectic approach in their one-to-one work. Understandably, inexperience and group work may induce anxiety and a need to hold onto a framework. However, as team coaches let go, they connect deeper with themselves and the essence underpinning team coaching. It is our experience that *letting go* can be relatively quick for those who have already been on the journey as a one-to-one coach. Clutterbuck (2020) outlined four levels of coaching maturity drawing on his previous work with Megginson(Clutterbuck & Megginson, 2011). Developed with one-to-one coaching, it suggests most coaches move through levels of coach maturity from (1) models-based, (2) process-based, (3) philosophy or discipline-based, and eventually (4) systemic-eclectic. Systemic-eclectic is described as the most liberating mindset, where coaches amass a wide range of ways of working and toolkits from multiple sources that they integrate into a self-aware, personalized *"way of being"* with the client. In guidance equally relevant to team coaching, Clutterbuck and Megginson (2011) suggested ideas about how a systemic-eclectic coach should work.

We have used these ideas to inform a series of reflective questions for team coaches (Table 15.1).

Table 15.1 Reflective questions

1. How attentive and relaxed are you and the client in allowing the issue and the solution to emerge in whatever way it chooses?

2. To what extent are you challenging yourself and asking if you need to apply any techniques or processes?

3. How confident and calm are you that you can find the right tool if you believe it is needed?

4. When you do use tools, how well are they subtly and almost seamlessly integrated?

5. How well would you describe your understanding of the origins and philosophy behind the frameworks, models, and techniques used?

6. To what extent are you using experimentation and reflexive learning to identify where and how a new technique, model, or process can fit into your philosophy and framework of team coaching?

7. To what level are you accessing new techniques, models, and processes based on client needs and not your own?

8. How well are you using co-team coaches and supervisors to challenge your coaching philosophy and as partners in experimenting with new approaches?

9. To what level are you taking a systemic and holistic view of the client, their environment/context and the coaching relationship, and subsequently exercising nuance in your approaches?

Overview of Frameworks and Models Used by Team Coaches

In the following chapters, we will explore five well-known team coaching frameworks/models, explaining their philosophical background, examining an overview of the model, and sharing how the frameworks/models may be applied. The frameworks/models selected to offer a variety of perspectives:

- The "Creating the Team Edge" framework (Chap. 16)
- The Five Disciplines of Successful Team Practice (Chap. 17)
- The PERILL Model (Chap. 18)
- The Six Conditions for Team Effectiveness Framework (Chap. 19)
- The High-Performance Team Coaching Model (Chap. 20)
- Team of Teams (Chap. 21)

The frameworks/models explored in Chaps. 16–21 are a sample of what team coaches may draw from. The remainder of this chapter will highlight some other team coaching frameworks/models/approaches that team coaches can explore.

Thornton (2016)

In the book *Group and team coaching: The secret life of groups* (2016), an emphasis is placed on psychoanalytic and systemic theories and approaches and how these can be helpful when working with groups, teams, and whole organizations.

Price and Toye (2017)

Based on their research with over 3000 teams, 16 drive factors were identified for teams to accelerate their performance. Each factor aligns with one of the four areas of their META framework (Mobilize, Execute, Transform, Agility). For each drive factor, there are drag factors that can hold a team back. Their research found that only 13% of teams were operating at the highest *accelerating* level.

Hauser (2018)

The *Shape-shifting model* identified four team coach role behaviors, including the (1) advisor, (2) educator, (3) catalyzer, and (4) assimilator. The model suggests that at the beginning of the work, a team coach is more likely to display advisor behaviors, compared to educator and catalyzer behaviors mid-way, and assimilator behaviors towards the end.

Leary-Joyce and Lines (2018)

The six lenses of a Systemic Team Coach highlight the systemic nature of team coaching and the need for team coaches to draw from various approaches to best serve the team. The six lenses that a systemic team coach needs to consider are proposed, including (1) individual, (2) interpersonal, (3) team dynamics, (4) team tasks, mission, and intent, (5) stakeholder interfaces, and (6) the wider systemic context.

Sandahl and Philips (2019)

Propose a model for great teams with seven keys to maximize productivity and seven keys to effective collaboration. In addition, five team coaching competencies are proposed, including (1) the ability to be system aware, (2) the ability to be tuned in—listening recalibrated, (3) the ability to be a reflective observer—the exquisite mirror, (4) the ability to be actively present—dance to the music, and (5) the ability to be committed—to stand in the fire.

Woudstra (2021)

The *TCS Team Coaching Wheel* has at its heart the team coach's Philosophy (world-view, principles, and values) and Stance (mantras that determine behavior). The next layer is described as the "transformational metaskills of presence, use of self and active experiments" (p. 131), with presence described as a coach's "distinctive *way of being*" (p. 99). The third layer relates to team coaching competencies organized in five clusters, which are: (1) Setting the Foundation, (2) Co-creating the Relationship, (3) Fostering Effective Communication, (4) Working with Systems and Dynamics, and (5) Facilitating Learning and Growth. At the wheel's outer edge are frameworks, models, tools, and techniques. In addition, Woudstra (2021), while encouraging team coaches to have their own way of approaching a team coaching journey, has outlined a typical team coaching journey, which includes initial meetings, a team engagement session, team discovery, team launch, team coaching, live action coaching, and a final review session. In between these stages, one-to-one coaching and "go/no-go" checkpoints can also play a role in the journey.

Woods (2022)

Outlines the *team Salient's six stages of team development*, which are (1) orientating, (2) resolving, (3) collaborating, (4) achieving, (5) excelling, and (6) reorientating. Each stage includes goals for the team to achieve, clarity on what the team needs during the stage, and practices to support the team coach, leader, and team.

Conclusion

The key message from this chapter is that while team coaching frameworks, models, and approaches are helpful, they are not the work. A team coach's "*way of being*" is paramount. It is important to note, that the frameworks, models, and approaches discussed in this book, both in detail in Chaps. 16–21 and in summary format in this chapter, while covering a lot of what has been written about team coaching, does not cover everything.

Chapter 16
The "Creating the Team Edge" Framework

Introduction

This chapter will explore the Creating the Team Edge model and approach, the research underpinning it, and how it can be applied as a process when working with teams in a coaching assignment.

Creating the Team Edge

The "Creating the Team Edge" model was developed by Lucy Widdowson and her colleagues at Performance Edge Partners Limited. The framework comprises a team effectiveness model with seven characteristics and a suggested team coaching roadmap (2018). Widdowson and Barbour (2021) further developed the framework, in particular highlighting the importance of a team coach's "*way of being.*"

Underpinning the framework is a study of five teams using the "Creating the Team Edge" model (Widdowson, 2018). The research reported how the model contributed to improvements in each team's performance:

- *Alignment on team purpose*
- Each of the teams agreed on a team purpose and collective team goals. To support the team purpose, they also decided on team values with associated behaviors, agreed on what team beliefs needed to be challenged, and a current and aspired to, team identity.
- *Developing psychological safety*
- Feeling safer in each other's company helped team members have more open and honest conversations. Team members reported giving each other meaningful feedback and becoming more at ease with showing vulnerability.

© The Author(s), under exclusive license to Springer Nature Switzerland AG 2024
J. Passmore et al., *Becoming a Team Coach*,
https://doi.org/10.1007/978-3-031-63546-5_16

- *Improvements in team learning*
- The team benefitted as individuals and collectively from sharing knowledge and best practices and reflecting on what worked well and what could be changed.

In addition, the study reported a broader impact, with the teams that were directly reporting to and working alongside the team-coached teams. These teams also reported improvements in performance (Widdowson, 2018).

The approach emphasizes that while frameworks, models, processes, tools, and techniques are helpful, a team coach's *"way of being"* is the most important. This *"way of being"* can be conceptualized under four headings, connection, confidence, courage, and continuing as follows (Widdowson & Barbour, 2021, 2021b):

- *Connection*
- Focusing on being deeply present, team coaches must retain awareness and continually attend to how well-connected they are with themselves, individual team members, the team, and the broader system.
- *Confidence*
- A team coach needs to develop inner confidence in their history (i.e., story), including successes and failures, while not being overconfident.
- *Courage*
- The team coach needs to stay present with themselves and the team in difficult moments and should be comfortable planning, letting go of the plans, and taking calculated risks in service of the team and its system.
- *Continuing*
- Never the finished article, the team coach should be committed to continuous learning, reflective practice, and team coaching supervision.

The Model

The "Creating the Team Edge" model consists of seven characteristics: team purpose, identity, values and beliefs, awareness, relatedness, ways of working, and transformation (see Fig. 16.1).

Each characteristic is considered essential for team effectiveness. Table 16.1 describes each element.

A Suggested Process for Team Coaches

Widdowson and Barbour (2021), when presenting what a team coaching process could look like, have stated that it is "indicative only of what we consider best practice" (p. 46). Chapter 24, on Team Coaching design, illustrates their example of a

Fig. 16.1 The "Creating the Team Edge" model for team effectiveness. Source: Widdowson (2018) with permission of Lucy Widdowson

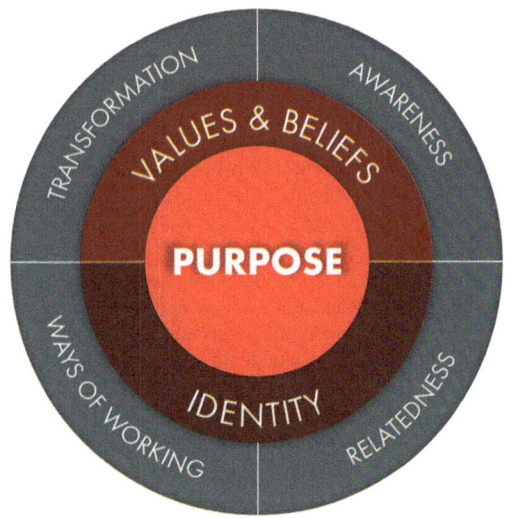

team coaching program (see Fig. 24.1). There are broadly five phases a team coach should consider.

Phase 1: Pre-Team Coaching Contracting

This phase is about initial contracting with critical stakeholders and the team leader. Some essential questions to consider include:

- Is it a team or a team in name only?
- What team development activity has occurred so far?
- What do the team leader and other relevant stakeholders know about team coaching?
- Does the team leader fully support the idea of team coaching?
- Is the team ready for team coaching? (team composition, context, etc.)
- If team coaching is unsuitable, are there other ways the team coach can support the team (e.g., coaching the leader)?
- Based on the available information, is team coaching the right team development intervention?
- If progressing, what are the objectives for the proposed work?
- How would you (we) know if you (we) have been successful?

Table 16.1 Creating the Team Edge descriptions of the seven characteristics

Purpose	Is about why the team exists. A team's purpose captures the spirit and essence of what it can only do, by working together to serve its organization and stakeholders. The team purpose only has weight when accompanied by collective performance goals.
Identity	The team works on developing their unique identity (i.e., their story). The identity binds them together and constantly reinforces the team's positive mindset, energy, and motivation. The team's identity should be recognizable and admired by those inside and outside the team.
Values and beliefs	Team values and beliefs provide a sense of right and wrong. The team explores and agrees on the culture it desires and its values, standards, and behaviors underpinning its efforts. The team regularly reviews and holds each other accountable for agreed behaviors. Belief in the team's purpose, identity, and values is essential for the team to perform.
Awareness	Teams develop an awareness of each other's strengths and personal preferences, and how to leverage these for the team's benefit. The team builds awareness and attends to how well they interact with their wider stakeholders.
Relatedness	Teams develop their connectedness and build mutual trust, support, and understanding. They invest time together in open and honest conversations. They proactively connect and build relationships with other teams and stakeholders within and outside their organization.
Ways of working	The team invests time in setting up the best systems and processes to enable its members to make confident and effective decisions. The team continually attends to the effectiveness of their communication and meetings and how well they work with other teams and stakeholders.
Transformation	Teams explore ways to challenge current performance while remaining future-focused. They apply innovative ways to think differently, have a learning culture that reflects and learns from mistakes, are diverse, practice inclusion, and attend to the team's well-being.

Source: Adapted from Widdowson (2018), Widdowson and Barbour (2021, 2021b)

Phase 2: Discovery Interviews, Team 360 Diagnostics, and Team Observation

Key activities to consider before designing a team coaching intervention include:

- *Discovery interviews*

- The team coach explains that the comments will support the co-design of the team coaching journey, be shared with the team in a summary format, and be non-attributable to any team member. While interviewing team members is the priority, talking to stakeholders within and outside the organization is also helpful. Interviews are usually scheduled for 30 minutes and will inquire about team effectiveness (using the seven characteristics), the team leader's role, and the team's context. They prioritize interviews over other forms of discovery. As well as the information and insights gleaned, interviews help the team coach build psychological safety, as the working alliance develops. Importantly, team members can express their hopes, fears, and concerns about the proposed team coaching journey.

- Before meeting the team, the coach will typically meet the leader and bring them through the summary. At this stage, the team coach is mindful of retaining the trust of the team leader and the team and must ensure confidentiality as promised. Deciding to share or not share the summary with the team before meeting them should be made on a case-by-case basis. If sharing before the meeting, asking each team member to reflect individually on some questions can be helpful. Alternatively, a team coach might share the summary for the first time when the team is together. The same decisions and approach apply to the Team 360 diagnostic.
- *Team 360 diagnostic*
- The "Creating the Team Edge" Team 360 consists of 42 questions, six questions on each team effectiveness characteristic. Responders can add verbatim comments on team strengths, development areas, and other "ideas for action." Up to 100 participants can complete the questionnaire across four groups. For anonymity purposes, having at least three responses per grouping is best. The four groups include:

    The team commissioner(s)—These are the people who inform the team's overall direction, for example, the corporate strategy and who may sign off on final budgets. It is essential to contract if there is only one team commissioner, as it would be impossible to maintain anonymity.
    The team members—This includes each team member and leader.
    Direct reports—These are the direct reports of the team members.
    Stakeholders—These can be internal and external stakeholders (e.g., peers, different teams, clients).

- *Team observation*
- Includes observing two or more members or the entire team when working. Team observation can also occur at any time agreed upon during the team coaching journey.

Widdowson and Barbour (2021) have suggested prioritizing discovery interviews and team diagnostics ahead of personality psychometrics for team coaching work. Other helpful sources during discovery include KPI reports, team correspondence, employee surveys and outputs from previous team development work.

Phase 3: Co-Designing the Team Coaching Journey

Some questions to consider:

- Who should be involved in co-designing? (e.g., team leader, team coach or coaches).

- What potential focus areas does the discovery work highlight?
- Who else needs to be engaged if considering a team of teams approach?
- What team coaching interventions could best support the team? (e.g., in-person, virtual, one-to-one coaching, team observation).
- What non-team coaching interventions could support the team as part of this journey? (e.g., team-building events, coaching skills, team training on other identified areas).
- How can team coaching effectiveness be measured?
- What do you need to co-design with the team leader, and what should be co-designed with the team?
- What would a first session potentially involve?
- What physical or virtual space is required to maximize the work's success?

Widdowson and Barbour (2021) are clear that one-to-one coaching of the leader, entire team, or selected team members can benefit and accelerate the work. They note, however, that careful contracting is required.

Phase 4: Team Coaching Interventions

Some questions to consider:

- How is the team taking ownership of their journey when together and apart?
- How well is the team coach staying in the moment and holding plans lightly?
- Is the team coach contracting before, during, and after each intervention?
- During and after the first workshop, how do you ensure you are continually co-designing the team coaching journey?

Phase 5: Evaluation

Some questions to consider:

- How can you best measure against the objectives agreed on in phase one?
- What changes are the team noticing?
- What changes are non-team members noticing?
- What changes are the team coaches noticing?
- How can the additional diagnostic interviews and repeats of the Team 360 diagnostic support evaluation? (e.g., during and after the work).

Conclusion

The "Creating the Team Edge" framework, first and foremost, promotes the centrality of a team coach's *"way of being"*. It also includes a research-based team effectiveness model and an example team coaching process that team coaches can adapt.

Chapter 17
The Five Disciplines of Successful Team Practice

Introduction

This chapter will explore the five disciplines of successful team practice, and how team coaches can use these to inform their work.

Five Disciplines

The five disciplines of successful team practice are drawn from the work of Peter Hawkins (2022). Hawkins, informed by the work of Peters and Carr (2013b), Hackman (2002), and others, has written extensively on teams and team coaching. Publications include *Leadership Team Coaching: Developing Collective Transformational Leadership* (Hawkins, 2021) and *Leadership Team Coaching in Practice* (Hawkins, 2022b).

Evolving themes in these texts include:

- Focus on external and internal relationships (Hawkins and Smith, 2006).
- Systemic team coaching for leadership teams (Hawkins, 2011).
- From systemic team coaching to eco-systemic team coaching (Hawkins, 2017).
- From high-performing teams to high-value creating teams (Hawkins, 2021).
- Beyond the team to a teaming and team of teams approach (Hawkins, 2022b).

When discussing team coaching, notwithstanding genuine differences, authors in team development occasionally use different words to describe a similar phenomenon, a point noted by Widdowson and Barbour (2021). Nevertheless, Hawkins' use of new terms and concepts allows team coaches to reflect on the essence of their work in a changing world.

J. Passmore et al., *Becoming a Team Coach*, https://doi.org/10.1007/978-3-031-63546-5_17

The spirit of Hawkins' work attends to the interconnectedness of everything, as evident from pandemics, conflict-related migration flows, and the human impact on our natural world. Eco-systemic challenges team coaches to reflect on what more they can do to support teams to think beyond traditional organizational boundaries. Likewise, a change in emphasis from high-performing teams to high-value-creating teams challenges team coaches to support teams in moving beyond a mechanistic view of performance, and to consider what sustainable beneficial value they can co-create with and for all their stakeholders. Finally, focusing beyond a single team towards a teaming and team of teams challenges team coaches to think more broadly about their work (See Chap. 21).

The Model

The five disciplines of successful team practice—also referred to as the five disciplines of value-creating teams (Hawkins, 2022b)—is a team effectiveness model with five domains: core learning, commissioning, clarifying, co-creating, and connecting (see Fig. 17.1).

Emphasizing an *outside-in* and a *future-back* focus, the model proposes that for teams to be effective, they must attend to each of the five disciplines. The model is non-linear, with the disciplines interconnecting in a continuous cycle. These five disciplines include:

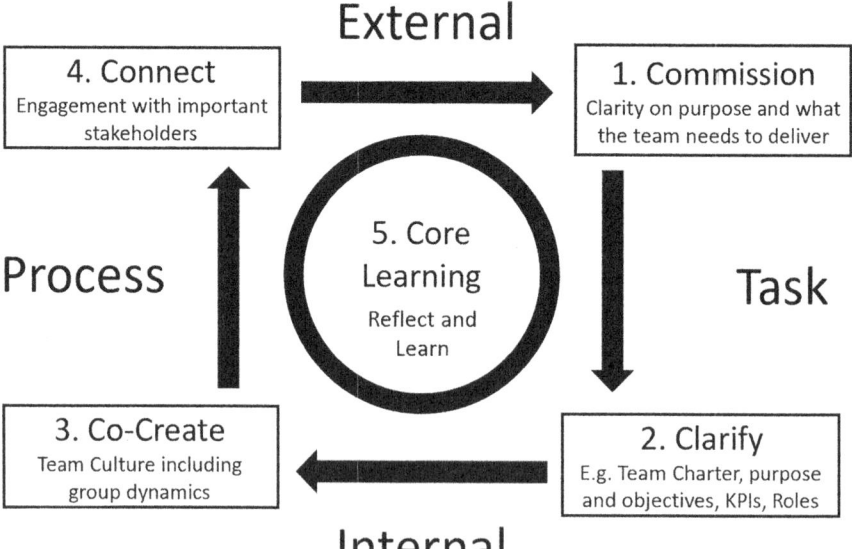

Fig. 17.1 The five disciplines of successful team practice. Source: Adapted from Hawkins (2021, p. 51)

Commissioning (Task/Outside Focus)

This discipline considers who brought the team into being and for what purpose. It comes from outside of the team. Some questions for a team to consider:

- What challenges do the team need to address?
- Who are our stakeholders, and what do they need from us?
- What stakeholders are we not noticing?
- What are the success criteria for each of our stakeholders?
- Who is the right leader, and who are the right team members to carry forward this commission?
- What support and resources are needed for the team to do its work?

Clarifying (Task/Inside Focus)

If it is not enough for a team to have a clear commission, they must also clarify what they wish to achieve together and how they want to go about their collective work. The clarity comes from inside the team. Some questions for a team to consider:

- What work can we do better together than apart?
- Have we agreed on a team charter that captures our purpose, vision, strategic narrative, collective performance goals and objectives?
- Have we agreed on team values that will direct our behavior when together and apart?
- How clear are we on agreed ways of working?
- How will we run our functional areas while attending to the work of this team?
- How aligned are the team and its members to the organization?

Co-Creating (Process/inside Focus)

Co-creating is about ensuring team agreements are not just a set of words but something that is living. If clarifying is about what the team wants to be and do, co-creation is about how well the team is doing it. Some questions for the team coach to use:

- Considering what was agreed while "clarifying"—how well is the team noticing, interrupting themselves, and course-correcting?
- How good is the team at collectively managing conflict?
- How effective and value-adding are team meetings?
- Is there enough trust in place for team members to work effectively together?

Connecting (Process/Outside Focus)

For a team to be effective, it must connect effectively with outside stakeholders. Some questions for a team to consider:

- Does the team have an updated stakeholder map?
- How well is the team connecting with each of its key stakeholders?
- How good are team members at representing the team, not just their function?

Core Learning

Core learning is at the model's center. Some questions for a team to consider:

- Are we dedicating enough time to reflect on what works well and what does not?
- How much do the team value individual and team learning?
- Is the team learning fast enough, given their context and environment?

A Suggested Process for Team Coaches

The five disciplines do not stand in isolation. Among other areas, the importance of systemic practice and team coach supervision is evident throughout Hawkin's work; areas explored further in Chaps. 14 and 28.

We are repeatedly asked a question from trainee team coaches: "What is a typical team coaching journey?" We agree with the statement that "there is no such thing as a typical team coaching journey, as every team is different, facing different challenges and dynamics, and thus every team coaching journey needs to be different" (Hawkins, 2022b, p. 412). Nevertheless, the team coaching process model, CID-CLEAR, can help team coaches explore a process that, while laid out under eight headings, is not linear and respects the idea that no two team coaching journeys are the same (Hawkins and Smith, 2006, 2013; Hawkins, 2011, 2014, 2017, 2021). CID-CLEAR stands for (C) contracting 1, (I) inquiry, (D) discovery, diagnosis, and design, followed by, (C) contracting 2, (L) listening, (E) explore and experiment, (A) action, and (R) review. The following section explains each stage.

Contracting 1

These are initial conversations, usually with those who have decided to explore team development work for their team (e.g., team leader, HR partner, team sponsor). Some questions to consider include:

- How have these initial conversations come about?
- What is the team's history regarding team development work?
- What challenges do the team face?
- What do the team's current and future stakeholders need from this team?
- What is the purpose of this team being a team?
- What level of understanding is there about team coaching?
- What would success look, feel, and sound like?
- How could success be measured?

Inquiry

This phase is about collecting data and impressions about the team. It can include one-to-one semi-structured interviews with team members and critical stakeholders, team 360 feedback (e.g., Team Connect 360), bespoke questionnaires, other feedback instruments (e.g., personality psychometrics), and existing sources (e.g., previous outputs from team development work, staff surveys, reports on team performance). Some important principles to consider include:

- One-to-one interviews are not just about data—they help establish relationships and a working alliance.
- Any data collected must be non-attributable to any team member.
- Do not overload the team with too many inquiry instruments.

Discovery, Diagnosis, and Design

It is essential at this stage "not to arrive at definitive conclusions about the team, but to develop emerging hypotheses, including the possible focus of the team coaching" (Hawkins, 2021, p. 92). There are two phases to this stage:

1. *Co-discovery and co-diagnosis*
   It involves meeting with the whole team and supporting them as they seek to understand the main points from the feedback. The team coach is essential in preparing the ground so the team approaches with curiosity and openness versus feeling judged.
2. *Co-designing the journey*
   The team coach and team start co-designing the team coaching journey at a high level.

Contracting 2

At this stage, the team coach and team contract on two key areas:

1. *Exploring the team coaching journey*

    The team coach and team explore what will likely be in the team coaching journey (e.g., workshops, team coach attending team meetings, stakeholder involvement, individual coaching). It can be helpful for the team coach to illustrate a typical team coaching journey.
2. *Relationship agreements between the team coach and the team*
    Areas to explore include:
    (a) Practicalities (e.g., location, times, place).
    (b) Boundaries (e.g., confidentiality on information flows, the nature of the team coach's supervision, confidentiality agreements on individual coaching).
    (c) Ethical considerations both parties may be subject to.
    (d) The working alliance (e.g., mutual expectations, ongoing feedback, and adjustments on the team coaching journey).
    (e) The contract with the broader organization (e.g., 360-degree feedback and/ or stakeholder interviews).

Listening

This stage concerns the team coach listening and sharing what they see, hear, and feel. Hawkins and Smith (2013) discuss engaging facts, behavior patterns, emotional patterns and assumptions, mindsets and motivations.

Explore and Experiment

Based on issues revealed so far, the team coach supports the team in exploring potential new ways to do things.

Action

This stage involves helping the team move from awareness to action, prioritizing, planning, and committing. It can be helpful for the team to rehearse new behaviors.

Review

A team needs to build a review process. Typical review methods include discussing progress during team meetings or involving the team coach in events or meetings. A key determinant of success will be, how well the team leader or team members take over the coaching roles.

Conclusion

In addition to the five disciplines of successful team practice, Hawkins continues to push the boundaries of team coaching.

Chapter 18
The PERILL Model

Introduction

This chapter will explore the PERILL model (Clutterbuck, 2020). We will first review the ideas that have informed this model from Clutterbuck's earlier work, then review the model and consider how team coaches can apply the model in their practice.

PERILL Model

David Clutterbuck has been an influential thinker in team coaching, his contributions include:

- *The distinctiveness of team coaching* (Clutterbuck, 2007)

- The first edition of *Coaching the Team at Work* was an early and influential text for team coaching. It proposed that facilitation is concerned with team dialogue management compared to the focus of team coaching on supporting a team to manage their own dialogue. In addition, this text challenged the efficacy of team building towards creating sustainable change.
- *The importance of tasks, learning, and relationships* (Clutterbuck, 2007)
- Suggested that a high-performing team needs to focus on tasks, relationships, and team learning and that no one area should receive focus over and above another.
- *Team coaching assumes professional characteristics* (Clutterbuck, 2019)
- *The Practitioner's Handbook of Team Coaching* provides a comprehensive overview of team coaching. It describes team coaching as an emerging discipline,

J. Passmore et al., *Becoming a Team Coach*,
https://doi.org/10.1007/978-3-031-63546-5_18

with differences in definition and approach expected and beneficial. The text also introduces the PERILL model.

- *Complex adaptive systems and the PERILL model* (Clutterbuck, 2020)
- The second edition of *Coaching the Team at Work* highlighted the systemic nature of team coaching, emphasizing the team as a complex adaptive system with multiple interacting elements linked to numerous other complex adaptive systems. The core of this second edition expands upon the PERILL model, which, among other areas, highlights the role of leadership and the team leader in particular.
- *Learning from practice* (Clutterbuck et al., 2022)

- *The Team Coaching Casebook* suggests that while there is increasing agreement on how team coaching is defined, it is also clear there are multiple approaches to what is complex work. These different approaches are considered strengths and brought to life through case studies. This text notes the maturing of team coaching evidenced by standards and emerging research.

The Model

The PERILL model, based on two decades of research and team observation, identifies five pillars of high-performing teams and one moderating factor. These include (P) purpose and motivation, (E) externally-facing systems, processes, and structures, (R) relationships, (I) internally-facing systems, processes, and structures, and (L) learning. A team may perform well or poorly on each, with (L) leadership considered to have a moderating effect (Clutterbuck, 2019, 2020). Figure 18.1 illustrates how each of the five pillars interacts to affect team performance and dysfunction, with Leadership Quality Behaviors (LQB) moderating in between.

Descriptions of each pillar and the leadership quality behaviors (LQB) element are as follows:

(P) Purpose and motivation

The team's purpose is about what the team exist to do. A helpful question to ask is:

- Why does this team exist?

(E) Externally-facing systems, processes, and structures
This pillar is about how effectively the team works with its external stakeholders. A helpful question to ask is:

- How aware are the team of their performance and reputation with each external stakeholder?

(R) Relationships
Relationships are about how team members work together. A helpful question to ask is:

IMPACT OF LEADERSHIP	Purpose and motivation	Externally-facing systems, processes and structures	Relationships	Internally-facing systems, processes and structures	Learning
Purpose and motivation	**IMPACT OF LEADERSHIP**	Strong alignment between the team and stakeholders	Positively working towards a shared purpose and goals	Focus on team clarity and delivery of collective goals	Strong focus on the benefits of team learning
Externally-facing systems, processes and structures	Poor alignment between the team and stakeholders	**IMPACT OF LEADERSHIP**	Collaborative and positive relationships with stakeholders	Timely and effective responses to issues identified	Examples of Improved systems and processes
Relationships	Team members pursuing their own agendas	Poor collaboration and conflict with stakeholders	**IMPACT OF LEADERSHIP**	Psycholoical safety underpinning open and honest conversations	Collaborative approach to learning
Internally-facing systems, processes and structures	Limited team clarity or focus on collective goals	Issues not identified or dealt with effectively	Lack of honest conversations with too much remaining unsaid	**IMPACT OF LEADERSHIP**	A culture that supports systems, processes and structure improvements
Learning	Emphasis on individual learning at expense of team learning	Lack of improvement in systems and processes	Competitive approach to learning	Emphasis on the status quo at the expense of change	**IMPACT OF LEADERSHIP**

Fig. 18.1 PERILL: Contexts of team performance and dysfunction. Source: Adapted from Clutterbuck (2020, p. 83)

- How well are team members respecting each other, having open and honest conversations, and creating an environment in which team members feel psychologically safe?

(I) Internally-facing systems, processes, and structures

This pillar is about how the team manages internal processes. A helpful question to ask is:

- How effectively is the team communicating, making decisions, and managing team workflows?

(L) Learning

Learning is about the team's ability to keep learning and responding to its changing environment. A helpful question to ask is:

- How effective is the team at reflecting and learning from successes and failures?

(L) Leadership

Leadership acts as a moderating influence for each of the pillars. As well as being about how the leader leads, it is also about the team's collective leadership. Notably, both of these exist within a dynamic system. A helpful question to ask is:

- What does the leader do that helps or hinders the team, in achieving its purpose?

A Suggested Process for Team Coaches

Clutterbuck (2020) outlined seven key steps involving the team coach and the team.

1. *Preparation*
    This phase is about understanding the team and its systems and can include:

    (a) *Interviews*—Involves interviews with each team member about the team and its context. The PERILL model can be used to inspire questions.
    (b) *Observation*—This can be a team meeting or interactions between two or more of the team. Two team coaches, one observing processes and dynamics and the other relationships and behaviors, can be helpful.
    (c) *Diagnosis*—Using a team 360, either off the shelf or created, this stage identifies potential focus areas for team coaching. Importantly, it is not about telling a team what is wrong with them. The importance of focusing on team strengths, including using strengths to work on weaknesses, is highlighted. Overuse of diagnostics up front may increase team resistance to team coaching.
    (d) *Integration and feedback*—Due to a large amount of potential data, the recommendation is to focus on critical themes. It prevents the team from getting lost in detail, which may be a technique to avoid discussing more challenging issues.
        Team readiness—Not every team will be ready for team coaching. Valuable questions to ask include:
        • Is it a team or a team in name only?
        • Is the team committed to a journey that includes open and honest dialogue?
        • Are there issues that need resolving before commencing a team coaching journey?

2. *Scoping and contracting*
    Contracting, more helpfully referred to as agreements, consists of two parts.
    Firstly, agreeing on what the team coaching should focus on, while recognizing this can change as the team's awareness develops. A helpful question to ask is:

    • What needs to be different for this team to become significantly more effective in delivering their team purpose?

    Secondly, agreeing on how different parties work with each other. Agreements to consider include, those between the coaches and leader, coaches and team, coaches and sponsors, leader and the team, team members with each other, and co-team coaches.

3. *Process skills development*
    This step is about supporting the team to co-coach each other by developing their listening, questioning, summarizing skills, use of silence and reflection time, and capacity to challenge each other and give genuine feedback. The team coach can help transfer responsibility for such processes by asking the team questions such as:

- What are we noticing about what is happening in the room?
- What question would it be helpful to ask ourselves right now?

Ultimately, an objective of the work is to support the team as they eventually start to ask themselves such questions.

4. *The team coaching conversation*

The conversation should go where it has to go. Nevertheless, a structure that a team coach might subtly use to support a team conversation could include (1) contracting for the session, (2) an overall goal for the session, (3) defining the issue, (4) uncovering the context, (5) redefining the issue based on a broader individual and collective understanding, (6) agreeing on mindset changes individually and collectively that may be required for progress to happen, (7) explore ideas to move forward, (8) deciding on next steps, and (9) recontracting based on learnings from the conversation.

5. *Process review*

It is essential to keep reviewing the team coaching work. Importantly, whether briefly at the end of a session or more formally after a few sessions, reviews should focus on what the team coach and the team need to do to make the work more effective. A helpful question for the team to reflect on is:

- How can we, as a team, make this work more effective?

6. *Process transfer*

To avoid team coach dependency, from the outset, the team coach should contract with the team that they will eventually withdraw, and for the work to be sustainable, the team will practice and learn the skills to coach themselves. Some helpful questions a team can ask themselves are:

- What did the team coach do that we are now doing?
- What is the team coach still doing that we can learn from and start doing ourselves?

7. *Outcomes review*

Working together, the coaches and the team review what has happened as a result of the team coaching. Some helpful questions to consider are:
- What has happened towards the goals agreed on at the start and those that emerged?
- What capability have we built as a team to help us perform in the future?

Conclusion

Clutterbuck's contribution to team coaching goes well beyond the PERILL model outlined in this chapter, as evidenced by the changes between the first and second editions of *Coaching the Team at Work*. His emphasis on the role of leaders and leadership within the team offers a helpful perspective for team coaches to consider.

Chapter 19
The Six Conditions for Team Effectiveness

Introduction

This chapter will review the work of Hackman and Wageman's Six Conditions for Team Effectiveness and explore how this framework can be used to inform team coaching.

The Six Conditions of Team Effectiveness

The Six Conditions for Team Effectiveness is a testament to the collaboration of Richard Hackman (1987, 2002) and Ruth Wageman (2001), who together proposed *A theory of Team Coaching* (Hackman & Wageman, 2005a). The theory was expanded upon further by Wageman et al. (2008), Hackman (2011a), and Wageman and Lowe (2019).

Some significant themes include:

- *Team design impacts coaching effectiveness*

- Wageman (2001) found that while good coaching by a leader modestly benefitted well-designed teams, it had an insignificant impact on poorly designed teams.
- *A three-dimensional definition of team effectiveness*
- In a definition that has become a benchmark in other research into team effectiveness, Hackman (2002, 2011a) and Wageman et al. (2008) articulated team effectiveness as:

  1. The team's output meets or exceeds the needs of those who use it (e.g., a client internally or externally).
  2. The team increases in capability as a consequence of its work.

3. The team contributes positively to the learning and personal well-being of its members.

- *A Theory of Team Coaching*
- One of the earliest contributions to the team coaching literature is Hackman & Wageman, (2005a), their theory proposes a focus on three areas:

   1. *Functions*–focus on the coaching functions that address a team's task performance, not interpersonal relationships.
   2. *Timing*—inspired by the work of Gersick (1988, 1989), beginnings, midpoints, and endings in a team's life each require different coaching activities.
   3. *Conditions*—group design and task and organizational constraints, if not addressed, will likely result in ineffectual team coaching.

- *A focus on conditions*
- Hackman's (2002) five-factor model ultimately became the Six Conditions. The six conditions for team effectiveness are (1) a real team, (2) a compelling direction, (3) the right people, (4) a solid team structure, (5) a supportive organizational context, and (6) competent team coaching (Wageman et al., 2008). An example of focusing on conditions is conflict, where they suggest that direct efforts to resolve team conflict can be wasteful when underlying conditions (or causes) are not addressed.
- Wageman et al.'s (2008) study on over 120 senior leadership teams revealed that only 21% of the teams could be described as outstanding. Notably, the teams found to be outstanding scored significantly better on the six conditions, which, when considered together, predicted 60% of the variance in team effectiveness. Hackman's (2011a) study reported that the six conditions accounted for 74% of the variance in team effectiveness.
- *Team Diagnostic Survey (TDS)*

- The peer-reviewed *Team Diagnostic Survey* (Wageman et al., 2005) has continued to develop since its inception. An example of this development is the assertion by Murphy and Sayer (2019) that the inclusion of a measure of psychological safety in more recent iterations "perhaps signals a move away from their earlier hypothesis that interventions focused on interpersonal relations do not improve performance" (p. 77).

The Model

The first three conditions, described as *the essentials,* are considered prerequisites for good team performance. The second three conditions, *the enablers*, allow a team to take full advantage of the foundational *essentials*.

The Essentials

1. *A real team*

In their research, the poorest-performing teams lacked clarity on team membership, were unstable, and had little interdependence (Wageman et al., 2008). In addition, teams with stable membership had healthier dynamics and performed better than teams that constantly dealt with new team members and leavers (Hackman, 2011a).

Some questions to consider:

- Are there clear boundaries that distinguish team members from non-members?
- Does the team have time for members to learn how to work effectively together?
- Are the team interdependent—i.e., do they genuinely need to share resources, information, and decision-making to complete tasks for which they can be held collectively accountable?
- Does the work need a team?

2. *A compelling purpose*

A team purpose, unique to the team and different from the organization's purpose, is essential to orientate and engage team members. The team's purpose should be challenging, consequential and provide clarity. While team purpose may be about an end state, it should be linkable to the team's actual work.

Some questions to consider:
- To what extent is the team's purpose challenging, consequential, and clear?
- What can this team uniquely do that other teams cannot?
- How well is the team's purpose linked to the actual work tasks of the team?

3. *The right people*

Wageman et al. (2008) when discussing leadership teams recognized that making changes to a team, especially if the team is inherited, is likely to be an iterative process. They describe team derailers as usually technically competent members who almost always lack people skills and competencies, such as empathy and integrity. In discussing integrity, they note that a derailer will often say one thing in public and another in private.

Some questions to consider:
- Does each team member have basic teamwork skills and a desire to collaborate?
- Does the team have the required knowledge, skills, and diversity level to help it achieve its purpose?
- If there are team derailers, is there an appetite to quickly challenge behaviors, support derailers on their self-development or ultimately, remove them from the team if necessary?

The Enablers

4. An Enabling Structure

    Three areas are considered necessary for an enabling structure, including (1) an appropriate team size of ideally no more than 6–8 people, (2) explicitly specified norms of conduct on what behaviors are acceptable and unacceptable when working together and apart, and (3) clarity on real team tasks that make sense for the team to work on together.

    Some questions to consider:

    - If the team is considered too large, how could it potentially be reconfigured?
    - How can the team keep their agreed norms alive when together and apart?

5. *A supportive organizational context*

    As teams operate within an organizational context, it is important to ensure that a team has support systems that promote effective teamwork.

    Some questions to consider:
    - To what extent does the reward system encourage team performance?
    - Do team members have the technical assistance or training available for knowledge, skills, or experience gaps?
    - How well does the organization's information system support the work of the team?

6. *Competent team coaching*

    If the first five conditions are in place, competent team coaching at the right times can support a team to become more effective. Wageman et al.'s (2008) research found that "outstanding teams had significantly more coaching, both from leaders and from one another, than did mediocre and struggling teams" (p. 160). External team coaches or a combination of external and internal team coaches can also provide team coaching.

    Some questions to consider:
    - Who can best provide team coaching for any given team and its context?
    - What training can support the coaching skills of the leader and team members?

A Suggested Process for Team Coaches

The article *Leading Teams When the Time is Right: Finding the Best Moments to Act* (Wageman et al., 2009) is helpful when considering a process for The Six Conditions for Team Effectiveness. Four times when the team's effectiveness can be most influenced are highlighted as (1) before the team exists, (2) at the team's launch, (3) at the mid-point of a performance period, and (4) at the end of a team's performance period. These four areas are supported by the findings in *A theory of Team Coaching* (Hackman & Wageman, 2005a), which highlighted the importance of carrying out appropriate coaching activities at the beginning, mid-point, and ending of a team's performance cycle. The following paragraphs will now consider each of the four areas.

1. *Before the Team Exists*

Before a team comes together, a leader, potentially with the support of an executive or team coach, should consider The Six Conditions for Team Effectiveness to ensure a high-quality team design. The significance of attending to a team's design is highlighted by the 60-30-10 rule (Hackman, 2011b; Wageman & Lowe, 2019). The rule proposes that when considering how well a team ultimately performs, condition-creating accounts for about 60%, the quality of the team launch 30%, and real-time team coaching only 10%.

The example is provided of a new CEO, who mistakenly might consider their direct reports to be the team, rather than exploring questions such as:

- Which of my senior leaders have the willingness and capability to collaborate to benefit the overall enterprise?
- What purpose would a leadership team serve?
- What enterprise-level tasks could be worked on better by a senior team rather than individually?

While the conditions should be attended to as comprehensively as possible before the team meet, there are areas where the team's input will be critical, for example, agreeing on team norms.

2. *Motivation Coaching at the Team Launch*

The next most important area is the team launch. Beginnings are described as "a unique opportunity for motivational coaching interventions that breathe life into a team's structural shell" (Hackman & Wageman, 2005a, p. 276). At the team launch, coaching should focus on helping the team move from names on a page to a real bonded team. The leader will share their purpose for the team, allowing the team to provide feedback and refine if necessary. Among other areas, the team will agree on how they will work together (team norms) and start orienting themselves towards their joint tasks. For established teams, a team relaunch can inject new impetus.

3. *Consultative Coaching at the Mid-Point*

The mid-point of a team's performance cycle offers an opportunity for consultative coaching where the team explores their work progress and decides on changes to better align with external demands and available resources.

4. *Educational Coaching at the Endpoint*

The end-stage provides the opportunity for educational coaching with a focus on the team taking time to reflect and learn. It is suggested that most teams are unlikely to take time for such reviews unless prompted to.

While the four areas discussed imply a structured approach, Wageman et al. (2009) highlight the need for a coach to sense systemic forces and judge when best to make real-time interventions.

Conclusion

The Six Conditions for Team Effectiveness have been a building block for developing team coaching. In particular, the emphasis on conditions and ensuring a team is ready for team coaching.

Chapter 20
The High-Performance Team Coaching (HPTC) Model

Introduction

This chapter will review Peters and Carr's High-Performance Team Coaching Model and explore how the model can be used to inform team coaching.

The High-Performance Team Coaching Model

Building on their Doctoral dissertation, practitioner researchers Dr. Jacqueline Peters and Dr. Catherine Carr (Carr & Peters, 2012) contributed significantly to an emerging team coaching literature through academic papers (Carr & Peters, 2013; Peters & Carr, 2013a), books (Peters & Carr, 2013b; Peters & Carr, 2013c), and book chapters (Peters, 2019, 2022; Peters & Carr, 2019).

Some themes that have emerged from their work include:

- *The importance of team working agreements, individual coaching, and team design and structure* (Carr & Peters, 2013)

- As well as establishing team working agreements, their research highlighted the usefulness of individual, peer, and team leader coaching, as part of a broader team coaching intervention. Another essential output from their work is the importance and opportunity for team coaches to support leaders and teams to reflect on their team design and structure. Indeed, their work is very clear about not taking on team coaching assignments which are likely doomed to failure due to issues regarding the design or structure of the team. In such cases, they advocate the merits of individual coaching, especially for the leader, to support addressing team design and structure issues as a potential precursor to broader work with the team. In this regard, their work is influenced and aligned with Wageman et al. (2008) and Hackman (2011a).

- *Team coaching effectiveness* (Peters & Carr, 2013a; Peters & Carr, 2019)
- A key theme of their work is a focus on team coaching effectiveness. While highlighting multiple benefits of team coaching, Peters and Carr's (2019) critique of seventeen academic/empirical studies on the efficacy of team coaching concluded, "team coaching demands more evidence of results" (p. 115). They noted an overreliance on case studies and self-reporting, as opposed to more objective business measures that could help strengthen the case for team coaching.
- *The High-Performance Team Coaching (HPTC) Model* (Carr & Peters, 2013)/ *System* (Peters & Carr, 2013b)

- Another output from their research was The High-Performance Team Coaching (HPTC) Model, a focus for the remainder of this chapter.

The Model

The High-Performance Team Coaching (HPTC) Model (Carr & Peters, 2013), also described as a system (Peters & Carr, 2013b), is an output of doctoral research carried out on two leadership teams, one government and the other corporate and a review of the available literature. The Model consists of five key elements, as follows:

1. *Three team stages*
   Influenced by Gersick's (1988) punctuated-equilibrium model, which emphasizes beginnings, midpoints, and endings as natural stages of a team's work together, the HPTC model suggests three times in a team's cycle when coaching has the most impact. Stating that team coaching is most effective at the beginning stage, they propose that creating events that focus on new beginnings (e.g., a project launch, new team members, a new strategy) can be helpful when working with an established team. The midpoint stage is mainly associated with the opportunity to review, whereas the ending stage is predominantly about integrating learning. They note that the ending stage does not necessarily mean a team is formally ending and can refer to reaching a natural milestone representative of an ending of sorts.
2. *Three coaching functions*
   Coaching functions are matched to the three coaching stages as follows: (1) define and initiate at the beginning stage, (2) review and realign at the midpoint stage, and (3) integrate at the ending stage. They noted that team coaching is more frequent at the beginning stage, with ongoing individual coaching a feature of the midpoint stage.
3. *Six team coaching components (phases)*
   Also referred to as phases, the six components are (1) assessment, (2) coaching for team design, (3) team launch, (4) individual coaching, (5) ongoing team

coaching, and (6) review of learning and successes. Phases 1–4 are primarily associated with the beginning stage (define and initiate), phase 5 with the mid-point stage (review and realign), and phase 6 with the ending stage (integrate). The six phases do not fit precisely into the team stages and coaching functions. For example, individual coaching may be a feature of the beginning stage (define and initiate) and the midway stage (review and realign). They also note that while the phases are part of a team cycle, a team coach or leader may decide to revisit any of the phases at the midpoint stage. For example, following assessment, an established team may decide on the need for a team relaunch.

4. *Safety*

Underpinning all coaching and at the core of their model is safety. They noted from their research the teams explicitly identified the importance of the team coach creating a psychologically safe space.

5. *Team effectiveness*

Their research pointed to team effectiveness improvements in three areas, including the (1) quality of outputs, (2) capability of the team to relate and work together effectively, and (3) level of individual engagement.

A Suggested Process for Team Coaches

As detailed in the previous section, The High-Performance Team Coaching (HPTC) Model (System) includes six components or phases (Carr & Peters, 2013; Peters, 2019, 2022; Peters & Carr, 2013b).

Critical areas to consider in each phase include:

Phase 1: Assessment

Before team coaching starts, it is essential to explore team readiness.

Wageman et al.'s (2008) conditions for team effectiveness (see Chap. 19) can help explore team readiness.

Areas to explore include:

- The extent to which it is a real team
- The existence or otherwise of a compelling team purpose
- If the team has the right mix of knowledge, skills, and talent to achieve the purpose
- How optimum the team structure is, including clarity of roles and responsibilities
- The degree to which the team exists in a supportive organizational context (e.g., information, time, resources).

Example questions to explore from Peters and Carr's (2013b) *Team Coaching Readiness Assessment* (p. 41) include:

- "Are there any team members who have performance issues that need to be addressed first or separately?"
- "Do you have goals that require all team members to participate in their success?"
- "Are there potential obstacles that might get in the way of the team participating in coaching? If so, what are they?"

Also, to help assess the team, the team coach can use:

- Team member interviews
- Team stakeholder interviews
- Validated team assessments
- Free screening tools—for example, the *High Performance Relationship and Team (HPR) Assessment* (Peters, 2015a), which assesses at an individual team level. (Available from https://app.assessmentgenerator.com/assessment/1913).
- Online surveys designed by the team coach
- Checklists—for example, the *Team Coaching Readiness Assessment* (Peters & Carr, 2013b)

If the team are ready for team coaching, the following steps are applicable.

- Introductory team coaching overview session—at this session, the team coach explains what team coaching is, what is involved, and how everyone can contribute.
- Pre-coaching debrief meeting on team assessment—the team coach presents information collated anonymously at this meeting. The team uses the information to decide for themselves their team strengths, development areas, challenges, opportunities, and potential areas of focus.

Phase 2: Coaching for Team Design

Since team structure and design contribute to 60% or more of a team's functioning (Hackman, 2011a), it is a judgment call if team coaching should proceed. Peters and Carr (2013b) state clearly that "without the right team design, coaching is unlikely to succeed" (p. 45). In such cases, they propose that the coach can support the team leader through individual coaching to see if it is possible to create the right conditions.

Phase 3: Team Launch

Activities viewed as necessary for a team launch or relaunch include:

- Putting aside adequate time, ideally offsite. Two to three days are suggested, with one day being the minimum.

- Co-creating a plan with the team leader, using team outputs from the assessment stage.
- Creating a safe reflective space for the team to think about their current state and ideal future.
- Developing an understanding and common vocabulary around team effectiveness. For example, the importance of safety, purpose, structure, camaraderie, repair, and success/results (Peters, 2015b).
- Supporting the team as they agree on a Team Charter, including its vision, purpose, values, working agreements, collective goals, and success measures.

Phase 4: Individual Coaching

Coaching can support the leader in reflecting on their team leadership behaviors and developing their team coaching skills. If coaching team members, it is essential that coaching helps team members develop individual goals aligned with the team goals.

Phase 5: Ongoing Team Coaching

The frequency of ongoing team coaching will depend on the team's needs. It can include the team coach attending a team meeting or specific team coaching sessions. Revisiting and reflecting on the Team Charter is integral to the ongoing coaching. Another important area is peer coaching. Peer coaching colleagues can provide "safe, deliberate, meaningful and skillful support to each other in order to help achieve their mutual and independent goals" (Peters & Carr, 2013b, p. 59). Training team members on coaching skills to support peer coaching can be helpful.

Phase 6: Review Learning and Successes

This phase is about supporting the team to reflect on the team coaching and, importantly, agree on how they will sustain momentum. It can be helpful to repeat assessments and team and stakeholder interviews. It is also a good opportunity for the team to reflect on how peer coaching and the Team Charter can help them sustain progress.

Conclusion

Based on a highly respected piece of doctoral research, The High-Performance Team Coaching (HPTC) Model, while presenting a process-driven approach, also allows the team coach to be flexible. A key emphasis of their work role is one-to-one coaching, especially for a leader, if the team is not ready for team coaching.

Chapter 21
Team of Teams: Team Coaching Within and Across Organizations

Introduction

This chapter will review the development of the concepts, team of teams and teaming, and how these ideas may be practically applied by the team coach.

The Challenge for Team Coaching

In making a case for team coaching, you will often hear about the danger of only focusing on executive coaching or the misplaced belief in the heroic team leader. What if today, despite its growth and professionalization, team coaching is placing too much hope in the power of individual teams to effect meaningful change? This chapter will contend that working with a team is often insufficient, even if the work is deeply grounded in systemic practice. We believe that team coaching can contribute to a more extensive conversation about how organizations can collaborate better. Firstly, team coaching needs to have a conversation with itself.

From published case studies (Clutterbuck et al., 2022; Hawkins, 2022) and our own experience as team coaches and team coach educators, it is evident that most team coaching, while systemic, supports single intact teams. Peters and Carr (2019) reviewed 17 studies that outline the benefits of team coaching while also calling for more robust evidence of the impact of team coaching. As team coaching effectiveness studies continue to emerge, we are confident, based on our experiences to date, that team coaching beyond the intact team, widely referred to as a "team of teams" or a "network of teams" approach, will be where team coaching can best prove its most meaningful value.

We hope this chapter challenges team coaches to think more broadly about their work and its potential impact. To help explore this topic, we will discuss different perspectives pointing to a new approach. While the thoughts presented may differ, we encourage team coaches to look for common threads and discover their unique way of engaging with this emerging work.

Teaming and Networks of Teams

In the book *Teaming*, Edmondson (2012) argued that a team, described as an "established, fixed group of people cooperating in pursuit of a common goal" (p. 13), is no longer enough. Instead, *teaming* is called for, which is described as "a dynamic activity, not a bounded, static entity" that is "largely determined by the mindset and practices of teamwork, not by the design and structures of effective teams" (Edmondson, 2012, p. 13).

The four pillars for effective teaming include (1) speaking up, (2) a collaborative mindset, (3) experimentation, and (4) ongoing reflection. In addition, four leadership behaviors to support teaming include (1) framing work as an opportunity for learning, (2) making it psychologically safe to team, (3) learning to learn from failure, and (4) supporting teams to span occupational and cultural boundaries. It is clear from the team coaching frameworks, models, and approaches discussed in Chaps. 14–20 that the concepts underpinning teaming are evident throughout.

In addition to teaming, Edmondson and co-authors, in the paper *No Team is an Island: How Leaders Shape Networked Ecosystems for Team Success* (Carboni et al., 2021), outline the reality of multiple reporting lines and overlapping teams. To align with what they describe as structural reality, they propose "switching focus to managing relationships among team members and between team members and external interests" (p. 6) rather than team building and stakeholder mapping exercises. We would argue that working with intact teams, networks of teams (a team of teams), and the ideas behind teaming are all essential.

Reflection questions for team coaches:

1. Where may I be too rigidly holding to the idea of an intact team as the unit of focus?
2. What ideas from *teaming* could further develop my team coaching practice, even when working with intact teams?
3. How can I support teams shifting from theoretical stakeholder mapping exercises, to actively managing relationships within and between organizations?

Team of Teams

In the article, *A Team of Teams World*, Drayton (2013) argues that traditional hierarchically structured organizations will continue to fail at an accelerating rate. Such organizational failure was apparent when General Stanley McChrystal took command of Iraq's Joint Special Operations Task Force in 2003. A combination of some of the best militaries in the world, including some of the best examples of teams (e.g., SEAL teams), were losing in the battle against al-Qaeda. The book *Team of Teams* describes setting aside a century of conventional wisdom, in a change they referred to as more about organizational architecture and culture than tactics or technology (McChrystal et al., 2015). Central to this change was addressing the *interface failures* between elite teams. When discussing this journey, McChrystal et al. (2015) and Fussell and Goodyear (2017) highlighted four key drivers:

1. *Developing Trust between Teams*—It was clear that trust within the best teams was strong, but trust between such teams was often lacking. An action taken to improve this was *representation*. A representative with good collaboration skills would get embedded, for a period, in another team. Not only did this increase understanding and respect, but it also supported the development of strong bonds and relationships across the task force. This initiative extended to external partner organizations (e.g., outside contractors).
2. *A Sense of Common Purpose*—They describe evolving their views from a "tribal small-team optic to a newfound feeling of higher purpose and calling" (Fussell & Goodyear, 2017, p. 19). For the task force, the aligning narrative shifted from talking about winning to discussing the changes required to win.
3. *Developing a Shared Consciousness*—This involved moving to a state where teams had an agreed understanding of the mutually shared problems, shared access to real-time information, and alignment on how to move forward. McChrystal et al. (2015) describe how this meant adopting an approach of "extreme transparency throughout our force and with our partner forces" (p. 163). They outline that at its peak, this involved up to several thousand people dialing into a video conference call, with General Stanley McChrystal and other senior leaders present, where anyone, irrespective of rank, could share.
4. *Empowering Execution*—The task force was still too slow. To address this, senior leaders pushed authority further down, albeit wisely, given the sensitive nature of the work. Importantly, they describe the results of quicker and better-quality decision-making.

Reflection questions for team coaches:

1. How can you best inspire and support trust building between teams, including teams external to the organization?
2. How can you support teams to reflect on how well their organizational purpose encourages within and across organization collaboration?
3. How can you best support multiple teams in developing a mutual understanding of their issues and potential ways forward?
4. How can you support leaders to reflect on how well they give autonomy and what they could do to improve?

Team of Teams and Agile Mindset Organizations

Widdowson and Barbour (2021) have outlined a shift from more siloed organizations towards what they describe as a *team of teams and agile mindset organizations* (see Fig. 21.1), commenting that "while there is little consistency on both the trajectory and speed of the journey, organizations are changing" and that "in truth, most organizations exist somewhere in-between" (p. 195). Maybe in-between is the desired destination. Supporting this view, when describing the Iraq Joint Special Operations Task Force as a hybrid structure, Fussell and Goodyear (2017) commented, "This hybrid structure harnessed the speed and information-sharing capabilities offered by the informal relationships found in networks while retaining the efficiency, reliability, and predictability of a bureaucracy" (p. 45).

To support an agile mindset, Widdowson and Barbour (2021) have highlighted the *agile values* outlined in The Agile Manifesto (2001) as helpful. Replacing the word software with product, these are (1) individuals and interactions over processes and tools, (2) working product over comprehensive documentation, (3) customer collaboration over contract negotiation, and (4) responding to change over following a plan. Supporting the importance of agile values, Kroll and Shea (2018) reported that teams that performed better were *being agile*, not just *doing agile* (e.g., agile methodologies such as Kanban and Scrum).

Twelve principles for organizations wishing to move towards a *team of teams and agile mindset organization* include (adapted from Widdowson & Barbour, 2021):

1. Has a purpose, vision, and values (behaviors) at an organizational and team level that prioritizes and rewards internal and external collaboration.
2. Purposefully builds capability through coaching, mentoring, team coaching, team-centric leadership development, process development training, and collaboration and relationship-related training for all employees.

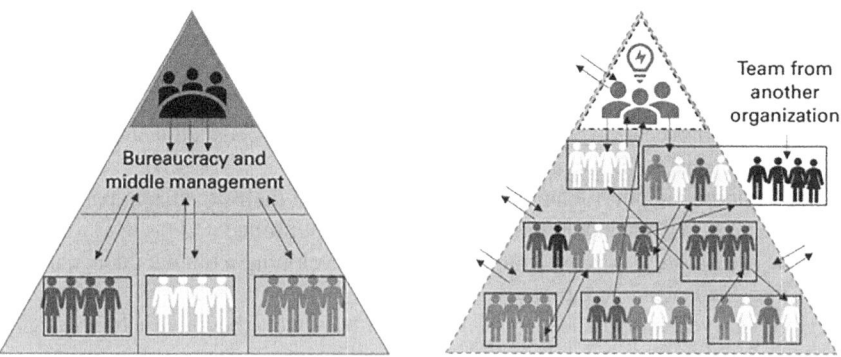

Fig. 21.1 Illustration of traditional siloed organizations and *team of teams and agile mindset organizations* (Source: Widdowson & Barbour, 2021, p. 195—With permission)

3. Appreciates diversity as a critical strength and proactively develops it.
4. Embraces approaches and techniques that maximize employee inclusion at an individual, team, and organizational level.
5. Understands the benefits and encourages different types of teams based on need (e.g., intact leadership teams, intact functional teams, cross-functional teams, project teams, self-led teams, agile teams, teams that come together and disband quickly—i.e., in-house teaming, multi-organization teaming).
6. Prioritizes reflection and learning, illustrated best by self-generated, colleague, organizational, and external partner feedback.
7. Encourages and provides opportunities for colleagues to take charge of their career development and growth.
8. Establishes planning, innovation, and business improvement processes that embrace longer-term and iterative approaches.
9. Creates time-sensitive information flows within the organization and with partners that support decision-making and action.
10. Agree on decision-making parameters for all employees that embrace empowerment, complement the organization's strategic intent, and maximize customer responsiveness.
11. View customers and other stakeholders as valued partners and proactively manage each relationship.
12. Embrace technology as a partner for the future (e.g., collaboration platforms, AI).

Exercise for Team Coaches to Support Teams and Organizations to Reflect on their Organizational Design

Explain each principle and ask the team to reflect and have a dialogue on the following:

- Based on your desired future state, how relevant is the statement?
- How well are you doing at present? (1 = poorly and 10 = brilliantly)
- What would better look like? (1 = poorly and 10 = brilliantly)
- What would be the benefits of improving this area?
- How can you move towards it?
- What could stop progress, and how could you overcome it?
- How can you measure progress?

For some, operating between a traditional hierarchical structure and a "team of teams and agile mindset" structure may not be enough. For those looking to explore a more radical perspective, see Laloux (2014), who, in the book *Reinventing Organisations*, describes the potential of organizations structured around self-organizing teams supported by coaches when needed.

Creating a "Teaming" and "Team of Teams" Culture

Hawkins (2022) presents a roadmap for creating a *teaming* and *team of teams* culture, which includes the following seven steps:

1. The right external team coaches are selected, viewing them as partners, not suppliers.
2. Developing internal team coaches, with support and supervision from experienced team coaches as required.
3. Through leadership development with team coaching at its core, develop leaders so they can coach their leadership teams.
4. Training managers to develop their teams, using technology to scale and give consistency.
5. Structure harvesting of organizational learning from team activities to ascertain company culture.
6. Team of teams coaching that is purposeful, based on a free flow of information, role-modeled by leaders and that addresses issues identified through organizational learning.
7. Teaming and partnering becomes how we do business with all our stakeholders.

Expected outputs from this approach include an increase in (1) team coaching provision, (2) effective teams, (3) organizational effectiveness, and (4) value creation through partnering with all stakeholders.

Reflection Questions for Team Coaches

To develop a *teaming* and *team of teams* approach within an organization:

1. What is your compelling narrative about the need for such an approach?
2. What development areas does this work highlight for you as a team coach?
3. Who might you need to partner with?
4. How can you use this road map as inspiration to co-create with an organization?

Moving Beyond Systemic to Meta-Systemic

As discussed in Chap. 14, Lawrence (2021a, 2021b) discusses five versions of how we can think about systemic, which include (1) First-order linear thinking, (2) First-order non-linear thinking, (3) Second-order thinking, (4) Complex adaptive systems, and (5) Meta-systemic (see Chap. 14, Table 14.2 for a description of each).

Lawrence (2021a) cautions against overidentifying with one or more of the five categories, highlighting the benefit of "the more ways of thinking I have access to, the more likely I am to be useful" (p. 10). Nevertheless, in thinking about working at an organizational level and beyond, there are critical areas Meta-Systemic thinking asks team coaches to consider, which include:

- *View the team as an imaginary construct—a social construct*

- The meta-aware team coach appreciates that considering the team as a unit can sometimes help simplify things, while knowing team members constantly dialogue with others inside and outside the organization. They value the position that "there is no inside or outside of a team or organization" (Lawrence, 2021b, p. 88).
- *Value other individual and team development perspectives*
- Team coaches must remain open to the essence of the work, which is about human collaboration. As team coaching tries to explain to others what it is and is not, it should be careful not to exclude other areas. Instead, a meta-systemic perspective asks for openness, curiosity, and partnering with whatever may support an organization to become more effective, "including perspectives that may not yet have shown up in the team coaching literature" (Lawrence, 2021b, p. 75).
- *Work beyond the team at an organizational or even a societal level*

- Operating at a meta-systemic level can result in a team coach focusing on supporting others to collaborate and team. It can involve introducing an educational element to the work and deciding to focus efforts at an organizational level.

Reflection questions for team coaches:
- What is your own developing theory of what systemic means for you and your work?
- How do you keep asking who else must be in the room, metaphorically or physically?

So Where Do You Go Next?

Reading these various perspectives could overwhelm any team coach and make them ask—Is this something I want to be involved in? And if so, where would I start? In the following section, we have outlined typical obstacles and our thoughts regarding each.

1. *"Surely, such cultural change can't be the sole responsibility of team coaching."*
   While true, team coaching is well-positioned to partner with other areas (e.g., organizational development) to consider the future of organizations.
2. *"It's hard enough (time, budget, etc.) getting one team to agree on a team coaching journey, never mind multiple teams."*
   In our experience, when you share the potential limitations of only working with one team, the question will often be asked: How would you approach this?

While the result of the conversation may not mean working at an organizational level, it can result in working with more than one team.

3. *"I'm not sure I have the confidence to start such a conversation, never mind engage in this work."*

Team coaching is, at its heart, about relationships and collaboration. We would encourage team coaches to explore, partner, and find confidence along with others.

4. *"There appears to be very little written about this. Where can I learn more?"*

While we wait for practitioner writing, research and theory to develop, explore what has been written and spoken on. Learn through co-creation with others and supervision of your work. Become a pioneer in this unfolding area rather than waiting to be taught.

Conclusion

We trust that this exploration of *team of teams—Team coaching within and across organizations* can inspire and support team coaches to think about how they practice today and what the future may require of them. As we wait for the literature to develop, we encourage team coaches to act as pioneers and practice with courage, creativity, and a heart of collaboration as we all work together to build a better future.

Part IV

Chapter 22
Using Coaching Tools for Team Coaching

Introduction

Coaching tools are often seen by coaches as a useful resource and within team coaching can provide a useful structure to a team coaching session. However team coaches need to have available a wide range of tools to be able to flex and adapt to meet team needs. In this chapter we will explore the role and value of tools within the team coaching session. Secondly, we will share some of our proven tools which we have used in team coaching assignments.

The Value of Coaching Tools in Team Coaching

As experienced team coaches we believe in an evidence-based and diverse approach. This means we look to draw into our practice a wide array of tools, techniques, models, and exercises to support the leaders and teams we work with. Some are tools we have developed, but most are drawn from courses, books, and conversations we have had along the way of the 20 plus years we have been coaching. In many cases, we cannot even remember the original source.

Our aim is to integrate these into what we each describe as our personal integrated coaching models. Most coaches have developed such an approach, and is the way they articulate their approach to coaching clients, which goes beyond a simple one- or two-dimensional label, such as "I am a cognitive behavioural coach" or "I use person centred and gestalt approaches," but is a sophisticated integration of years of experience and training (see Passmore, 2021 for an example).

These tools fall into the same category, they are drawn from multiple approaches and can be integrated into a wider approach, with the aim of creating a seamless experience for clients.

J. Passmore et al., *Becoming a Team Coach*, https://doi.org/10.1007/978-3-031-63546-5_22

They are offered here with the intent you will adapt and integrate them into your wider coaching practice, taking into account your own professional competence, preferences, and curiosity, and in making selections of which tool to use when, you will deeply consider both the situation and the team who you are working with.

It is worth remembering that tools are not a replacement for a strong client relationship, a sound evidence base for your work and selecting the right tool to fit the team and the context or challenge they are exploring.

In deciding which tool to use it may be helpful to reflect on the following questions:

- Have I developed rapport with this team?
- Do I have sufficient time to use this tool within the time we have agreed for this session, and what else we need to achieve?
- Do I have permission from all of the team to use the tool?
- Do the team members understand the tool and what they have been invited to do?
- Have I positioned the tool in a way which allows them, me or the tool to "fail" (one way of doing this is to introduce the tool as an "experiment".)
- Have I positioned the tool in a way which encourages not only short-term benefit, but which also encourages deeper reflection on the process, after the team coaching session?

Team Coaching Tools

Tool 1: Potholes and Hedges

Hedges and potholes offer a metaphor to consider the risks that could occur on projects. Hedges are clearly observed risks which are known and can be planned for. Potholes are unforeseen risks, which if not planned for, can derail a project.

When working with a team we usually start by describing the metaphors: hedges and potholes. We then encourage the team to list the Hedges (foreseen risks), followed by generating their plans to mitigate or manage these risks. Secondly, to move to potholes (unforeseen risks,) and consider these (previously unforeseen) risks. While the first comes to mind easily, the latter requires challenge and provocation for the team to think more broadly and creatively to identify these (unforeseen) risks. Finally moving to generate mitigation and management plans for each risk.

Tool 2: Coat of Arms

The Coat of Arms technique is a great way to explore the team's or organization's values. A coat of arms is a hereditary emblem, usually displayed on a shield or flag. It was used in the Middle Ages to represent a family and was widely adopted by most noble families across Western Europe. Each symbol on the coat of arms represents a key attribute or aspect about the family.

The tool involves inviting each team member to produce their own personal coat of arms and then to explain their Coat of Arms to the rest of the team. The exercise can be extended by inviting the team to produce a Coat of Arms for the team.

It is a great tool when a new team has come together, or is seeking a change in direction, and focusing it on values provides an opportunity for a deeper conversation about what each member of the team considers important and which guides their behavior.

Tool 3: Disney Model

This technique was developed by Robert Dilts (1995). It encourages greater creative thinking by providing a space by encouraging team members to adopt three different perspectives: dreamer, critic, and realist. It can be used in a variety of contexts. The model works in a sequence, with team members invited to act as the "dreamer" or visionary. In this role there is no need for individuals to consider what is practical or possible, but to instead generate a vision of what could be. In the case of Walt Disney this reflects his vision for Epcot.

Once the creativity has been exhausted, the team can move to the second stage: to act as the realist. How could these visions be turned from drawing board fantasy to reality: action plans, resources, and how much time would be needed.

The final phase of using the tool with the team is to invite team members to act as critical friends. In this role the aim is to evaluate the ideas, examining in detail both roadblocks, limitations and weaknesses.

Tool 4: Constellations

The constellations process was developed by Bert Hellinger, a German psychotherapist, originally for use in family systems (Hellinger, 2003). The technique works well with a team, using pebbles, Lego characters, or chess pieces. Each team member is invited to create a spatial representation of their current situation by mapping it out using the chess piece or pebbles, with each piece representing a person in their system.

The coach explores with the team member where they had placed the chess piece (pebble), enquiring what the position represents for them and its relation to other team members. The individual is then invited to physically move the pieces to new positions to an ideal or desired relationship, and again exploring what is preventing it, and how the actors could make changes to enable this new position (relationship) to come about.

At each stage individuals can be invited to record with photos the maps they have created and to note, or discuss in twos or threes the relationships and barriers which are preventing the ideal position (relationships).

Tool 5: Empty Chair

This is a technique drawn from Gestalt Therapy but is used in a number of different approaches. It can be used one-to-one or can be used in a team session. A member of the team is invited to have a conversation with a stakeholder who is not present, but where there is a challenging and difficult relationship. The client is invited to sit facing the empty chair and describe the client and then to talk to them as if present. They can be invited to move to the chair and act as if the person is present, and acting as they give a response. Finally, the client can be invited to move away from the two chairs to the side of the room, firstly by themselves and then by inviting the group to contribute to share perspectives on the conversation, and ways the client may adapt their approach to this relationship.

Tool 6: Six Thinking Hats

This technique was developed by Edward de Bono (1985) to assess options from different angles/viewpoints. Most teams are dominated by one or two mindsets (hats). By using this technique a more rounded perspective can be achieved. The members of the team are invited to analyze the option using different lenses (hats), one at a time.

The technique may start by clarifying the idea or option before the coach invites different team members to adopt a specific hat, or perspective. It can be particularly fun if the coach has available six different colored caps.

Most people have come across the concept before, but it is worth the coach reminding the team what each color represents:

1. White hat: Facts—What is the data available? What are past trends?
2. Red hat: Emotions—What does your intuition say, what is your gut reaction and emotions? How will other people react? In group settings, this can be done on a piece of paper: everybody votes and hands in their paper.
3. Black hat: Risks—Why might it not be a good option? What may go wrong? Why might proceeding with caution be recommended (dangers and difficulties)?
4. Yellow hat: Positive aspects—Positive aspects, optimistic outcomes, strengths, values, and benefits.
5. Green hat: Opportunities—Creative solutions/brainstorming. Free thinking with little criticism. What are the possibilities, alternatives, and new ideas? New life.

6. Blue hat: Plans—Process control or thinking more about the future.

Tool 7: Fancy-Dress Party

We all like dressing up whether it is for a special occasion or for a fun party. When we do so we can take on the identity of another person, be this a space explorer, a baby, or a person from a different country. These dressing up games allow us to test out different roles and consider how they may affect our relationships. This tool revolves around an imagined fancy-dress party. Like many coaching tools, it starts with a single question, If you were going to a fancy dress party, what (or who) would you go as, and who from the team would you go with (and who would they go as?). Team members can write their answers independently and then share.

The coach can use the shared story to explore the relationship between the two people and what the characters they have chosen might represent.

The tool can be either used one-to-one as part of team coaching, or be used in the team coaching session, with team members sharing their dressing up plans.

Tool 8: Blob Tree

The "Blob Tree" was developed by Pip Wilson for use with children to explore their emotional states (Wilson, 2018). It can be used in team coaching as a light-hearted, fun way to raise self and team awareness about where people may sit in relationship with others in the team.

The coach can share the picture (see Wilson, 2018) and then ask people to select a character (each charter on the tree has a number) and explain why they consider themself to be at that place.

The coach can extend the exercise to ask where the person would like to move to and who might help them to traverse from their current branch or position to their new location on or by the team.

There are multiple versions of the Blob Trees available on the Internet and the coach can select one which best suits their client and the situation.

Tool 9: Seventh-Generation Thinking

Most people accept that the world faces an existential crisis. The evidence concerns the fact we are witnessing an unprecedentedly rapid change in the earth's climate. While the earth's climate has cooled and warmed multiple times over the billions of years of earth's history, what is different this time is that instead of this happening over several centuries as a gradual process, it is happening over several decades, and will bring devastation to low lying areas as waters rise, to food production as temperatures rise, and to ecology across the planet threatening many species' already fragile existence. On top of this, humanity is consuming finite resources at an unsustainable pace, whether that is rare earths or precious metals. In short we cannot go on like this for another 1000 years: we need to change.

Some of the largest controllers of the planet's wealth, and the largest uses of these finite resources are the companies we coach. In our view it would be remiss of us if we did not introduce the ideas of sustainability, as it would have been remiss if we were coaches 200 years ago working with cotton farmers in the USA or shipping companies in the UK and had neglected to mention the slave trade.

Seventh-generation thinking is an idea drawn from native peoples and encourages individuals and teams to take the long view. By this we do not mean 15 or 25 years (about one generation), we mean 200 years, or around seven generations.

When one of the editorial teams' daughters was born they planted a tree in their garden. Ten years on, the small knee high spindle (2 foot) has grown into a 20 foot high tree. In a further 10 years, it may be 30 feet, and, in 60 years, it will cast shade across the garden for her own children to play under. But maybe in 100 years after this, after you and I, reader are dead and forgotten, that tree will still be casting shade for your great, great, great, great grandchildren, who have come to play on the swing which then hangs for that majestic tree, with my great, great, great, great grandchildren.

In essence the decisions and actions we take today cast long shadows. Inviting teams to think about how future generations, not just today's investors, will view their actions. Seventh-generation thinking urges current leaders to live and work for the benefit of the future generation, as custodians of their organizations and of our planet, not owners, paying regards as they do so for our planet's finite resources and the billions of sentient species which share this planet with us.

As the Iroquois people said: "*In all of your deliberations... look and listen for the welfare of the whole people and have always in view not only the past and present but also the coming generations, even those whose faces are yet beneath the surface of the ground—the unborn of the future*".

Tool 10: Neil's Wheel

Neil's wheel was developed by Neil Scotton for people to use to "*easily and consistently open up deeper, inspiring and transformative conversations*" (Scotton, 2020).
The team coach can put it to use when:

– They are working on the early stages of a new team.
– They want to explore meaning, purpose, making change happen, or more.
– Alignment and clarity are needed. Such as regarding team culture, goals, priorities, team identity, etc.
– After a conflict to re-establish trust.

– They need to connect what is going on outside of the team with what matters to the team.

There is no one single way to use the wheel. The team coach can share the picture of the wheel and observe how the team explores the segments, what they say, or to which segment they are drawn and which they avoid.

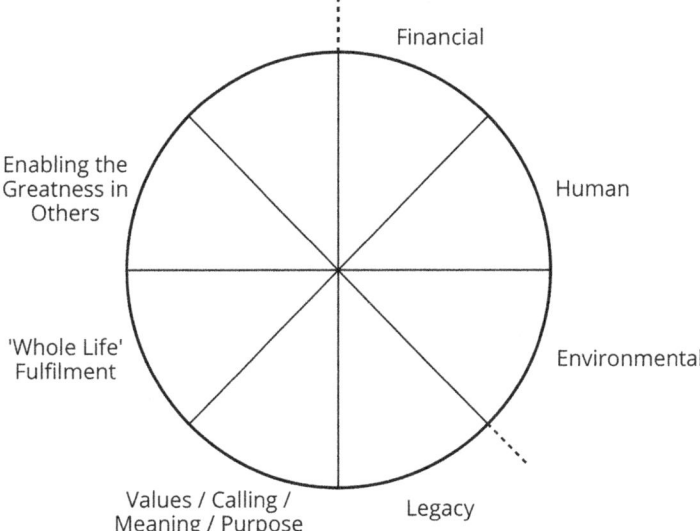

Source: neilswheel.org, © Neil Scotton, 2020 (Used with permission of Neil Scotton)

There are seven (7) segments named and one blank. The team decides what is missing for their own wheel/system. Each segment can be explored distinctly, in combination with another, or all segments together. The team can look at all the segments in one session or explore each segment in different sessions. The team members can "score" the wheel collectively, or they can do this individually and compare scores and further reflect on similarities and differences. Another way to use it can be for the team to divide further the segments, with subdivisions, or to explore the importance of each segment.

Some questions the team coach can ask are:

– Is there a segment you avoid exploring?
– What are you most drawn to?
– What is included in each segment?
– How do all the pieces feel together?
– What questions do you want to ask yourselves and each other, as you walk through the segments?
– What thoughts, feelings, or new ideas arise?
– What questions emerge for the team?

Neil's Wheel is a simple and free tool with two main advantages: it is neutral, which means that the coach does not guide the team's thinking, and it invites a range of perspectives from the team on each segment.

Conclusions

We have set out in this chapter how tools can be useful to the team coach and share just a small selection of coaching tools and techniques which we use in our work. A fuller selection of team and individual teams is available and we direct readers to these resources (Passmore et al., 2021, 2022, 2023).

Part V

Chapter 23
Developing Your Team Coaching Business

Introduction

This chapter will discuss how to develop your team coaching business as an internal or external team coach. The chapter will outline five foundational principles for team coaching business development and a 12-step business development process. For the most part, we will not separate internal or external, as the principles and steps can apply to both areas.

The Five Foundational Principles

Principle 1: Reframing Business Development

Many of us do not like the idea of the highly trained salesperson exuding warmth, repeatedly using our name while asking brilliant questions that can be hard to say no to. For example, someone selling income protection insurance asks, what would you miss doing if you could not work? The prospective client shares openly. Pauses. The salesperson then gently asks if anything else comes to mind. As the prospective client keeps talking about the things they love but can no longer afford, their mind starts wondering about the merits of income protection insurance. If the insurance salesperson is considered genuine and with good intent, the chances of a sale increase the more the prospective client talks about their concerns. You might ask, what is wrong with this? The answer is nothing, if the prospective client has concerns about what happens to them if they can no longer work, was connected to the insurance salesperson through a recommendation and requires help working out what they need.

J. Passmore et al., *Becoming a Team Coach*,
https://doi.org/10.1007/978-3-031-63546-5_23

Selling, or being influenced, is a part of everyday life. A brilliant salesperson with a great product can be extremely useful as we navigate a complex world. Unfortunately, sales or business development can get a bad name from unscrupulous salespeople, selling what, on some occasions, is not needed. For example, a message from a stranger on a social media platform, with no coaching experience evident, with a statement like—I've noticed your excellent work here. I would love to know how you feel about increasing your coaching business × 10 through a simple 6-step plan. If only it were that easy.

Thankfully, with team coaching, there is an opportunity to move past the idea of selling or even business development. Instead of selling or business development, we prefer exploring *partnership* opportunities. A conversation among equals, attempting to determine if a partnership is worth pursuing. The client explores how to best develop their team with the support of a team coach curious about the same question.

Reflective Question for the Team Coach
- If I have not already, how can I reframe business development?

Principle 2: Human Connection Before Process

Widdowson and Barbour (2021), when discussing teams highlight the importance of *connection before work,* even with significant deadlines pending. Education specialists talk about *connection before correction.* Similarly, the term *connection before business development* is equally applicable when developing a team coaching business.

In sales training, the mantras *people buy people* or *always be connecting* are common. So, what does a great connection look like? Norcross (2010) has outlined the relationship elements with the strongest correlation to successful therapeutic outcomes. Extrapolating the factors, we believe some of the most helpful to reflect on in the context of business development are:

- *Being empathetic*—means absorbing yourself in the client world and showing, to some extent, that you understand and appreciate something of their experience.
- *From the outset, discussing a joint purpose*—means using language like, if it suits to work together, it would be great if we can partner on creating something that makes a lasting difference.
- *Having positive regard*—means observing and not judging. It means accepting the client's world as not broken, just different. It means being warmly curious.
- *Being genuine with appropriate self-disclosure*—means being okay with being you. It means sharing our concerns, fears, and hopes. It means a rare form of honesty. For example, saying to a prospective client, "My most significant concern with everything we are talking about is that most of this type of work lacks impact due to short-term thinking. I'm only interested in partnering to make lasting change."

Reflective Question for the Team Coach
- What are my connecting strengths and development areas?

Principle 3: Why Coaches Should Be Naturally Brilliant at Business Development

There are several reasons why coaches should excel at business development, including the reality that coaches:

- Are, in many cases, drawn to coaching due to a desire to help and make a difference.
- Are trained on the importance of chemistry (connection) before work.
- In their work, listen deeply and ask questions that illuminate awareness.
- Listen beyond the words, investigate patterns and develop hypotheses.
- Are predisposed towards seeing clients grow and take ownership of their journey.

When running business development simulations during team coach training, we regularly witness team coaches realize that the skills they need are already there. Often, what is missing is confidence.

Reflective Question for the Team Coach
- Do I believe I have the skill set to be brilliant at business development, and if not, what stops me from thinking this?

Principle 4: Deciding on Your Team Coaching Business Model

Some of the business model choices faced by a team coach include:

When working as an employee of an organization:
- Team coaching while attending to other duties.
- Full-time in-house team coach. It may include training others, supervising, and working with external partners.
- Working in-house while developing your team coaching practice, to eventually practice externally.

When working as an external team coach:
- Developing a business focused on team coaching.
- Working as an associate for a team coaching business.
- Developing the team coaching practice in an established coaching business.

In our experience, a team coach is more likely to be involved in more than one of these models. A fundamental choice for external team coaches is balancing the investment required to develop a sustainable business, versus working as an associate. In addition, as team coaching grows, many practicing team coaches are also involved in team coaching education, supervision, or research.

Reflective Question for the Team Coach
• Who can I speak to, to explore the best career development journey for me as a team coach? (e.g., from your network, supervisor, coach, team coaching focused businesses, employer, potential employers).

Principle 5: Developing your Team Coaching Brand

Developing your personal team coaching brand is essential regardless of your business model. A brand is effectively a story, an essence, a personality, and a collection of behaviors that attract or repel. Brands know who they target and how to engage their audience in dialogue. Whoever your potential buyers are, you must find ways to enter their consciousness. Some team coaches target a niche market, whereas others take a broader approach. We have seen both working.

Before telling the world about your story, it is essential to understand who you are as a coach. Bachkirova (2021) suggests looking at this from three levels. These are:

Level 1—Self-inventory. It is about completing an honest assessment of your capabilities, qualifications, and commitment to ongoing development.

Level 2—Self as an instrument. Referring to the importance of connecting with others, as discussed in Principle 2, they have suggested that when a coach realizes they are the main instrument in the work, it reveals a new level of understanding. This thinking aligns with our emphasis on a team coach's *"way of being"* as central.

Level 3—Fully professional self. "At this new level, coaches see themselves not only as an instrument that is part of a complex dynamic system with a client, but also as being part of a much wider set of social relationships that are at play when they coach" (Bachkirova, 2021, p. 43). At level 3, some key areas of importance include co-experimentation, collaboration, creativity, resilience in dealing with issues, being at ease that the criteria for success might not be evident, having a thought-out philosophy and not mindlessly following others, knowing your purpose, being clear about the process you follow and having good supervision.

Reflective Question for the Team Coach
• What unique value as a team coach do I bring to the world, and how can I courageously share this with those I wish to partner with?

The Twelve-Step Business Development Process

While presented sequentially, the following proposed business development process is much more complex and agile. Depending on the situation, steps can change order and also be repeated.

Step 1: Putting Yourself in the Shop Window

If working internally, this can mean:

- Advocating for the difference that team coaching can make
- Building successful case studies
- Creating ambassadors for your work
- Ensuring you are getting in front of the decision-makers

If working externally, this can mean:

- Developing your social media presence (e.g., LinkedIn)
- Designing a website (even if not heavily used, the process brings clarity)
- Developing case studies, requesting testimonials, and asking for referrals/ introductions
- Seeking networking, speaking, and writing opportunities

Whether working internally or externally, telling your brand story can take courage. For example, it is common knowledge that a short video on LinkedIn will have significantly more reach than a standard post. Nevertheless, many team coaches would shy away from the discomfort of speaking on camera. Developing your brand will mean becoming *comfortable with discomfort*.

Step 2: Connecting with Potential Clients

By putting yourself in the shop window, opportunities to connect with clients will emerge. Once they do, some of our top tips include:

- Irrespective of who contacts whom, act professionally, showing appreciation at all times, even with someone you know
- Be concise in your communication, always finishing with a proposed next step (e.g., time slots you are free to speak next)
- Move the conversation from writing to speaking as soon as possible. You leave so much of who you are behind if you only communicate through the written word.

Step 3: The Initial Conversations

Some top tips include:

- Do your homework. Know as much as possible about the person and company you are meeting.
- Keep it short. The initial call or meeting is about establishing if there is a more extensive conversation worth having.
- Add value without expecting anything in return (e.g., share a helpful insight from your work with teams).
- Be confident in your capability as a team coach, even if you doubt yourself.
- Ask about them and the teams they work in and lead.
- Get across what drives you to do this work (your purpose) without getting into too much detail on the how.
- Ascertain if there is value in having a further conversation.
- Agree on the next step, including who else should be included (e.g., you might share some information about team coaching or agree on a time to have a more extensive conversation).

Step 4: Being Prepared for the Long Game

Putting it simply, people are busy. As humans, we spend much of our lives over-thinking what others are thinking. When someone does not reply or get back to us, we can believe they must not be interested or even judge them as rude. In our experience, it is essential to:

- Remain patient—clients often return after an extended period, normally apologetically.
- Be compassionate—we have no idea what is happening in people's lives.
- Stay on their radar—it could be saying hello at a conference or simply liking a LinkedIn post.

Step 5: Exploring Client Needs Using a Coaching Approach

Use all your coaching skills to learn about the team's needs, including their needs as a leader. Some examples of questions and statements include:

- What journey has your team been on so far?
- Tell me about what your team are great at and what needs work.
- Based on the challenges you have mentioned, what would be the consequences of not addressing them?

- What difference could developing your team make for you, the team, and those who rely on it?
- Based on what you know about my (our) work, what can I do to support you?
- How would you see yourself involved if we partnered together?
- What question have I not asked that you would maybe like to think about?
- Would the following be an accurate summary of what you have shared?
- What else comes to mind?
- Based on this discussion, I'm confident I can design a proposal that should interest you. What are your thoughts on that?
- If rapport is strong, ask—Would you have any guide on a budget?
- Ideally, we would meet to discuss the proposal. However, I'm happy to be guided by you.
- Would the following be a fair summary of the steps agreed upon?

Note that at no point have you jumped in with a solution. You want the client to look forward to seeing the proposal.

Step 6: The Team Coaching Proposal—First Submission

There is no one way to structure a proposal document. The following ten steps are a guide only.

1. *Cover page*—Use imagery that tells your story and, ideally, a brand tagline that explains the value you bring to the world. Ensure you use the correct client company logo.
2. *Who we are*—An opportunity to briefly tell your story of why and how you add value.
3. *Needs identified so far*—Summarize the client needs you have identified so far. Check to see what may have changed if presenting in person or online.
4. *Why team coaching*—Explain briefly what team coaching is, evidence of its impact, what it involves, and what benefits it could offer the client, based on their needs.
5. *Why team coach with us*—An opportunity to share a relevant case study and testimonial(s).
6. *A potential team coaching journey*—Outline graphically what a team coaching journey for the client would look like (see example in Fig. 24.1). Ask the client for initial feedback on it.
7. *Investment proposal*—Outline the investment required, either broken down into components or as one overall package (please note, there are differing views on these two approaches, and it is a matter of personal preference). Different packages (e.g., Gold, Silver, and Bronze) can be helpful.
8. *The team coaches*—Images and profiles of the team that would deliver the work.
9. *Appendices*—Share anything else you think is relevant. For example, it could be further case studies or testimonials.

10. *Next steps and thank you*—Be brave in saying you would like to partner with the client. Agree on the next steps.

Step 7: The Feedback Conversation

Ask—What is working for you, and what are you unsure about? Welcome any resistance as helpful information. Hardingham (2021) helpfully comments when writing about resistance, "It is the part of our client that protects what they are, the part of our client that is not yet ready to risk change." They further state, "If we can embrace our client's resistance when we experience its push-back, then our client will be reassured at a deep level that we are safe and mean them no harm" (p. 55).

Step 8: The Team Coaching Proposals—Second Submissions or More

It is usual for a proposal to be amended based on client feedback and other needs you identify. It is good practice to ensure version control. In addition, it is also good practice to only share proposals in pdf format. For larger contracts, multiple meetings are likely.

Step 9: The Commercial Negotiation

In theory, the more the client buys into the proposal, the easier the negotiation. Best-in-class negotiation includes considering each negotiation variable. Some examples include the engagement length, design and delivery commercials, payment terms, cancellation policy, travel, resources, and the number of team coaches. Having an optimum, desirable and essential for each variable is helpful. The optimum refers to the ideal world (e.g., a year-long engagement). Desirable refers to what you would be happy with (e.g., a six month engagement). The essential refers to your bottom line (e.g., two days, with the promise to discuss a second phase).

Step 10: Agreeing a Partnership

Agreements to work together can be formal or informal. It is best practice to outline what each party agrees to do throughout the engagement period. It is common practice for clients to request the signing of an NDA (Non-Disclosure Agreement).

Step 11: Implementing a Partnership

Maintaining a partnership requires constant dialogue and contracting, as discussed in Chap. 8. A simple technique to use with a client is WWW (what worked well) and EBI (even better if). When disagreements or challenges present, it is essential to keep listening, engaging, and working towards a joint resolution.

Step 12: Preparing Your Shop Window Refresh

Asking for client testimonials helps refresh your shop window. It is essential to agree with the client on how you will use it and what names will appear on it. In addition, with similar agreement from your client, case studies can be beneficial. If a client is unwilling or unable to do either, they may be willing to recommend you to a colleague or contact or act as a reference.

Conclusion

If team coaches stay focused on connection before business development, identifying clients' needs and tapping into their coaching skills, best-in-class business development will follow.

Chapter 24
Designing a Team Coaching Program

Introduction

Knowing how to design a team coaching program is a key skill when working with teams. Team coaching programs will flex to the needs of the team; however, the team coach will need to understand how to structure and design a team coaching journey. Usually, the design will be co-created with the team leader and team following a range of diagnostic interventions. These will be discussed in more depth within this chapter, however, they may include one-to-one interviews with team members and or a team 360 questionnaire. The diagnostic interventions help the team coach gain clarity on what are the outcomes the team want to achieve from the team coaching journey, the strengths of the team, and opportunities for further development.

What to Consider Before Designing a Team Coaching Program?

Before starting the design, it is important to consider the following:

- What outcomes does the team want from the program?
- What will be their measures of success?
- Who is the team and what is the size of the team?
- Who are their key stakeholders, customers, etc.?
- How long will a team coaching program be?
- How many team coaches should be involved?
- What diagnostics should be used?

J. Passmore et al., *Becoming a Team Coach*, https://doi.org/10.1007/978-3-031-63546-5_24

- What type of interventions will be included in the program? For example, team coaching workshop sessions, one-to-one coaching, observing the team in action, team development.
- Will team coaching sessions be held face-to-face, virtually, or a hybrid of both?
- What is the location for the interventions, and will these be suitable for team coaching?

What Could a Team Coaching Program Look Like?

Widdowson and Barbour (2021) suggested a five-phase process (Fig. 24.1):

Phase 1—Contracting and understanding the need, objectives, and readiness for team coaching.

Phase 2—Discovering areas of strengths in the team and opportunities for development, using diagnostic one-to-one interviews and team 360 questionnaires.

Phase 3—Co-designing the program in partnership with the team leader, team, and key stakeholders.

Insights gained from phases one to three will then help the team coach to identify the objectives and areas of priority for the team to focus on.

Phase 4—A series of team coaching workshops will take place. These will, however, flex and adapt depending on the needs of the team.

Phase 5—Evaluation of the team coaching program—reviewing measurements agreed in Stage 1.

It is important to note that this is only an indicative example and team coaching design will often vary depending on the needs of the team. However, conducting some form of diagnosis is essential to understand where the team is currently and what should be prioritized.

Contracting is explored in Chap. 8, Sect. 2, therefore, the other phases involved in the design will be explored further below.

What Diagnostics Can Be Conducted?

There are a number of different ways to diagnose the health and effectiveness of a team. These include:

- *One-to-one interviews* with team members and stakeholders. Interviews are extremely helpful in engaging team members in the team coaching journey, answering any questions they may have and building relationships. They enable the team coach to understand what is working well in the team, what can be improved, and what team members would like to achieve from the team coaching program.

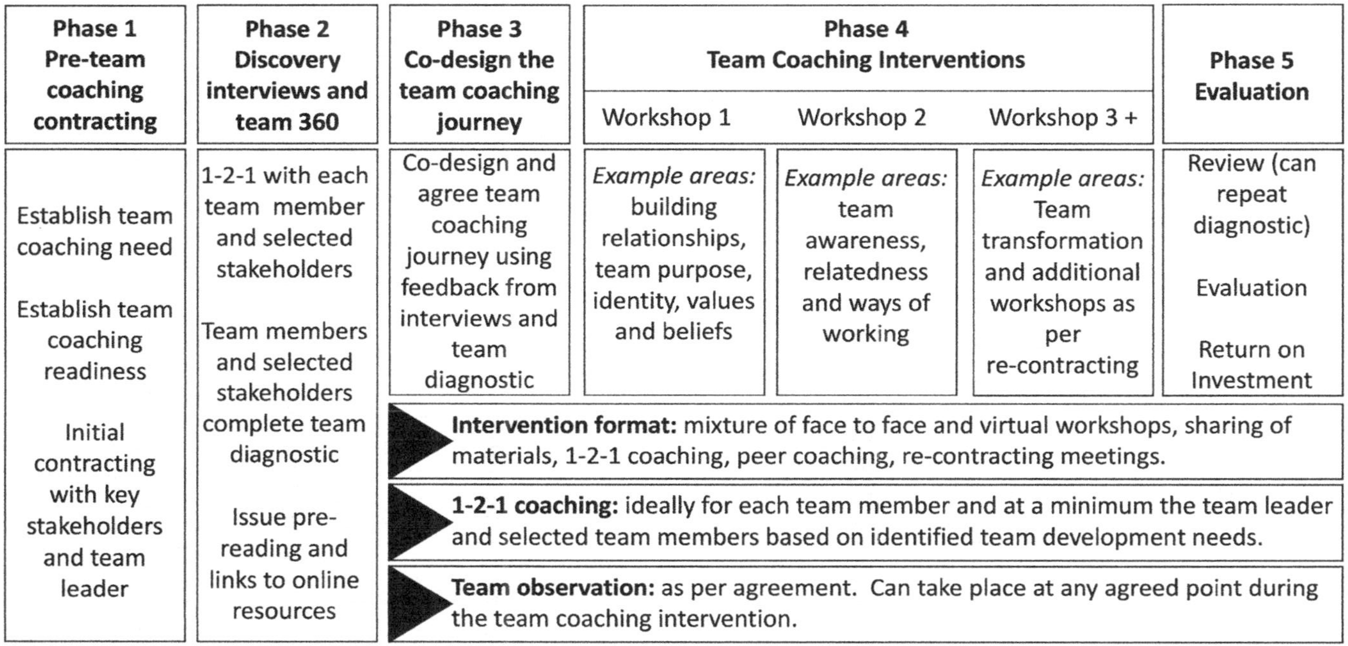

Phase 1 Pre-team coaching contracting	Phase 2 Discovery interviews and team 360	Phase 3 Co-design the team coaching journey	Phase 4 Team Coaching Interventions			Phase 5 Evaluation
			Workshop 1	Workshop 2	Workshop 3 +	
Establish team coaching need	1-2-1 with each team member and selected stakeholders	Co-design and agree team coaching journey using feedback from interviews and team diagnostic	*Example areas:* building relationships, team purpose, identity, values and beliefs	*Example areas:* team awareness, relatedness and ways of working	*Example areas:* Team transformation and additional workshops as per re-contracting	Review (can repeat diagnostic)
Establish team coaching readiness	Team members and selected stakeholders complete team diagnostic					Evaluation
Initial contracting with key stakeholders and team leader	Issue pre-reading and links to online resources					Return on Investment

Intervention format: mixture of face to face and virtual workshops, sharing of materials, 1-2-1 coaching, peer coaching, re-contracting meetings.

1-2-1 coaching: ideally for each team member and at a minimum the team leader and selected team members based on identified team development needs.

Team observation: as per agreement. Can take place at any agreed point during the team coaching intervention.

Fig. 24.1 Adapted from "Creating the Team Edge" (Widdowson, 2018; Widdowson & Barbour, 2021)

- *Team questionnaires*, including Team 360 diagnostics. Many of these were discussed in Sect. 3, Approaches; including the Five Disciplines (Hawkins, 2011); PERILL (Clutterbuck, 2019, 2020); High-Performance Team Coaching System (Peters & Carr, 2013b); and Creating the Team Edge (Widdowson, 2018);
- *Individual and Team Psychometrics*. These may include, for example, Lumina Spark and Lumina Team, Insights, Strengths Finder, and Myers Briggs. Psychometrics can help create awareness about styles and preferences within the team; however, are unable to give a clear picture of team effectiveness and performance.

Team diagnostics can provide useful data at the start, during, and end of a team coaching program for the team and team coach and provide a view of where the team is at these points in time. Team coaches will, however, need to agree with the team leader and team, the most appropriate diagnostics to use and when.

What Interventions Will Be Included?

Team coaching programs can include a number of different types of intervention over a number of months:

- Team coaching workshops
- One-to-one coaching
- Team observation
- Team skill development

Team Coaching Workshops

The number of team coaching workshops will depend on what has been contracted with the client and the client's budget. The key is to have a series of workshops with time in between for the team to be able to take any actions made, embed them, and sustain their learning.

There is no set pattern to the number and length of workshops; typically they may fall into one of the following patterns:

- A number of 2-day team coaching workshops
- A series of half or 1-day sessions
- A combination of 1-day, 2-day sessions
- Any mix of the above

One-to-One Coaching

There are differing schools of thought about whether you should offer one-to-one coaching in parallel to team coaching. The reason for the debate is due to the view that there could be a conflict of interest if you are coaching the team and individuals within it. Whatever you decide, careful contracting is needed between the team coach, team, and team members regarding confidentiality and what is in and out of scope.

Thinking about the question of how many sessions, once again this can vary from six one-to-one sessions to a one-off session at the beginning, middle, or end of the program.

Team Observation

Observing the team doing their "real work" can offer some helpful insights. Team observation can take place for example, during their usual meetings or when working on important decisions. The role of the team coach is to help the team assess their own effectiveness, review their dynamics, and consider areas of strength and improvement. The team coach can also provide a "mirror" for the team, illuminating helpful and unhelpful behaviors.

How Will the Impact of the Team Coaching Program Be Evaluated?

The final stage of the team coaching program offers an important opportunity to evaluate the impact of the team coaching journey. Methods for evaluating the impact could include:

- Re-run the Team 360 diagnostic to review what has changed or areas that still need further development
- Conduct one-to-one interviews with team members and stakeholders to ask what changes they have noticed
- Review measures of success agreed at the contracting stage, for example, these could include the team's key performance indicators, employee engagement surveys, team objectives, etc.

How Many Team Coaches Should Be Involved?

In an ideal scenario, it is recommended to partner with a fellow team coach, even when working with small teams. This is because working with teams is complex and multi-dimensional, presenting a demanding task for the team coach. Collaborating with a co-team coach offers many advantages, outlined below. Although there can be a few drawbacks, the benefits definitely seem to outweigh the challenges.

What Are the Benefits of Partnering with a Co-coach?

- One can hold the room and the other observes the dynamics and behaviors of team members.
- The opportunity to bring different approaches to design.
- Team coaches can role-model how teams work together—both when aligned and where there are differences.
- The ability to support each other.
- Contingency planning and cover.
- To bring different perspectives and increase creativity regarding design.
- Joint problem-solving.
- Increased focus on clients/team members (e.g., during breakout exercises or one-to-one conversations).
- More access points for clients/team members to build a relationship with the team coaches.
- To give each other feedback—positive and developmental.
- A second set of eyes in the room.
- Enjoyment of working alongside someone whose values you share.

What Are the Drawbacks?

- Increased investment for the client of two team coaches.
- Risk of overcomplicating an intervention, for example, if the co-coaches have contrasting styles.
- Conflict and tension if coaches are not philosophically aligned (Widdowson & Barbour, 2021).

Conclusion

It is important to be aware that there is no exact science of how to design a team coaching program. For many team coaches, the design will start to form when the team receives the results of their diagnostics and agrees for themselves on their objectives for the program.

Chapter 25
Best Practices for Co-Coaching a Team

Introduction

In Chap. 24, we saw that in an ideal scenario, it is recommended to partner with a fellow team coach, even when working with small teams. The element of Co-Coaching is present in three of the ICF Team Coaching Competencies: Competency 3, Competency 5, and Competency 6.

Co-Coaching Partnership

The impact of successful co-coaching partnership is undeniable and one of its keys is in the contracting between the two team coaches.

Competency 3 confirms the partnership starts with the agreement. The co-coach is one of the relevant parties with whom the team coach needs to partner and create clear agreements about their coaching relationship as well as the team coaching engagement.

Competency 5 explains that working with a co-coach allows the team coach to be more present in the session. More specifically, working with a co-coach can:

- Take pressure off the singular team coach, given the significant amount of information emerging during team coaching sessions
- Can help to observe team dynamics, team and individual behavior patterns
- Provide alternative perspectives
- Model team behavior

We learn more about modeling of behavior in Competency 6: the two team coaches model effective, confident, and fluid communication and collaboration for the team members to experience even as observers. But as we saw in Chap. 24, the

© The Author(s), under exclusive license to Springer Nature
Switzerland AG 2024
J. Passmore et al., *Becoming a Team Coach*,
https://doi.org/10.1007/978-3-031-63546-5_25

value of working with a co-coach expands beyond modeling behaviors as the co-coach can offer additional:

- Eyes to notice what is happening in the room
- Ears to listen to what is being said or what is not
- Perceptual abilities of what is happening in the room
- Perspectives
- Voices
- Support, especially in more complex programs and/or duration that are physically, mentally, and/or emotionally demanding
- Skills and expertise
- Diversity in coaching approaches and styles that ultimately enrich the entire coaching experience for the client's benefit

How to Create a Successful Co-Coaching Partnership

Britton (2013) introduces the *Co-facilitation Arc*, in which conversations are sustained at the beginning, during design and implementation, as well as post-program, to achieve successful co-facilitation. Kanelidou and Rog (2021) argue that successful co-coaching requires preparation and ongoing work from both team coaches:

1. Good contracting and alignment
2. Clarity of the roles, responsibilities, commitments, and flexibility
3. Strategy and approach for any potential challenges with the team, individual members, or one another
4. Review, sharing reflections and observations
5. Regular meetings and supervision
6. Awareness of their dynamic as a team and their impact

In the next section, we will explore how team coaches can organize this work and create a successful co-coaching partnership.

Step 1: Selecting the Right Co-Coach

The first step is the selection of the right co-coach. The most common mistake here is to assume that having good chemistry or rapport is enough to create a good co-coaching partnership. This is a list of factors to take under consideration when choosing the right co-coach for a specific team coaching engagement:

- The team coaching training of the co-coach, their experience in team coaching and/or working with teams in any other capacity: trainer, consultant, facilitator, mentor.

- The background. Some team coaches prefer co-coaches who have a similar background to theirs; others prefer the diversity of the background and knowledge. Also, in some cases, the experience or knowledge of the client's specific industry.
- Differences in terms of strengths, skills, and expertise. Do these differences complement each other or create significant challenges?
- The ability of the co-coach to bring different perspectives and cover blind spots.
- Mindsets, philosophies, and vision of the co-coaching partnership and how much these are aligned.
- Diversity factor: gender, cultural, racial, sexual, generational, disability, religious. Either because we need to balance the dynamics in the team, or we need to have an ally within the coaches' team, or because the co-coach would understand better or speak the language of the team's own diversity.
- Chemistry is of course an important factor, as well as the energy the two co-coaches can create together as a team.
- Personal motivations for this partnership and the team coaching assignment.

Choosing our co-coach is a very personal process. Feeling comfortable with the co-coach, trusting one another, and forming a good partnership that will be a model for the team members are must haves.

Once the right co-coach is identified, some questions that the coaches can explore together are:

- Do we trust each other?
- Are we able to have open communication and difficult conversations?
- In what way is our mindset aligned?
- Do we have fun working together?
- Will our different ways of thinking help us and the team, or is it being an obstacle?

Step 2: Managing the Process

The second step is regarding the processes we can follow before, during, and after the team coaching engagement in which we will collaborate.

Before the Team Coaching Engagement

Before the team coaching program, the two coaches should discuss and clarify all the administrative and professional aspects about the team coaching and their partnership:

- When and where the sessions will take place.
- When and where the two coaches as a team meet.

- How do they collect data from the sponsor and the team (assessments, meetings, others).
- How will they use the above data to calibrate the design and process of the team coaching.
- Terms of payments.
- Purpose of the team coaching program.
- Personal and collective purpose and value of the co-coaching partnership.
- Roles and responsibilities of the different stakeholders.
- Clarify their own roles and responsibilities inside and outside of the sessions.
- Who handles content vs process and when.
- How they communicate with each other inside and outside the sessions.
- Review of models, tools, other activities used, to ensure clarity and understanding.
- When and how to give feedback to one another.

The psychological contract between the two co-coaches is equally important. That is when the two coaches openly share what they need from one another, any possible underlying issues, expectations, hidden agendas, hopes, desires, concerns, and set the ground rules of their collaboration. Anticipate situations and have agreements in place for how to handle them:

- How to manage disagreements, conflict, surprises.
- What to do if one of them gets stuck.
- How we handle difficult team dynamics in the moment.
- How to step in if anything gets missed in the moment or to add value.
- How to ask for support and play to our strengths in our interactions with the team.

During the Team Coaching Engagement

During the team coaching program, the co-coaches have a process in place on how they prepare as a team before each session, and how they debrief after each session.

They can set aside time to calibrate with each other, review their roles, reflect on expectations and outcomes, and check emerging assumptions about each other and the team.

Another important element to consider is if the co-coaches receive supervision individually, or if they engage in joint supervision as a team.

Some of the questions that co-coaches can explore in their meetings or their debriefs are:

- How do we feel regarding the progression of the coaching?
- Are there any insights on team and individual behaviors to leverage and watch out for?
- What is working best, and what is not working well?

- How do we feel with our own interactions, collaboration, and behaviors with each other?
- How do we feel concerning our interactions with the team?
- What do we perceive in one another and how do we think this affects the team coaching assignment?
- How are we contributing to or derailing the team's agenda?
- Should we change or adjust something, e.g. tools, approach, or recontract with the team?
- How do we request feedback from the team/team members?

After the Team Coaching Engagement

After the team coaching program has finished, the co-coaches should have the opportunity to consider the following:

- Final feedback for each other.
- Review and reflect on the feedback or evaluation received from the team regarding the coaches as a team.
- Whether the initial objectives were achieved.
- Other outcomes achieved through the program.
- Effectiveness of the program on the team and on themselves personally.
- Opportunities for their continuing development as a team and individually.
- Evaluation of the resources used: materials, online platforms, etc.

The feedback we request from each other is an opportunity to really reflect on the effectiveness of our partnership; on what we brought to the table and how to enhance future collaborations.

Some of the questions the co-coaches can explore are:

- What worked well in our interactions with each other?
- What worked well in our interactions with the team?
- What didn't work well? What needs improvement?
- What goals were achieved? (These goals can be about our assignment/the team's goals, and about our partnership/performance).
- What have we learned as coaches? How can we include these lessons in future work?
- What can we do differently next time? What should we keep the same?
- How do we see our partnership moving forward?

When to Work with a Co-Coach

Although the ideal scenario is to always have a co-coach, this is not always feasible or preferable. Increased budget costs for the client or overcomplicating an intervention can direct us to work without a co-coach.

When it comes to choosing when to partner with a co-coach, different team coaching practitioners have different strategies. For some it is just a matter of numbers: if the team members' number is larger than say eight, for example, the team coach will bring onboard a co-coach and they include that in the contract with the sponsor. This number is personal to the team coach and can depend on the size that the team coach feels comfortable coaching.

Other team coaching practitioners consider various factors aside from the size of the team.

These factors can include:

- The duration of the sessions. Team coaching is a very intense process that requires the full attention of the coach, the alertness of their senses, and even physical endurance, if the sessions are going to be lengthy. With that in mind, the presence of a second coach who can take the lead at times (based on the agreement and the roles of the two coaches) can give space for the other coach to take a much needed mental break while still being present.
- The budget. If the sponsor has a healthy budget, bringing a co-coach can always enrich the process.
- The focus areas/topics that the team wishes to work on, or the industry. If the team coach is not familiar with the industry and its language or ways of processing, or the topics that the team needs to focus on their work, having a co-coach who is familiar with these can prove to be helpful. Similarly, the same would be true in respect to challenges that are observed in the initial conversations with the sponsor and the team leader. If, for example, team dynamics is going to be a challenge in an assignment and the team coach does not feel they are the best expert on such dynamics, they can opt to have a co-coach who is expert in such team dynamics.
- The functionality or dysfunctionality of the team. Coaching a mature team that is already functioning progresses in a smoother manner than coaching a team where dysfunctions or toxic patterns are observed. The presence of a co-coach can be critical in such cases as any projections from team members to the coaches would be less tense or avoided. It would also serve the purpose of modeling the new desired behaviors.
- How advanced they are. Beginner team coaches opt to partner with more experienced team coaches. That way they provide a better experience for the team and at the same time they learn from each other.
- The team coach's background/ diversity. In this point, team coaches want to be intentional: do they need a co-coach with complementing or similar background? What would be more meaningful working with a specific team? It is important to note here that when working with a co-coach who is very different, more

emphasis needs to be given to ensure alignment and clarity on roles and processes, and avoid conflict.
- Above all, the key factor is what will serve the team better.

Conclusion

In this chapter, we have explored the practice of co-coaching and how the team
coach engages collaboratively with a co-coach to help them deliver the coaching
assignment, along with exploring the factors which are best agreed upon between
the coaches to enhance the collaborative partnership between the two coaches.

Chapter 26
Going Deeper on Team Dynamics

Introduction

In discussing "Embodies a Coaching Mindset" (Chap. 7), the supplementary competency, *remains objective and aware of the team dynamics and patterns,* was introduced. This chapter will delve deeper into some of the dynamics experienced in teams and between teams, examples of how they can manifest, and ideas on how a team coach can best remain objective. As discussed in Chap. 1, while not all groups are teams, every team is a group. Therefore the terms, team and group dynamics are used interchangeably throughout the chapter.

Group dynamics are "all the invisible and emotional forces and communications between individuals in a group, which lead groups to behave in much more extreme ways than any of the individuals would have done on their own" (Hardingham et al., 2004, p. 168). While the team coach is not a team member, they are part of the group, and despite the need to remain objective, they are also part of the invisible and emotional forces. The team coach needs to be able to notice as much as possible of what usually remains unnoticed within themselves, the team, and between teams.

Where to Start

Compared to one-to-one coaching, understanding group dynamics is essential for the team coach. However, the sheer volume of material, albeit mainly from a group therapeutic setting, can be overwhelming. Thankfully, there is a reprieve. We would contend that while a good knowledge of group dynamics is essential, expertise is not. Based on our review of the extensive group dynamics literature, we would suggest the team coaching approaches described in this book negate many of the most harmful aspects of the group dynamic. In any case, an attempt to cover such a broad

© The Author(s), under exclusive license to Springer Nature
Switzerland AG 2024
J. Passmore et al., *Becoming a Team Coach*,
https://doi.org/10.1007/978-3-031-63546-5_26

topic in one chapter will likely fail. Therefore, this chapter will focus on concepts we have witnessed students struggle with in our role as team coaching educators.

Reflective Question for the Team Coach

How is my team coaching likely to benefit from a deep knowledge of group dynamics, and what drawbacks are there, if any, from going deeper?

The Importance of Context

Learning about the organization, team readiness enquiries, one-to-one interviews, team 360 diagnostics, observation, co-design, and contracting are each likely to happen before you ever meet the team. In attending to these areas, the team coach will already have significant data about the group dynamic. For example, information about the team's history, membership, diversity, size, experience, purpose, identity, behaviors, relationships, inclusiveness, leadership, reward structure, governance, tasks, anxieties, and hopes, which all can support a team coach in developing initial hypotheses about the group dynamic. However, a health warning! Group dynamics occur mainly under the surface, at an unconscious level. So, while understanding context is essential, it can never substitute for being with a team.

Reflective Question for the Team Coach

Based on my understanding of a new team I am working with, what initial hypotheses do I have about the group dynamic?

The Importance of Human Needs

What if many of the behaviors we consider unhelpful are expressions of unmet needs? Berne (1966) contended that humans need stimulus (intimacy), recognition, and structure. Similarly, Deci and Ryan (2004), in the context of human intrinsic motivation, proposed humans need to feel in safe communion with others (relatedness), perceive themselves to be the source of their behavior (autonomy), and believe they have the opportunities to develop their potential (competency). Linked to these deeper needs, Heron (1999) describes how group members can feel acceptance, orientation, and performance anxiety.

Reflective Question for the Team Coach

How can I best attend to the deeper needs of the team and support the team to do the same?

The Importance of Roles and Existing Group Membership

Roles and existing group memberships are some of the most visible reminders about the systemic nature of a team. Individuals simultaneously operate in multiple roles and groups (parent, sibling, partner, caregiver, colleague, leader, community, etc.). In addition, team members can be in several teams simultaneously, which may challenge who they represent at any time. Intertwined with roles is human identity, the story we tell ourselves about our past, present, and future.

Beyond official roles, team members are also usually unconsciously given or take on other positions within the team. Beneath-the-surface roles in teams include enforcer, caretaker, clown, dreamer, rebel, follower, and bystander (Anand & Barsoux, 2023). Even in how we communicate within groups, we can assume different roles. Kantor (2012) describes four action stances that group members can take up, one or more of. They include move (initiates communication), follow (supports others), oppose (challenges), and by-stand (reflects without agreeing or disagreeing).

Reflective Question for the Team Coach

How can I get the team to focus on their conscious and unconscious roles and existing group memberships and how these may be helping and hindering the team?

Exploring Group Processes

Every team has group processes, many of which remain invisible to the untrained. Thornton (2016) outlined nine of the most significant group dynamic processes. Table 26.1 describes each group process alongside questions for a team coach to reflect on.

Table 26.1 Group dynamic process and corresponding reflective questions for a team coach

Group dynamic process	Reflective questions for the team coach
Group matrix. The team's total communication, history, and shared heritage.	To what extent do I support a team honoring its present and past? (e.g., past achievements, previous team members, length of service, culture, context).
Communication. Everything that we can attach a meaning to, not just words. Examples: The message itself, expressions, tone, who speaks and who does not, animation, adherence to time, focus, energy, use of technology, and arrivals and departures.	How well am I bringing to the team's awareness, with curiosity, compassion, and courage, patterns of communication that might be helping or hindering the team's effectiveness?
Translation. The process of bringing together conscious and unconscious communications into words?	How can I, through example, support the team to develop the capacity to articulate with words what may be below the surface?
Mirroring. How we unconsciously compare current experiences with experiences from the past. It includes projection and transference, which we will explore in the next section.	Based on the premise that multiple perspectives from the group can help improve understanding of the present, which can help individuals disentangle present reality from their past (Thornton 2016), how can I best ensure multiple perspectives are heard?
Exchange. When the experience of something new helps a group gain fresh information.	Based on the understanding that self-generated feedback is extremely beneficial, how can I maximize individual and team self-reflection and feedback?
Resonance. Happens when a group member speaks, and others find shared meaning or resonance from what is being said (e.g., stories).	Without forcing team members to share (i.e., inspire courageous sharing for the team's benefit while giving a choice), how can I best use the power of team member storytelling?
Condenser phenomena. Refers to the emotional shift or release of tension in a group when something that previously remained unsaid or out of consciousness gets shared.	How can I create and maintain psychological safety so team members feel safe to take risks when sharing?
Location. Describes the idea that everything that happens in a group, even if located in one or two people, has meaning for the entire group. For example, one person takes on a role no one else wants, which could lead to scapegoating at a later date.	How can I, with curiosity, compassion, and courage, check if what happens with one or two team members has greater significance about how the team functions?
The reflection process. This occurs when a team member tells a story or recalls a conversation, and the group picks up on a dynamic or feeling that the storyteller was previously unaware of.	How can I create opportunities for team members to learn and reflect on what each other shares?

Adapted from Thornton (2016)

Unconscious Processes and Defense Mechanisms in Teams

To avoid mental conflict, humans implement various psychological defense mechanisms. Lee (2003) describes these as conscious (e.g., denial, intellectualization, and rationalization) and unconscious (e.g., repression, projection, and splitting). He notes that even if someone is aware that they are adopting unproductive behavior, they may be powerless to change if the emotions defended against remain unconscious. As our unconscious past, mainly attributable to childhood and life experiences, arrives in the unconscious present, our choices of helpful behavior can be limited.

Team coaches must develop group emotional literacy if they are to have any chance of noticing what is happening to themselves and the team while staying objective. To help build this literacy, we will explain some key concepts that can exist at an individual and collective (team) level. While this list is not exhaustive, we recommend exploring the sources referenced in this chapter to learn more.

Splitting defined

"The process of dividing the individuals and groups into polarized entities of good or bad; specific qualities are perceived as being contained in one and their opposites in another individual or group" (McRae & Short, 2010, p. 60).

Examples of Splitting

A team member viewing other team members as "for" the team effort or "against." Or a team that thinks of themselves as collaborative compared to a team they consider obstructive. In both cases, others or situations get viewed as opposite, with little thought given to what they have in common. You might notice the similarity of "them" and "us" thinking in our societal divisions (e.g., right or left, progressive or conservative, Christian or Muslim). By splitting, humans can avoid the discomfort of exploring areas like their unspoken feelings, the impact of their position on others, and potential similarities with the other.

Projection defined

Often accompanying splitting, projection "involves projecting onto other individuals or groups one's own unacceptable desires and impulses" (McRae & Short, 2010, p. 60).

Examples of Projection

An argumentative team member who does not consider themselves the cause of arguments while highlighting a colleague as an antagonist. Or a team that takes no responsibility for a project delay while ascribing blame to another team.

Projective identification defined

"Refers to the unconscious interpersonal interaction in which the recipient of a projection reacts to it in such a way that their own feelings are affected: they unconsciously identify with the projected feelings" (Halton, 2019, p. 16).

Examples of Projective Identification

For example, the team member highlighted as antagonistic believes themselves to be so, whether true or not. Or the team blamed for the project delay absorbs responsibility for the delay. In both cases, the individual or team may start to act out some of the behaviors projected onto them.

Transference defined

"The unconscious re-enactment of the past in the present" that is either positive (positive transference) or emotionally conflictual (negative transference). Furthermore, *transference as a projection* is when "a person unconsciously transfers and projects onto a person in the present, earlier experiences of a similar person or context in the past" (Lee, 2003, p47).

Examples of Positive Transference

During a team coaching session, a team member(s) keeps positively comparing the current team coach or the team coaching to prior experiences or team development activities they did not like. In this example, they may be subconsciously seeking approval from the team coach. This could include approval they are not getting from others, which may include the team leader.

Examples of Negative Transference

During a team coaching session, a team member(s) keeps negatively comparing the current team coach or the team coaching to prior experiences or team development activities they did like. In this example, the team member(s) might be trying to communicate deeper unmet needs, such as team coaching being unnecessary, poorly timed, the wrong team coach, or dissatisfaction with the leader. The negative transference might unconsciously be expressed in what Heron (1999) describes as active resistance, denigration, sabotage, or rivalry, which in this example, could be with the team coach, leader, or others.

Countertransference defined

"Refers to the feelings, bodily sensations, thoughts and behaviors that are evoked in a person by someone else" (Lee, 2003, p. 48). Projective identification, as described earlier, underpins countertransference.

Examples of Countertransference

In the positive transference example, the team coach may suddenly feel happiness about themselves and their work, even though what the team has communicated may have nothing to do with them. In identifying with the positive transference, the team coach may be getting needs met, like feeling appreciated, which they may not be getting from others. In the negative transference example, the team coach may suddenly feel inadequate and sad, even though what the team communicated may have nothing to do with them. The sudden feeling of inadequacy or sadness could result from an earlier problematic team coaching assignment and have nothing to do with the current work.

What Can a Team Coach Do About Such Unconscious Processes and Defense Mechanisms?

Below are four ideas as to what a team coach can do to support themselves and the team:

1. *Know enough to illuminate*

   This involves the team coach educating themselves about group dynamics. In a topic that could create a lifetime of study, the team coach must know enough to be self-aware and support a team. Training a team on key group unconscious processes and defenses capable of sabotaging their effectiveness can also be helpful.

2. *Notice with curiosity*

   This involves the team coach becoming more aware of when patterns or moments in a group dynamic, without warning, impact their feelings, bodily sensations, and thinking. It is about noticing what you notice in such moments and being curious instead of judgmental. Cardona and Damon (2019) refer to using feelings as data in such instances. It is also essential to support a team to become more aware of themselves individually and collectively. To help, there are multiple approaches a team coach can use to develop awareness. Some examples include constellation work (see Whittington, 2020), drawing socio-grams or similar (see Anand & Barsoux, 2023), and story-work (see Hill, 2017).

3. *Exploring the self in the context of your past and present*

   This is about exploring and learning from your past and how it impacts your present. Reflective practice, speaking to friends, loved ones, or a trusted colleague (which may include a co-team coach), or team coaching supervision can all help with such explorations. Similarly, it is also essential to create a safe and reflective space for teams, to reflect on what from their past may be appearing in their present and what this means for the future.

4. *Act with compassion in service to self and others*

   This is about using your intuition, wisdom, and experience to act or not act on patterns noticed, both in yourself and the team. The following are examples of dialogue a team coach could have with a team, a co-team coach and their supervisor.

   With a team

   "I want to invite you each to reflect individually on three questions. After your reflection, I invite you to share what you are comfortable sharing with the team."

   1. "What are you noticing about your and each others' contributions/interactions during this session?"
   2. "How is it similar or different from how you normally interact?"
   3. "What are you learning about how you are when together and apart?"

   "Earlier, when xx said (or did) xx, I felt xx, and I'm curious whether that has something to do with me, this team or both. I believe there could be a benefit in exploring it together if you are ok with that."

"I've noticed a pattern in how the team xx, and I would be keen to get your reflections on its significance or otherwise."

"I'm wondering, and I could be wrong, if xx."

"I have got a hypothesis that I'd like to test with the team, with your permission."

With a co-team coach

"I sensed some tension when we discussed xx with the team. I'm wondering if we should explore it together."

"I would be keen to discuss the pros and cons of jointly going to a supervisor on xx topic."

"I've been working with xx team and have been getting xx feelings that I'd like your perspective on."

With your supervisor

"During a recent team coaching session, xx happened when the team did xx. It left me feeling very xx. I decided it had more to do with me than the team, and I would be keen to explore it today."

Towards Team Maturity

A significant contributor to working with the unconscious processes in groups is psychoanalyst Wilfred Bion. According to Bion (1961), groups function either as a highly functional *work group,* where each member contributes to a task, or a *basic assumption group*, where dynamics of an emotional nature occur, which can obstruct, divert, and impede group functioning (McCrea & Short, 2010).

Stokes (2019) has commented that when under the influence of a basic assumption, "group members lose their critical faculties and individual abilities, and the group as a whole has the appearance of having some ill-defined but passionately involving mission" (p. 31). What others outside of the group might consider trivial, the group unconsciously sees as matters of life or death as they manage anxieties linked to their psychological survival. Stokes (2019) outlines the basic assumptions from the work of Bion (1961) as:

Basic assumption dependency
The group views its primary task as the welfare of its members. The leader's role is to help team members feel good, not focus efforts on real work or a joint purpose. Instead of facing their anxieties, group members are happy for the leader to absorb them on their behalf. When team coaching, behaviors to look out for include the team not addressing difficult agenda items, resisting organizational change, and the stifled growth and development of team members due to an over-reliance on the leader.

Basic assumption fight-flight
To help manage their anxieties, the group focuses on a danger or enemy that should be attacked or fled from. Heron (1999) also refers to the idea of group submis-

sion. When team coaching, behaviors to look out for include (adapted from Heron, 1999):

In attack mode: Team coach and team coaching resisted, authority or competence challenged, and competition for control in the group. Also, the scapegoating of others may be evident, including irrational blaming, invalidating, criticism, accusing, labeling, and stereotyping.

In flight mode: Irrelevant theorizing and generalizing, jocularity, gossip, persistent talking about non-team issues, rescuing others from self-disclosure, collusive pairing, insisting on a more precise task and conventional goals.

In submission mode: Passive behaviors dominate, including dependence on others, mindlessly following, and permission seeking. Also, withdrawal or shutdown, powerlessness, and a loss of identity may be evident.

Basic assumption pairing (hope)

"Is based on the collective and unconscious belief that, whatever the actual problems and needs of the group, a future event will solve them" (Stokes, 2019, p. 30). Originally described as the group focusing on two leaders pairing to act as saviors for the group, Stokes (2019) has proposed that *basic assumption hope* would be a more accurate description. When team coaching, behaviors to look out for include focusing on the future at the expense of current challenges, decisions not being made, and believing that what lies ahead will improve the team's situation.

Complementing the team coaching approaches described in this book, McRae and Short (2010), referring to how to avoid or deal with basic assumption group behaviors, have proposed that in mature work groups, members:

- Work jointly towards a common task or group goal (Bion & Rickman, 1943).
- Develop trust in the group and the leader, sharing aspects of themselves, taking risks, and openly sharing how they feel about each other.
- Feel a sense of inclusion and belonging to the group, valuing what each other contributes.
- Work with conflict that surfaces in the group. It can mean, at times, after a respectful and robust discussion, agreeing to disagree. Edmondson (2012) has suggested that conflict will likely increase in psychologically safe teams as team members feel more secure expressing themselves.
- Respectfully confront each other on specific behaviors in the spirit of learning and performance. Widdowson and Barbour (2021) have commented that despite the challenges of team members giving each other feedback, "it is an essential element to any great team" (p. 176).
- Take risks in sharing uncomfortable information, behaving in new ways, and taking up different roles.
- Recognize, acknowledge, and work with their differences and similarities, with diversity embraced as a strength.
- Take time for reflection and self-examination concerning their role and interactions in the group.

Team exercise for the team coach
- Turn each statement into a question, e.g. how well as a team do we xx.
- Ask each team member to reflect on their answers individually.
- Ask each team member to score their response between one and ten, with one equalling low and ten high.
- Collect the scores anonymously and reveal the average for each question.
- Invite the team to have a dialogue about what *better* could look like.

Conclusion

In summary, we hope this chapter has given you a deeper insight into group dynamics. As authors, we believe any section of this chapter could have merited a chapter on its own. We trust that going deeper into group dynamics has helped you reflect on yourself, the groups you spend your life in, and your work as a team coach.

Chapter 27
Navigating Systemic Challenges and Opportunities as a Team Coach

Introduction

This chapter aims to help team coaches reflect on their level of awareness and state of their practice, regarding some of our time's main challenges and opportunities. The four areas we will discuss include (1) team engagement and wellbeing, (2) team diversity and inclusion, (3) team coaching, climate change and our broader ecology, and (4) team coaching and the technological revolution.

Team Engagement and Wellbeing

The *Gallup Global Workplace 2023 Report* (Gallup, 2023a) offered good and bad news. The good news is that since the survey's inception, the number of engaged employees has increased yearly, except for a dip in 2020, rising from 9% in 2009 to 23% in 2022. The 23% of engaged (or thriving) employees "find their work meaningful and feel connected to the team and their organization." Of the 23% of workers who are engaged, those who work solely remotely are the most engaged (30%), followed by hybrid (24%) and then on-site only (21%). The bad news is that 77% of employees are not engaged. Non-engaged employees, who make up 59%, are described as "psychologically disconnected from their employer," and actively disengaged, who make up 18%, are referred to as those who "take actions that directly harm the organization, undercutting its goals and opposing its leaders" (Gallup, 2023a, p. 4).

Regarding wellbeing, 44% of the workers reported feeling a lot of stress the previous day, with 21% feeling a lot of anger (See Table 27.1). Remote-only workers are experiencing high stress and anger levels, with on-site-only workers reporting the least, albeit still at a high level. Anyone looking for solace in hybrid may be

J. Passmore et al., *Becoming a Team Coach*, https://doi.org/10.1007/978-3-031-63546-5_27

Table 27.1 Stress, anger, and intent to leave summary from the Gallup Global Workplace 2023 Report

	Feeling stressed a lot the previous day	Feeling anger a lot the previous day	Intent to leave
Manager	41%	23%	51%
Individual	43%	20%	51%
Remote only	43%	27%	50%
Hybrid	45%	21%	58%
On-site only	38%	19%	42%
Average	*44%*	*21%*	*51%*

Source: Adapted from Gallup (2023a)

disappointed as they reported the highest stress levels and intention to leave (Gallup, 2023a).

But there is hope! The report also found in best-practice organizations, 72% of employees are engaged (Gallup, 2023a). So what can organizations do? Firstly, stop being preoccupied with work location and focus on culture. The Gallup analysis found that "engagement has 3.8 times as much influence on employee stress as work location. In other words, what people experience in their everyday work—their feelings of involvement and enthusiasm—matters more in reducing stress than where they are sitting" (Gallup, 2023a, p. 8). Secondly, we would say, follow the science. The areas of focus proposed by Gallup to increase engagement align with what we have written in this book. The report notes, "by switching to proven, science-based management, organizations could change the course of the economy—and world history" (Gallup, 2023a, p. 1). We agree, however, there is another opportunity. While reviewing the Gallup approach to developing engagement, Widdowson and Barbour (2021) stated, "while we agree with each of the points on this list and particularly welcome the emphasis on coaching and purpose, we believe that coaching in the context of individuals and teams would be an important addition" (Widdowson & Barbour, 2021, p. 168). The statement that "one of Gallup's biggest discoveries: the manager or team leader alone accounts for 70% of the variance in team engagement" (Gallup, 2023b) is hopefully pointing towards a future where team coaching, alongside one-to-one coaching, will add to the armory of ways to transform employee engagement and wellbeing.

Reflection Questions for the Team Coach
- How can I get the teams I coach to focus more on engagement and wellbeing?
- How can I get the organizations I coach in to focus more on engagement and wellbeing?

Team Diversity and Inclusion

Too often, diversity and inclusion are considered a corporate matter. While this is true, it is equally a team and individual matter, including us individually as team coaches. As team coaches and team coach educators, we are increasingly coming across issues relating to gender, disability, culture, neurodiversity, mental health, race, personality preferences, and diversity among team coaches, to name only some.

What Can Team Coaches Do?

Firstly, it is about trusting the work of team coaching, as described in this book. When discussing inclusion, Whittington (2020, p. 271) has commented, "If you don't feel safe, either psychologically or physically, you can't learn, you can't love, you can't lead and you can't follow." In our work as team coaches, we find that when you create a safe container and share your own or other stories relating to diversity and inclusion, team members start to share what, for many, has remained unsaid. However, there is a note of caution. For some, sharing is too traumatic. As team coaches, we need to balance courage with compassion.

Secondly, as team coaches, we must all become more aware, proactively seek out training opportunities and bring areas of concern to supervision. When we reflect on awareness, some of the diversity challenges are stark, for example:

- Roche and Passmore's (2021) finding that within coaching "there is a gap, a silence, a blind spot in our profession when it comes to race."
- 73% of dyslexic people hide their dyslexia from employers (Made by Dyslexia, 2017).
- Only 16% of autistic adults are in full-time paid work (The Professional Association for Social Work and Social Workers, 2016).
- 29% of senior management is female, and only 33 Fortune 500 companies are led by female CEOs (Darina, 2023).

Thirdly, we must support team leaders and teams to lead on diversity and inclusion. We know from research that just building a diverse team is not enough. Mannix and Neale (2005) reviewed nearly 50 years of social science research on diversity, from which they powerfully commented, "To implement policies and practices that increase the diversity of the workforce without understanding how diverse individuals can come together to form effective teams is irresponsible" (p. 32). We are clear that team coaching offers one of the best opportunities to support teams in building genuinely diverse and inclusive workplaces.

A helpful piece of research to enable team coaches to get practical on team diversity and inclusion is the research on inclusive leadership. From their systematic review of 107 papers on inclusive leadership behaviors, Korkmaz et al. (2022) have proposed a multi-level model with four dimensions, which are (1) fostering employees' uniqueness (e.g., promoting diversity), (2) strengthening belongingness within a team (e.g., building relationships), (3) showing appreciation (e.g., recognizing efforts and contributions), and (4) supporting organizational efforts (e.g., promoting the organizational mission on inclusion). Regarding the team element, they summarize *strengthening belongingness within a team* as attending to the relationship between the leader and the team and among the team members. Korkmaz et al. (2022) have proposed four focus areas to do this, which include:

1. *Supporting employees as individuals* includes team leaders paying attention to team members' feelings, offering guidance, and exhibiting availability.
2. *Promoting diversity* includes recognizing team member differences, valuing each person's unique characteristics, and actively helping team members contribute.
3. *Empowering employees* includes enabling team members to take action on their own, team decision-making, and team members sharing ideas on how each executes their role.
4. *Serving employees' learning and development* includes team leaders explicitly stating they are interested in team members' needs for growth, providing feedback, supporting employees when mistakes are made, and paying attention to team member training.

While the four areas have been proposed mainly from a team leader perspective, we suggest they offer even more significant potential if considered at a collective team level.

Reflection Questions for the Team Coach
- What is my learning edge on diversity and inclusion?
- What else can I do to create an even safer space for teams?
- On team diversity and inclusion, what does acting with courage and compassion mean for me?

Team Coaching, Climate Change, and our Broader Ecology

Hawkins (2021, p. 255) shares, "many coaches have asked me why I increasingly stress the importance of attending to the ecology in every coaching and every team coaching relationship they undertake. They said it was not their responsibility and they had been taught that they should not bring their own agenda into the coaching room. But the ecological issues are by their very nature everyone's agenda and the ecology is already in every coaching room. It is the air we breathe, the food we eat etc.". Building on the point that the ecology is already there, Hawkins and Turner (2020) suggest the coach's role is to uncover, surface, and explore. Whybrow et al. (2023) point to Sir John Whitmore's reflections when defining the purpose of coaching. Whitmore (2009, p. 225) states, "coaches are midwives at the birth of a new social order, one in which compassion for all people and for all of nature and our only home, form the core theme. What more rewarding challenge could there be?"

Despite this latest thinking and the heightened focus within the coaching profession, we know from our roles as team coach educators that many team coaches are still uncomfortable bringing what they view as their agenda into the room. Recognizing this challenge for coaches, Cox and Flynn (2022) have noted the importance of transparency and clear contracting, commenting that "charged conversations require more permission" (p. 82). Hawkins (2021) highlights the importance of undertaking our own, often non-linear journey and has proposed the eco-consciousness cycle. The five stages are eco-curious, eco-informed, eco-aware, eco-engaged, and eco-active.

While we would always encourage a team coach to be authentic and courageous, we would caution against believing or acting in a way that team members automatically share your worldview. Each of us will have experienced moments in life when a person, through their words or deeds, *loses the room*. The team coach must be clear with the client on who they are as a team coach and how they like to work.

Reflection Questions for the Team Coach
- What is my journey as a team coach regarding climate change and our broader ecology?
- Tapping into my *"way of being"*, how can I bring climate change and our broader ecology into the room in a way that only I can?
- What else do I need to reflect on in this area, and how can supervision support this?

Team Coaching and the Technological Revolution

Isaacson (2021) commented that "the exponential development of technology is creating a permanent sense of instability, bringing delight and disquiet depending on the technology in particular, our personal preferences, our age, and our background" (p. 10). The question that comes to mind reading this quote is, what if, irrespective of our preferences, age, or background, we have no choice but to embrace technology? Before we discuss this further, it is helpful to consider that the technologies, transforming how we coach, differ. Isaacson (2022) uses the terms *coachtech* and *CoachTech* to explain. He argues that *coachtech* is any existing technology a coach can adopt and use, whereas *CoachTech* is developed with coaching in mind.

Firstly, we will consider *coachtech*. It is hard not to forget the impact of COVID-19. Team coaches worldwide had to shift their practice from in-person to video conference. Even within this group of authors, there were different speeds of adoption. Like many reading this book, we quickly became experts on video conferencing, video conference meeting invites, screen sharing, breakout rooms, sharing via chat, messaging groups, sharing and working on joint files in the cloud, polling tools, and virtual whiteboards. As an author group, we promptly concluded that online team coaching could be as connected and impactful as in-person. We also quickly concluded that while technology was never the essence of what is profoundly human work, it was an excellent support act.

While we are unaware of any research on virtual team coaching outcomes, it is worth noting that Michalik and Schermuly (2023), in the context of one-to-one coaching, could not find any significant outcome differences between in-person and digital approaches, although she found differences in blended approaches. Whatever the future research confirms, it is evident that some team coaches and many teams are not convinced. In our experience, post-COVID-19, nearly all our one-to-one coaching work has remained virtual, whereas much of our team coaching work has become a blend of virtual and in-person. For team coaching, areas such as business development, team one-to-one diagnostic calls, 360 team diagnostic tools, review meetings, one-to-one coaching that is part of the team coaching program, and some observation and shorter sessions with teams have mainly remained virtual. In comparison, more extended periods with the team, from one day to *a* week, have a high chance of being in person, even for global teams.

Another example of *coachtech* is ChatGPT. In experimenting with ChatGPT for this book, we asked it two questions: (1) Can you outline an example team coaching journey? and (2) I am working as a team coach, and two team members are not speaking to each other. Both answers were extremely impressive and, with some small amends, could have been used for client work. Its ability to summarize data collected from one-to-one diagnostic interviews was even more special. We anonymized the text (i.e., removed all names and any company-sensitive information) from ten 30-min interviews. We asked it to combine the text into critical themes for the team to reflect on. With a couple of additional prompts, ChatGPT produced a summary report, which would have usually taken a few hours to create, in minutes.

However, we encourage caution in the use of AI tools. We note Passmore and Tee's (2023) work where hallucinations are common, as well as wider question marks about bias, IP, and confidentiality. We too recommend that all users should verify content before including the outputs and be sensitive to the other risks associated with the technology.

While *coachtech* is now clearly embedded with team coaching and will only increase in use, it would appear that *CoachTech*, is still, for now, primarily focused on one-to-one coaching. Isaacson (2021) has broken the rise of coaching platforms into three groups:

1. *Coaching administration platforms*—helps coaches to manage coaching engagements.
2. *Coaching management platforms*—allows organizations to make coaching accessible to more employees—benefits such as scale, cost-effectiveness, data collection, measurement and reporting, and targeted resources are all noted.
3. *Digital coach brokers*—act as an online marketplace where clients can select independent coaches.

Another example of *CoachTech* is the rise of the AI Coach. Reflecting on their experience, Isaacson (2021) suggests "the existing AI coaches act like a conversational veneer on a standardized, engineered process flow" (p. 110). This sounds a far cry from the working alliance at the heart of coaching (De Haan et al., 2016, 2019) and team coaching effectiveness (Murphy, 2023).

Reflection Questions for the Team Coach
- How am I innovating and integrating new technologies into my team coaching work?
- What ethical concerns do I have about *coachtech* or *CoachTech,* and how can I explore them and influence the conversation?
- What could the future hold that I need to be mindful of? (e.g., VR, AR, AI developments).

Conclusion

In conclusion, while some of the areas discussed could cause overwhelm, each needs attention. In our experience, the literature and team coaching training providers are increasingly attending to these areas. However, as highlighted in Chap. 28, team coaching supervision is essential for team coaches to explore whatever is emerging in their work.

Chapter 28
Team Coaching Supervision

Introduction

Supervision allows team coaches to reflect on their practice, notice patterns of behavior, and explore who they are, forming a fundamental role in their personal and professional development. It is seen as important for coaches; however, it can be argued that it is essential for team coaches, who manage multiple dynamics, increased complexity, and the broader systemic context when working with teams. The importance of supervision is reflected in the requirement for evidence of supervision to achieve ICF ACTC team coaching credentials, and we are also now seeing some organizations requesting that team coaches actively engage in supervision.

As suggested by Shohet and Shohet (2020), supervision also helps us when we are unsure what to do; "…when we are most stuck, we can grow if we have a space to reflect with another who will both support and challenge us" (Shohet & Shohet, 2020, p. 3).

This chapter builds on Passmore and Sinclair (2024), which focuses on supervision in one-to-one coaching and expands on this in the context of team coaching. It will explore what supervision is, how it works in practice, how to find a suitable supervisor, and how to get the best out of supervision.

What Is Supervision?

Several writers have offered definitions of supervision (de Haan, 2012; Hawkins & Smith, 2013; Hodge, 2016; Passmore & McGoldrick, 2009) along with the coaching professional bodies. The ICF (2019) defines supervision as: "a collaborative learning practice to continually build the capacity of the coach through reflective dialogue for the benefit of both coaches and clients."

J. Passmore et al., *Becoming a Team Coach*,
https://doi.org/10.1007/978-3-031-63546-5_28

To the ICF, "Coaching supervision focuses on the development of the coach's capacity through offering a richer and broader opportunity for support and development. Coaching supervision creates a safe environment for the coach to share their successes and failures in becoming masterful in the way they work with their clients" (ICF, 2019).

Much of the foundation of thinking regarding supervision has derived from the helping professions, specifically social work and psychotherapy. Similar to coaching, the relationship between supervisor and supervisee is critical. Therefore, supervision is a co-created learning relationship, enabling the supervisee to reflect and develop. It also offers a safe space for the supervisee to focus "on their emotional and professional wellbeing and growth" (Hodge, 2016, p. 89).

As mentioned previously, the work of a team coach is complex and can be challenging. Team coaches will draw upon their capacities, capabilities, and knowledge when coaching teams, and it will take many years of practice to be "masters of their craft" (Hawkins, 2021, p. 326). Hawkins (2021) suggests that supervision supports the team coach to help them:

Maintain the boundaries of working closely with the team whilst being independent of team dynamics and culture

Be aware of the systemic dynamics within and between the team and the broader system to which the team belongs

Be able to sense and make sense of these complex system dynamics

Develop as a team coach

How Can Supervision Help Me?

When engaged in team coaching work with clients, team coaches face many different relationships, dynamics, and systemic aspects to navigate. Working with their supervisor can help to unpick some of the complexities and challenges they may be experiencing. We discussed some examples of topics a team coach can bring to supervision in Chap. 7. Developing this further, team coaches can seek supervision on a wide range of topics, for example:

- Contract with the client, the organization, and the wider system
- Relationship with the team leader, team, stakeholders, and organization
- Relationship with the co-coach
- How to stay independent of the team dynamics and culture
- Managing their own well-being
- Exploring triggers and patterns of behavior for themselves and the team
- Seeking support
- Discussing their own development in relation to ICF Core Competencies, capacity as a team coach, knowledge
- Exploring limitations and vulnerabilities
- Ensuring professional standards and ethics are maintained

- Partnering with the team, team leader, and organization
- Team coach cases (i.e., with organizations, teams, team sessions)
- Working with a co-coach

Supervision, therefore, can encompass many different aspects. We will further explore three key areas of supervision (Passmore & Sinclair, 2024) that are also aligned with the common themes suggested by Turner and Palmer (2019) shared in Chap. 7, where supervision can be of help:

Support

As suggested by Hodge (2016), supervision also provides much-needed support for the team coach regarding their professional and emotional well-being. It helps them to feel nurtured, safe, and trusted, supported in exploring their fears and vulnerabilities and gives them confidence in their work and clarity about their practice (Hawkins & Smith, 2013; de Haan, 2008). Additionally, it helps them gain different perspectives, a space to be re-sourced, and an opportunity to explore the many relationships in the system (Turner & Palmer, 2019).

Learning and Development

A core element of supervision is to help the team coach learn, grow, and further develop on their path to mastery. The ICF Team Coaching Competencies are a useful reference to explore areas of skill, including strengths and areas the team coach may want to further develop. The team coach may also want to discuss the Being, Doing, and Knowing of team coaching discussed in Chap. 10 (Widdowson et al., 2020). This may include exploring their knowledge of team dynamics, models, and frameworks, the system in which the team exists and their "*way of being*" relating to their ability to build empathy and relationships with the team, stakeholders, and their co-coach. Actively engaging in supervision will help the team coach build and develop their reflective practice and self-awareness.

Safety and Standards

In Chap. 6, "Demonstrates ethical practice," we considered the ethical and professional standards a team coach needs to be aware of and maintain. The supervision relationship is an ideal space to help team coaches explore and gain clarity on their professional and ethical practices. The ICF's Code of Ethics and core values of professionalism, collaboration, humanity, and equity provide the foundation for the supervisor and supervisee conversation.

Approach to Supervision

Passmore and Sinclair (2024) summarize the triangulated approach to supervision (Fig. 28.1), which has evolved from many different models of supervision.

It is evident that there are different approaches to supervision. These broadly fall into the three areas described in Table 28.1.

How Does Supervision Work in Practice?

Supervision for team coaches, Hawkins (2021), states that it can take place in a number of different ways:

1. One-to-one supervision

    1. Focus is on coaching and team coaching
    2. Only team coaching

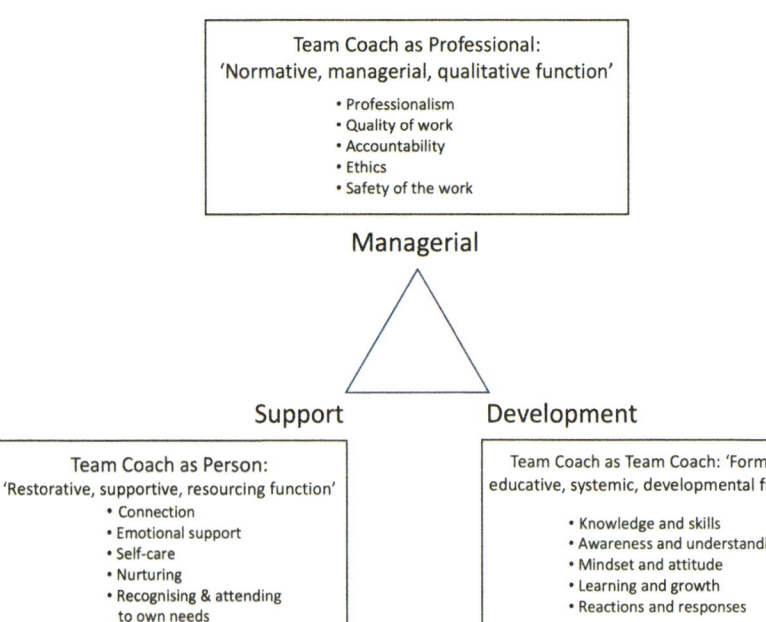

Fig. 28.1 Triangulated approach to supervision

Table 28.1 Functions of supervision

Functions of Supervision			
Kadusin and Harknes (2002)	Proctor (2000)	Hawkins and Smith (2013)	Newton and Napper (2007)
Managerial	Normative	Qualitative	Accounting
Supportive	Restorative	Resourcing	Nurturing
Educative	Formative	Developmental	Transformative

Used with permission of Passmore and Sinclair (2024, p. 237)

2. Group supervision

   1. Focus within the group is on both coaching and team coaching
   2. Only team coaching

3. Joint supervision

   1. Two co-coaches coaching the same team

4. Team of team coaches or consultants together

   1. Team of team coaches or consultants who are all coaching teams within the same organization

5. Team leader coaching

   1. Focus is on how the team leader coaches their own team

The best approach will depend on the amount of team coaching the supervisee is undertaking and whether the supervisor is experienced in supervising team coaching. Hawkins continues to suggest if team coaching is a substantial part of the team coach's practice, then supervision solely focusing on team coaching would be beneficial.

The supervision relationship, as mentioned earlier, is focused on building rapport and a safe, trusting space. The supervisor and supervisee will agree:

- How will they work together?
- How will they share if the supervision is working or not working for them?
- Boundaries of confidentiality
- What is in the scope of the discussion?
- What the supervisee would like from the supervision
- Regularity of sessions and duration
- Location of sessions
- Costs of the sessions and relevant terms
- Ethical and legal obligations

The supervisor will usually provide a supervision agreement so both parties are clear on the parameters of the relationship.

How Can I Find a Suitable Supervisor?

With the development of competencies for team coaches and the ICF team coaching credential, supervision is now viewed as a key requirement for team coaches. However, there is still a need for further supervisors who are trained and experienced in coaching teams.

In seeking a supervisor, team coaches may find the following questions useful to ask:

- What experience do you have in coaching and team coaching?
- What experience do you have in supervising coaches?
- What experience do you have in supervising team coaches?
- What are your qualifications and accreditations as a coach?
- What are your qualifications and accreditations as a team coach?
- What are your qualifications and accreditations as a team coach supervisor?
- How many hours of experience do you have supervising team coaches?
- What is your approach to supervision?
- What types of supervision do you offer? (i.e., one-to-one, group supervision, joint supervision).
- What supervision do you have as a supervisor?
- What do you do to keep up-to-date with the latest developments in team coaching and supervision?
- What is your knowledge of the ICF Team Coaching Competencies?
- What is your knowledge of the ICF Code of Ethics?

Getting the Best from Supervision

Before engaging in supervision, for the supervisee to gain the maximum benefit they need to consider:

- *Chemistry with the supervisor*: The team coach needs to feel safe to share with their supervisor their successes, proudest moments, fears, vulnerabilities, blind spots, and challenges. Therefore, it is essential that they have a deep level of rapport, connection, and trust.
- *Chemistry with the group*: Where the team coach is engaging in group supervision, it is also important that they feel safe to explore their own questions for supervision and be willing to offer observations, reflections, and enquiries for other group members.
- *Preparation for the supervisee*: Prior to a session, the supervisee will need to consider what question they want to explore at supervision, what they want from the supervisor or group, what is the right location for the session, and how they will capture their learning.

- *Frequency and duration of supervision*: There are many different views about the length and frequency of sessions and these will also vary from one-to-one supervision to group supervision. This can range from monthly one-to-one team coaching supervision, to quarterly group supervision. The amount of supervision needed may depend on the volume of team coaching you are engaged in. The key is to ensure that it is regular enough for the team coach to have adequate time for reflection, exploration, and growth.
- *Contract*: As discussed earlier in this chapter, it is important to ensure that you and your supervisor are clear on your contract and how you will work together.
- *Co-create*: The heart of supervision is the relationship between the supervisee and supervisor to co-create, explore together both the known and unknown, and learn and grow.
- *Reflect on your learning*: Taking time to reflect and review your learning following supervision sessions will help you to further develop your reflective practice, consider how you will incorporate new learning into your practice; and other areas you would like to bring to future supervision sessions.

Conclusion

It is evident that supervision plays a vital role in supporting a team coach in their practice, learning, and journey to mastery. Carroll (2001, p. 77) suggests that supervision is much more than a function, it is a "way of life" where we explore who we are, what is within us and beyond us, and what brings the best out of us. Carroll notes: "It is possible that adopting a supervisory attitude, viewing supervision as a reflective process that allows participants to think deeply and vulnerably about life and values, work and career, relationships and connections, might make an immense difference in how participants live" (Carroll, 2001, p. 77).

Chapter 29
Continuous Professional Development for Team Coaches

Introduction

Team Coaching is one of the fastest growing disciplines in the coaching profession and an increasingly important intervention. As a result, more organizations—private corporations, government agencies, and non-profit/charities—are resorting to team coaching to harness the power, energy, and wisdom of the team, and to work towards sustainable results and continuing development. As the demand of team coaching increases, team coaches desire to differentiate themselves and showcase their reliability as partners, equipped with the complex skills for effective team coaching.

The development of the team coaching practitioner, similarly to the development of the one-to-one coaching practitioner (Passmore & Sinclair, 2024), is constant. Section II of the ICF Code of Ethics includes Standard 16 *Commit to excellence through continued personal, professional and ethical development*.

In this chapter, we are going to present some of the available continuous professional development opportunities of the team coaching practitioner.

Advanced Certification in Team Coaching

To set the standard for team coaching practice, ICF Credentials and Standards has developed the ICF Team Coaching Competencies model, as we saw in Chap. 5. At the same time, this model serves as the foundation for the ICF Advanced Certification in Team Coaching (ACTC), designed to recognize the knowledge, skill, and competence of advanced team coach practitioners.

The ICF began accepting applications for the Advanced Certification in Team Coaching operational pilot program in December 2021, and the first ACTC earners who participated in the operational pilot received their certifications in August 2022.

© The Author(s), under exclusive license to Springer Nature
Switzerland AG 2024
J. Passmore et al., *Becoming a Team Coach*,
https://doi.org/10.1007/978-3-031-63546-5_29

In January 2023, the ACTC was fully launched and ICF began accepting applications from individual team coaches. Simultaneously, ICF Coaching Education launched the Advanced Accreditation in Team Coaching in January 2023.

While the number of certified team coaches remains small in comparison to general coaches, it continues to grow reflecting the wider growth of team coaching.

Earning an ACTC gives additional credibility while providing an excellent opportunity for team coaching practitioners to pursue their continuous professional development.

Further on, we are going to present the Team Coaching Certification requirements. Please note these established requirements are in effect running at the time of writing this book; for any future modifications please visit the ICF website, granting no changes are anticipated in the immediate future: https://coachingfederation.org/credentials-and-standards/team-coaching.

Requirements Overview

For both paths the requirements' categories are similar (see Table 29.1):

- ICF Credential
- Team coaching education
- Team coaching experience
- Coaching supervision
- Team Coaching Certification Exam

Table 29.1 Eligibility requirements

	Option 1	Option 2 (AATC path)	Option 3 (Credit for prior learning)
1. ICF credential	ACC, PCC, or MCC	ACC, PCC, or MCC	ACC, PCC, or MCC
2. Team coaching education	60+ h completed	60+ h completed	30+ h completed
3. Team coaching experience	At least five team coaching engagements within the last 5 years	At least five team coaching engagements within the last 5 years	Completion of ten team coaching engagements, with at least three engagements completed 5 years or more prior to the date of application
4. Coaching supervision	At least 5 h	At least 5 h	At least 10 h
5. Exam	Passing score	Passing score	Passing score

Application Paths

There are three paths that a team coach can follow in their application:

- Option 1
- Apply using at least 60 h of team coaching education, without credit for prior learning
- Option 2
- Using completion of an ICF Advanced Accreditation in Team Coaching (AATC) program
- Option 3
- With credit for prior learning for long-term team coach practitioners

Credit for Prior Learning (CPL)

This is Option/Path 3 for long-term team coach practitioners.

To be eligible for this application, applicants must meet all of the following criteria:

- Completion of ten team coaching engagements, with at least three engagements completed 5 years or more prior to the date of application
- Completion of at least 10 h of coaching supervision with an eligible supervisor
- Completion of at least 30 h of team coaching education

ICF Credential

Hold an *active* ICF Credential at the Associate Certified Coach (ACC), Professional Certified Coach (PCC), or Master Certified Coach (MCC) level.

Team Coaching Education

Depending on the path they will follow, applicants are required to have completed 30 or 60 h of Team Coaching Education (Table 29.2).

In addition, team coaching education needs to be: aligned with the ICF Team Coaching Competencies, ICF Core Competencies, and ICF Code of Ethics, and completed through one or more ICF-accredited or non-accredited providers.

Table 29.2 Team coaching education

For application with Option 1:	For application with Option 2: (AATC)	For application with Option 3: (credit for prior learning)
Applicants must document completion of at least 60 h of team coaching education	Applicants will have received the required 60 h of Team Coaching education through their AATC	Applicants must document completion of at least 30 h of team coaching education.

Table 29.3 Team coaching experience

For application with Option 1:	For application with Option 2: (AATC)	For application with Option 2: (credit for prior learning)
At least five team coaching engagements within the last 5 years.	At least five team coaching engagements within the last 5 years.	A total of ten engagements as follows: • Five of the engagements must have been started within the 5 years prior to the application creation date. • Three of the engagements must be completed at least 5 years prior to the application creation date. • Two of the engagements may have been done at any time.

Applicants submitting non-ICF accredited education will be required to provide a program syllabus or course outline with their application. Educational curricula may be reviewed to ensure alignment with ICF standards.

Team Coaching Experience

Applicants must complete at least five (5) or ten (10) team coaching engagements within a specific time frame (Table 29.3).

A team coaching engagement includes all activities and sessions completed as part of a team coaching agreement. Engagements may include other team development activities (team training, consulting, facilitation, team building, etc.), but must include team coaching sessions to be eligible.

Team coaching delivered with teams of more than 15 members must include a co-coach.

Applicants are required to submit a letter of verification for two team coaching engagements. The letter of verification may be provided by a team member, team leader, authorized representative of the sponsor organization, or a third-party coaching body.

Letters should be signed, submitted on company letterhead (unless prohibited by a confidentiality agreement) and include the following elements:

• Name and contact information of the authorized representative
• The representative's role within the organization or team

- Name of the ACTC applicant
- Total hours of the team engagement
- Start and end dates of the engagement
- Number of team members

Coaching Supervision

Depending on the path they will follow, applicants are required to have completed at least five (5) or ten (10) hours of supervision (Table 29.4).

An applicant's coaching supervisor must meet at least one of the following criteria:

1. Hold an active coaching supervision certification, credential, or accreditation by a coaching or coaching supervision professional body.
2. Have completed a coaching supervision education program of at least 60 h and have at least 120 h of coaching supervision experience.
3. Be an eligible ICF Mentor Coach with 60 h of coaching supervision education and at least 120 h of coaching supervision experience.

Team Coaching Certification Exam

Achieve a passing score on the ICF Team Coaching Certification Exam.

Passing score is 460 (of 600). The exam consists of 62 items across four sections, which must be completed in 150 min. Sections 1 and 3 contain multiple-choice questions testing knowledge of topics that are foundational to the team coaching competencies, while Sections 2 and 4 contain scenario-based questions testing judgment and decision-making in realistic team coaching situations.

Table 29.4 Coaching supervision

For application with Option 1: Applicants must document completion of at least five (5) hours of Coaching Supervision or guided reflective practice with an eligible supervisor.*	For application with Option 2: (AATC) Applicants will have completed the Coaching Supervision requirements through their AATC program and will not have to document it separately	For application with Option 3: (credit for prior learning) Applicants must document completion of at least 10 h of Coaching Supervision or guided reflective practice with an eligible supervisor.*

Sample Questions

ICF provides sample questions from both categories: multiple-choice and scenario-based. These questions can be found at: https://coachingfederation.org/credentials-and-standards/team-coaching/exam.

Below we are going to present these questions with a brief explanation of the correct answers.

Multiple-Choice

Question 1

Which of the following best describes a key difference between team mentoring and team coaching?

A. Team mentoring is often completed in a single session, while team coaching extends over several years
B. Team mentoring focuses on developing individual team members, while team coaching supports the team as a whole
C. In team mentoring, the mentor is the expert and shares their knowledge with the team. In team coaching, the team is the expert

Correct answer: C

Explanation: See Team Development Modalities table in ICF's Team Coaching Competencies: Expert; Ownership in Team Mentoring is the Mentor, in Team Coaching is the Team (page 3). See also Chap. 5, Table 5.3.

Question 2

Which of the following best describes the parties that should be involved in the development of a team coaching agreement?

A. The team coach and one representative from the sponsor organization
B. The team coach, all team members, the team leader, and the sponsor organization
C. The team coach, the team leader, all current team members, and anyone who has left the team in the last year

Correct answer: B

Explanation: See Competency 3, in ICF's Team Coaching Competencies, supplementary competency b: "Partners with all relevant parties, including the team leader, team members, stakeholders, and any co-coaches to collaboratively create clear agreements about the coaching relationship, processes, plans, development modalities, and goals" (page 9). See also Chap. 8, Box 8.2 (b).

Question 3

A team coach can best help resolve conflict among team members by:

A. Acknowledging the conflict and inviting team members to share how they would like to address it as a team.
B. Addressing the conflict with members of the team individually outside of the team coaching session.
C. Sharing ideas with the team about what the coach sees as the main reasons that the team is experiencing conflict.

Correct answer: A

Explanation: See Competency 4, in ICF's Team Coaching Competencies, supplementary competency g: "Partners with the team to identify and resolve internal conflict" (page 12). See also Chap. 9, Box 9.2, (g).

Question 4

Asking the team questions is a technique used most effectively by a team coach to:

A. To break the tension when the team is discussing a challenging topic
B. Discover potential areas of conflict that the team should avoid
C. Encourage the team to engage in internal dialogue and reflection

Correct answer: C

Explanation: See Competency 7, in ICF's Team Coaching Competencies, supplementary competency b, Background: "questions and other techniques should be used to enhance team development, but in team coaching the work should also foster internal team dialogue and processing" (page 17). See also Chap. 12, Box 12.2, (b).

Question 5

How can a team coach most effectively support the team in summarizing learning and insight within a session?

A. Recap the reflections and learning that the team coach heard from team members throughout the session
B. Invite team members to share their reflections and learning with the team at the end of the session
C. Ask each team member to email the team leader with their learnings from the session

Correct answer: B

Explanation: See Competency 8, in ICF's Team Coaching Competencies, supplementary competency Background: "Team dialogue and reflection is essential in order to take full advantage of all team members' knowledge and skills" (page 19). See also Chap. 13: At the close of sessions.

Scenario-Based

Question 1

A team coach was hired to work with a company's senior management team, including the Chief Executive Officer (CEO), the Chief Financial Officer (CFO), the Chief Operating Officer (COO), and the Chief Human Resources Officer (CHRO). The team coaching agreement includes five monthly coaching sessions to support the team as they plan an upcoming company reorganization. The team coach has previous experience as the CHRO of a company in the same industry, where the coach also supported a reorganization effort. After the first session, the CEO asks the team coach to provide recommendations for the reorganization that the team should consider and discuss during the next session. What should the coach do?

Best action: Clarify the difference between team coaching and team consulting and refer the CEO back to the team coaching agreement.

Worst action: Offer to meet directly with the CEO to provide suggestions about organizational changes the CEO may want to consider.

Explanation: This is touching on two team coaching competencies: 1 "Demonstrates Ethical Practice"—supplementary competencies b and e—and 2 "Establishes and Maintains Agreements"—supplementary competencies (a) and (b)—See ICF's Team Coaching Competencies (pages 5, 6, 9), and Chaps. 6 and 8. Since it is a team coaching agreement that the team coach has with the management team, the request from the CEO is outside this agreement.

Question 2

A team coach is working with a senior management team that includes the CEO of the organization and directors from five different departments. During the initial session, it is clear to the team coach that there is conflict between the CEO and one of the department directors. The CEO and director avoid eye contact throughout the session and cross their arms when the other one speaks. Towards the end of the session, the CEO rolls their eyes at an idea the director shares, and the director responds with a rude remark to the CEO. The other members of the team seem uncomfortable, watching in silence or looking down at the floor. What should the coach do?

Best action: Invite the team to reflect on how conflict impacts the team's progress and how the team can best address conflict when it occurs.

Worst action: Ask the CEO and director to leave the room and continue their conversation elsewhere.

Explanation: See ICF's Team Coaching Competency 4, supplementary competency g (page 12) and Chap. 9: "Partners with the team to identify and resolve internal conflict." Conflict within a team is inevitable; the background of this supplementary competency is about the importance of bringing conflict to the surface and dealing with it in a manner that promotes learning and growth.

Question 3

A team coach has been working with a team for six months to support their goal to collaborate more effectively. The team members live and work in various time zones around the world and have few opportunities to interact directly with one another. The team members seemed uncomfortable during the initial sessions. Over time, however, the coach saw the team members develop a greater level of trust and familiarity. During a session midway through the scheduled engagement, the coach presents a challenging exercise to the team and the team members quickly partner to complete the exercise. As the team finishes this activity, the coach observes the significant improvement in the team's collaboration skills over the six month team coaching engagement. What should the coach do?

Best action: Invite the team members to share their reflections on the team's collaboration.

Worst action: Share that the team has achieved its goal of improving collaboration and announce that no additional team coaching sessions are needed.

Explanation: See ICF's Team Coaching Competencies 5—supplementary competency c—and 8 (pages 13, 19), and Chaps. 10 and 13: The team coach encourages to pause and reflect how they are interacting in team coaching sessions, and takes full advantage of all team members' insights. Additionally, in team coaching the ownership is of the team and the team can decide if they have achieved their objectives; it's not for the coach to decide and to stop the engagement.

Question 4

A team coach is supporting an organization's senior leaders to develop a clear long-term strategy to increase profitability. The team includes a newly hired Chief Executive Officer (CEO), the Chief Operating Officer (COO), the Chief Financial Officer (CFO), and the vice presidents for marketing and sales. During the third session, the team engages in a discussion to collectively define a new strategy to improve the organization's sales figures. Members of the team seem actively engaged in the conversation, however the coach notices the CEO frequently looking at their phone and scrolling through emails. The coach senses that the other team members are becoming increasingly frustrated and the conversation stalling. What should the coach do?

Best action: Invite the team members to share what they need to move towards the development of a clear, unified strategy.

action: Ask the CEO to put their phone away and focus on the discussion.

Explanation: See ICF's Team Coaching Competencies 7—supplementary competency b—and 8 (pages 17, 19), and Chaps. 10 and 13: The team coach uses questions to foster internal team dialogue and processing, and to encourage full participation.

Question 5

A coach is working with an executive team to improve their workplace's culture, following complaints of poor treatment by staff. During a recent coaching session, the team brainstorms strategies to improve the culture, including developing clear organizational values. The director of human resources expresses concern about senior leaders identifying values for the organization without the staff's input. Other team members respond that the HR director's idea is impractical because collecting staff input would take too long and delay the team's progress. Frustrated, the HR director asks the coach to share their thoughts on the best approach. What should the coach do?

Best action: Remind the team that it is their role to determine the best approach for their organization, and ask the team what would support them to move forward.

Worst action: Share what the coach would do in this situation, but indicate that it is ultimately the decision of the team.

Explanation: This also touches on two team coaching competencies: Competency 1 on ethical practice Competency 7 on awareness (pages 5, 17), and more specifically on facilitating the team's ownership. See also Chaps. 6 and 12.

Other Continuous Professional Development for the Team Coach

Coombs and Ahmed (1974) proposed three types of learning:

- Formal education
- Non-formal learning
- Informal learning.

The formal education of the team coach could be reflected in completing training programs and certifications on team related topics, team coaching, team coaching models, assessments and more in the pursuit of post-graduate degrees, and academic research on team coaching.

Non-formal learning opportunities are increasing thanks to technology and the possibility to attend webinars from anywhere makes them more accessible. Seminars, workshops, labs, conferences on team coaching related or specific topics are available for the team coaching practitioner. The ICF Team & Group Coaching community of practice, along with team coaching communities of practice of local chapters, are an example of such a resource where the team coach can attend webinars, panel conversations, presentations, workshops, and network with other team coaches of different geographic locations, background, expertise, and experience.

Informal lifelong learning for the team coach can be achieved from a variety of opportunities and sources:

Reflective Practice/Supervision

As viewed earlier in Chaps. 7 and 29, coaching supervision is one of the resources for the development of the team coach. From covering gaps in the coaching training (Hawkins & Smith, 2013), to gaining different perspectives, a space to be re-sourced (Turner & Palmer, 2019) is one of the most valuable ways to maintain and expand our skills and sharpen team coaches supervision (Walter, 2023).

Peer Support

In the form of mentoring, peer networks, and peer groups. The benefits of peer-to-peer conversations cannot be undervalued. From accountability partners to having another reflective practice structure—other than supervision—where team coaches can share resources and ideas, reflect on what goes well, what does not go well, what might be missing, and more.

Self Study

Books, articles, podcasts, educational videos.

Organizing self-study in an intentional and critical way. For example, reading a book the team coach can reflect on these questions:

- What do I recognize from the knowledge shared?
- What will I be able to apply?
- How could I apply it?
- What would or should I say no to?
- What would I like to explore further or discuss with my peers?

Other

Involvement in group activities with a learning or self-development purpose, new hobbies, volunteer work, team sports, community work, and other ongoing experiences in groups are some examples of opportunities for shaping values, attitudes, behaviors, and skills, and expanding our insights about teams.

Practice

This includes the practice of team coaching, but also other practices like teaching about team coaching, writing articles, doing research, interviewing experts, and any other opportunity that allows us to sharpen our skills, enrich our knowledge, expand our perspectives, and improve our mindset.

Courage

Thornton (2019) refers to the attribute of humility for the development of a team coach. Taking it a step further we can talk about the courage to be humble and know our limits, the courage to experiment and step into new things, the courage to unlearn and learn again, the courage to face our own biases, seek support, and lean into the discomfort that often happens in team coaching.

Conclusion

In this chapter, we have reviewed the alternative options for continuing your journey as a team coach, originating with securing formal accreditation from the ICF for your practice to enhancing and maintaining your practice through continuous professional development (CPD) and coaching supervision.

References

Allworth, E., & Passmore, J. (2008). Using psychometrics and psychological tools in coaching. In *Psychometrics in coaching: Using psychological and psychometric tools for development* (pp. 7–24). Kogan Page.

Anand, N., & Barsoux, J.-L. (2023). *Fixing a self-sabotaging team. How to spot and counter dysfunctional group behavior*. [online] Retrieved November 3, 2023, from https://hbr.org/2023/03/fixing-a-self-sabotaging-team

Anderson, M., Anderson, D., & Mayo, W. (2008). Team coaching helps a leadership team drive cultural change at Caterpillar. *Global Business and Organizational Excellence, 27*(4), 40–50. https://doi.org/10.1002/joe.20212

Athanasopoulou, A., & Dopson, S. (2018). A systematic review of executive coaching outcomes: Is it the journey or the destination that matters the most? *The Leadership Quarterly, 29*(1), 70–88. https://doi.org/10.1016/j.leaqua.2017.11.004

Bachkirova, T. (2021). Understanding yourself as a coach. In J. Passmore (Ed.), *The coaches' handbook: The complete practitioner guide for professional coaches* (pp. 39–47). Routledge.

Berne, E. (1966). *Principles of group treatment*. Grove Press.

Berne, E. (2016). *Games people play: The psychology of human relationships*. Penguin.

Bion, W. R. (1961). *Experiences in groups and other papers*. Routledge.

Bion, W. R., & Rickman, J. (1943). Intra-group tensions in therapy; their study as the task of the group. *The Lancet, 242*(6274), 678–682.

Blake, A. (2018). *Your body is your brain: Leverage your somatic intelligence to find purpose, build resilience, deepen relationships and lead more powerfully*. Tokay Press.

Britton, J. J. (2013). Co-facilitation, partnering and collaboration: Who has your back. In *From one to many: Best practices for team and group coaching*. Wiley.

Burt, D., & Talati, Z. (2017). The unsolved value of executive coaching: A meta-analysis of outcomes using randomised control trial studies. *International Journal of Evidence Based Coaching and Mentoring, 15*(2), 17–24. https://doi.org/10.24384/000248

Cannon-Bowers, J. A., Bowers, C. A., Carlson, C. F., Doherty, S. L., Evans, J., & Hall, J. (2023). Workplace coaching: A meta-analysis and recommendations for advancing the *science of coaching*. *Frontiers of Psychology*. https://doi.org/10.3389/fpsyg.2023.1204166

Carboni, I., Cross, R., & Edmondson, A. C. (2021). No team is an island: How leaders shape networked ecosystems for team success. *California Management Review, 64*(1), 5–28.

Cardona, F., & Damon, S. (2019). Family patterns at work. How casting light on the shadows of the past can enhance leadership in the present. In A. Obholzer & V. Z. Roberts (Eds.), *The unconscious at work: A Tavistock approach to making sense of organisational life* (pp. 11–18). Routledge.

Carr, C., & Peters, J. (2012). *The experience and impact of team coaching: A dual case study* (Doctoral dissertation). Middlesex University, UK.

Carr, C., & Peters, J. (2013). The experience of team coaching: A dual case study. *International Coaching Psychology Review, 8*(1), 80–98.

Carroll, M. (2001). The spirituality of supervision. In *Integrative approaches to supervision.* Jessica Kingsley.

Clark, T. (2020). *The 4 stages of psychological safety: Defining the path to inclusion and innovation.* Berrett-Koehler Publishers.

Clutterbuck, D. (2007). *Coaching the team at work.* Nicholas Brealey.

Clutterbuck, D. (2014). Team coaching. In E. Cox, T. Bachkirova, & D. Clutterbuck (Eds.), *The complete handbook of coaching* (pp. 271–284). Sage.

Clutterbuck, D. (2019). Towards a pragmatic model of team function and dysfunction. In D. Clutterbuck, J. Gannon, S. Hayes, I. Iordanou, K. Lowe, & D. MacKie (Eds.), *The practitioner's handbook of team coaching* (pp. 150–160). Routledge.

Clutterbuck, D. (2020). *Coaching the team at work: The definitive guide to team coaching* (2nd ed.). Nicholas Brealey.

Clutterbuck, D., Gannon, J., Hayes, S., Iordanou, I., Lowe, K., & MacKie, D. (2019). Introduction. In D. Clutterbuck, J. Gannon, S. Hayes, I. Iordanou, K. Lowe, & D. MacKie (Eds.), *The practitioner's handbook of team coaching* (pp. 1–8). Routledge.

Clutterbuck, D., & Megginson, D. (2011). *Coach maturity: An emerging concept.* [online] Accessed December 27, 2019, from https://www.davidclutterbuckpartnership.com/wp-content/uploads/Coach-maturity.pdf

Clutterbuck, D., Turner, T., & Murphy, C. (2022). *The team coaching casebook.* McGraw-Hill.

Coombs, P. H., & Ahmed, M. (1974). *Attacking rural poverty: How non-formal education can help.* Johns Hopkins University Press.

Covey, S. (2004). *The 7 habits of highly effective people.* Free Press.

Cox, C., & Flynn, S. (2022). *Climate change coaching: The power of connection to create climate action.* Open University Press.

Darina, L. (2023). *Shocking male vs female CEO statistics 2023.* [online] Retrieved August 31, 2023, from https://leftronic.com/blog/ceo-statistics/

de Bono, E. (1985). *Six thinking hats: An essential approach to business management.* Little Brown.

De Haan, E. (2008). *Relational coaching: Journeys towards mastering one-to-one learning.* John Wiley & Sons.

de Haan, E. (2012). *Supervision in action: A relational approach to coaching and consulting supervision.* Open University Press.

De Haan, E., Grant, A. M., Burger, Y., & Eriksson, P. O. (2016). A large-scale study of executive and workplace coaching: The relative contributions of relationship, personality match, and self-efficacy. *Consulting Psychology Journal: Practice and Research, 68*(3), 189–207.

De Haan, E., Gray, D. E., & Bonneywell, S. (2019). Executive coaching outcome research in a field setting: A near-randomized controlled trial study in a global healthcare corporation. *Academy of Management Learning & Education, 18*(4), 581–605.

de Haan, E., Molyn, J., & Nilsson, V. O. (2020). New findings on the effectiveness of the coaching relationship: Time to think differently about active ingredients? *Consulting Psychology Journal: Practice and Research, 72*(3), 155–167. https://doi.org/10.1037/cpb0000175

de Haan, E., & Nilsson, V. O. (2023). What can we know about the effectiveness of coaching? A meta-analysis based only on randomized controlled trials. *Academy of Management Learning & Education.* https://doi.org/10.5465/amle.2022.0107

De Meuse, K. P., Dai, G., & Lee, R. J. (2009). Evaluating the effectiveness of executive coaching: Beyond ROI? *Coaching: An International Journal of Theory, Research and Practice, 2*(2), 117–134. https://doi.org/10.1080/17521880902882413

Deci, E. L., & Ryan, R. M. (Eds.). (2004). *Handbook of self-determination research.* University of Rochester Press.

Dilts, R. (1995). *Strategies of genius.* Meta Publications.

Douglas, T. (1995). *Survival in groups. The basics of group membership*. Open University Press.

Drayton, B. (2013). A team of teams world. Although this organizational model still dominates, it is failing. *Stanford Social Innovation Review, 11*(2), 57.

Druskat, V. U., & Wolff, S. B. (2001). Building the emotional intelligence of groups. *Harvard Business Review, 79*(3), 80–91.

Duijts, S. F., Kant, I., van den Brandt, P. A., & Swaen, G. M. (2008). Effectiveness of a preventive coaching intervention for employees at risk for sickness absence due to psychosocial health complaints: Results of a randomized controlled trial. *Journal of Occupational Environmental Medicine, 50*(7), 765–776. https://doi.org/10.1097/JOM.0b013e3181651584

Edmondson, A. C. (1999). Psychological safety and learning behavior in work teams. *Administrative Science Quarterly, 44*(2), 350–383.

Edmondson, A. C. (2012). *Teaming: How organizations learn, innovate and compete in the knowledge economy*. Jossey-Boss.

Edmondson, A. C., & Lei, Z. (2014). Psychological safety: The history, renaissance, and future of an interpersonal construct. *Annual Review of Organizational Psychology & Organizational Behavior, 1*(1), 23–43.

Edmonson, A. (2020). *Creating psychological safety at work*, podcast. Retrieved November 5, 2023, from https://www.youtube.com/watch?v=SkFohYhIaSQ

EMCC. (2020). *Team Coaching definition*. Retrieved March 9, 2023, from https://www.emcc-global.org/accreditation/tcqa/

Fontes, A., & Dello Russo, S. (2021). An experimental field study on the effects of coaching: The mediating role of psychological capital. *Applied Psychology: An International Review, 70*(2), 459–488. https://doi.org/10.1111/apps.12260

Forsyth, D. R. (2014). *Group dynamics* (6th ed.). Wadsworth Cengage Learning.

Foy, K. (2021). Contracting in coaching. In J. Passmore (Ed.), *The coaches handbook: The complete practitioners guide for professional coaches* (pp. 344–354). Routledge.

Fussell, C., & Goodyear, C. W. (2017). *One mission: How leaders build a team of teams*. Macmillan.

Gallup. (2023a). *The Gallup Global Workplace 2023 Report* [online]. Retrieved August 31, 2023, from https://www.gallup.com/home.aspx

Gallup. (2023b). *What Is Employee Engagement and How Do You Improve It?* [online]. Retrieved August 31, 2023, from https://www.gallup.com/workplace/285674/improve-employee-engagement-workplace.aspx

Gersick, C. J. (1988). Time and transition in work teams: Toward a new model of group development. *Academy of Management Journal, 31*(1), 9–41.

Gersick, C. J. (1989). Marking time: Predictable transitions in task groups. *Academy of Management Journal, 32*(2), 274–309.

Gordy, C. (1937). Everyone gets a share of the profits. *Factory Management & Maintenance 95*, 82–83.

Grant, A. M. (2009). *Workplace, executive and life coaching: An annotated bibliography from the behavioural science and business literature*. Coaching Psychology Unit, University of Sydney.

Grant, A. M., Passmore, J., Cavanagh, M. J., & Parker, H. M. (2010a). The state of play in coaching today: A comprehensive review of the field. In G. P. Hodgkinson & J. K. Ford (Eds.), *International review of industrial and organizational psychology 2010* (pp. 125–167). Wiley Blackwell. https://doi.org/10.1002/9780470661628.ch4

Grant, A. M., Passmore, J., Cavanagh, M., & Parker, H. (2010b). The state of play in coaching. *International Review of Industrial & Organizational Psychology, 25*, 125–168.

Graßmann, C., Schölmerich, F., & Schermuly, C. C. (2020). The relationship between working alliance and client outcomes in coaching: A meta-analysis. *Human Relations, 73*(1), 35–58. https://doi.org/10.1177/0018726718819725

Griffiths, C. R. (1926). *Psychology of coaching: A study of coaching methods from the point of view of psychology*. Charles Scribner.

Hackman, J. R. (1987). The design of work teams. In J. Lorsch (Ed.), *Handbook of organizational behavior* (pp. 315–342). Prentice-Hall.

Hackman, J. R. (2002). *Leading teams: Setting the stage for great performances*. Harvard Business School Press.

Hackman, J. R. (2011a). *Collaborative intelligence: Using teams to solve hard problems*. Berrett-Koehler Publishers.

Hackman, J. R. (2011b). Walking on three legs. In S. A. Mohrman & E. E. Lawler III (Eds.), *Useful research: Advancing theory and practice* (pp. 103–110). Berrett-Koehler.

Hackman, J. R., & Wageman, R. (2005a). A theory of team coaching. *The Academy of Management Review, 30*(2), 269–287. https://doi.org/10.2307/20159119

Hackman, J. R., & Wageman, R. (2005b). The theory of team coaching. *Academy of Management, 30*(2). https://doi.org/10.5465/AMR.2005.16387885

Halton, H. (2019). Some unconscious aspects of organizational life. Contributions from psychoanalysis. In A. Obholzer & V. Z. Roberts (Eds.), *The unconscious at work: A Tavistock approach to making sense of organisational life* (pp. 187–195). Routledge.

Hardingham, A. (2021). Understanding your clients. In J. Passmore (Ed.), *The coaches' handbook: The complete practitioner guide for professional coaches* (pp. 48–57). Routledge.

Hardingham, A., Brearley, M., Moorhouse, A., & Venter, B. (2004). *Coach's coach: Personal development for personal developers*. Chartered Institute of Personnel and Development.

Hastings, R., & Pennington, W. (2019). Team coaching: A thematic analysis of methods used by external coaches in a work domain. *International Journal of Evidence Based Coaching and Mentoring, 17*(2), 174–188. https://doi.org/10.24384/akra-6r08

Hauser, L. L. (2014). Shape-shifting: A behavioral team coaching model for coach education, research, and practice. *Journal of Psychological Issues in Organizational Culture, 5*(2), 48–71.

Hauser, L. L. (2018). Team Coaching Operating System (TCOS): The intersection of evidence-based research and Gestalt principles. *Gestalt Review, 22*(2), 208–225.

Hawkins, P. (2011). *Leadership team coaching: Developing collective transformational leadership*. Kogan Page.

Hawkins, P (2014) *Leadership team coaching: Developing collective transformational leadership* (2nd ed.). Kogan Page.

Hawkins, P. (2017). *Leadership team coaching: Developing collective transformational leadership* (3rd ed.). Kogan Page.

Hawkins, P. (2021). *Leadership team coaching: Developing collective transformational leadership* (4th ed.). Kogan Page Publishers.

Hawkins, P. (2022). Foreword: Maps, models, and muddles! In D. Clutterbuck, T. Turner, & C. Murphy (Eds.), *The team coaching casebook* (pp. 65–68). Open University Press.

Hawkins, P. (Ed.). (2022b). *Leadership team coaching in practice: Case studies on creating highly effective teams* (3rd ed.). Kogan Page.

Hawkins, P., & Smith, N. (2006). *Coaching, mentoring and organizational consultancy, supervision and development* (1st ed.). Open University Press.

Hawkins, P., & Smith, N. (2013). *Coaching, mentoring and organizational consultancy: Supervision, skills and development*. OUP.

Hawkins, P., & Turner, E. (Eds.). (2020). *Systemic coaching: Delivering value beyond the individual*. Routledge.

Heimbecker, D. (2006). *The effects of expert coaching on team productivity at the South Coast Educational Collaborative*. Boston University.

Hellinger, B. (2003). *Farewell: Family constellations with descendants of victims and perpetrators*. (C. Beaumont, Trans.). Carl-Auer-Systeme Verlag.

Heron, J. (1999). *The complete facilitator's handbook*. Kogan Page.

Hicks, B. (2010). *Team coaching: A literature review*. IES.

Hill, S. (2017). *Where did you learn to behave like that? A coaching guide for working with leaders*. CreateSpace Independent Publishing Platform.

Hirsch Pontes, E. (2024) *Supervision. In Foundations of Team Coaching training guide*, Team Coaching Global Alliance.

Hodge, A. (2016). The value of coaching supervision as a development process: Contribution to continued professional and personal wellbeing for executive coaches. *International Journal of Evidence Based Coaching and Mentoring, 14*(2), 87–106.

Hubble, M. A., Duncan, B. L., Miller, S. D., & Wampold, B. E. (2010). Introduction. In B. L. Duncan, S. D. Miller, B. E. Wampold, & M. A. Hubble (Eds.), *The heart and soul of change: Delivering what works in therapy* (2nd ed., pp. 23–46). American Psychological Association.

Hullinger, A., & DiGirolamo, J. (2020). *The state of coaching supervision research.* International Coaching Federation. Retrieved November 5, 2023, from https://researchportal.coachingfederation.org › Document › Pdf › 3537.pdf

Huston, R. E. (1924). Debate coaching in high schools. *Quarterly Journal of Speech Education, 10*, 127–143. https://doi.org/10.1080/00335632409379481

ICF. (2019). *Definition of Supervision.* Accessed November 25, 2023, from https://coachingfederation.org/credentials-and-standards/coaching-supervision

ICF. (2020a). *Team coaching competencies.* Retrieved January 29, 2024, from https://coachingfederation.org/app/uploads/2021/01/Team-Coaching-Competencies-4.pdf

ICF. (2020b). *ICF code of ethics.* Retrieved November 5, 2023, from https://coachingfederation.org/app/uploads/2020/01/ICF-Code-of-Ethics_final_Nov12.pdf

ICF. (2023a). *Definition of coaching.* Retrieved 12, 2023, from https://coachingfederation.org/about

ICF. (2023b). *Definition of team coaching.* Retrieved January 12, 2023, from https://coachingfederation.org/credentials-and-standards/team-coaching

Innegraeve, M. (2023). Dancefloor to the balcony. In J. Passmore, M. Grieve, J. Flower, C. Day, & J. Moon (Eds.), *Coaching tools* (Vol. 3). Libri Publishing.

Isaacson, S. (2021). *How to thrive as a coach in a digital world: Coaching with technology.* Open University Press.

Isaacson, S. (2022). *Superhuman coaching: Ten technologies that expand coaching beyond what's humanly possible.* Hanwell Publishing.

James, J. M., & S. & Corlett, S. (2020). A framework of modes of awareness for team coaching practice. *International Journal of Evidence Based Coaching and Mentoring, 18*(2), 4–18.

Jones, R., Napiersky, U., & Lyubovnikova, J. (2019). Conceptualizing the distinctiveness of team coaching. *Journal of Managerial Psychology, 34*(2), 62–78. https://doi.org/10.1108/JMP-07-2018-0326

Jones, R. J., Woods, S. A., & Guillaume, Y. R. (2015). The effectiveness of workplace coaching: A meta-analysis of learning and performance outcomes. *Journal of Occupational and Organizational Psychology, 89*(2), 249–277. https://doi.org/10.1111/joop.12119

Kadusin, A., & Harknes, D. (2002). *Supervision in social work* (4th ed.). Columbia University Press.

Kanelidou, K. (2023). *Embodying a coaching mindset in team coaching in Foundations of team coaching training guide*, Team Coaching Global Alliance.

Kanelidou, K., & Rog, E. (2021). *Co-coaching a team: When and how?* WBECS Social Impact Coaching Community of Practice.

Kantor, D. (2012). *Reading the room: Group dynamics for coaches and leaders* (Vol. 5). Wiley.

Katzenbach, J., & Smith, D. (1993). *The wisdom of teams.* Harvard Business Press.

Kirkpatrick, D. L. (1959). Techniques for evaluation training programs. *Journal of the American Society of Training Directors, 13*, 21–26.

Kline, N. (1999). *Time to think: Listening to ignite the human mind.* Hachette.

Korkmaz, A. V., Van Engen, M. L., Knappert, L., & Schalk, R. (2022). About and beyond leading uniqueness and belongingness: A systematic review of inclusive leadership research. *Human Resource Management Review, 32*(4), 1–20.

Kozlowski, S. W., & Ilgen, D. R. (2006). Enhancing the effectiveness of work groups and teams. *Psychological Science in the Public Interest, 7*(3), 77–124.

Kriek, H. S., & Venter, P. (2009). The perceived success of team building interventions in South African organisations. *Southern African Business Review, 13*(1), 112–128.

Kroll, C., & Shea, C. (2018). The Agile evolution, it's more than process. *Workforce Solutions Review, 9*(2), 22–25.

Laloux, F. (2014). *Reinventing organizations*. Nelson Parker.

Lanz, K. (2016). Team coaching. In J. Passmore (Ed.), *Excellence in coaching: The industry guide* (pp. 313–326). Kogan Page Publishers.

Lawrence, P. (2021a). *Coaching systemically: Five ways of thinking about systems*. Routledge.

Lawrence, P. (2021b). Team coaching: Systemic perspectives and their limitations. *Philosophy of Coaching: An International Journal, 6*(1), 52–82.

Lawrence, P., & Whyte, A. (2017). What do experienced team coaches do?: Current practice in Australia and New Zealand. *International Journal of Evidence Based Coaching and Mentoring, 15*(1), 94–113.

Leary-Joyce, J., & Lines, H. (2018). *Systemic team coaching*. AoEC Press.

Lee, G. (2003). *Leadership coaching: From personal insight to organisational performance*. Kogan Page.

Made by Dyslexia. (2017*). Connecting the dots*. [online] Retrieved August 31, 2023, from http://madebydyslexia.org/assets/downloads/connecting_the_dots_2019.pdf

Mannix, E., & Neale, M. A. (2005). What differences make a difference? The promise and reality of diverse teams in organizations. *Psychological Science in the Public Interest, 6*(2), 31–55.

Maseko, B. M., Van Wyk, R., & Odendaal, A. (2019). Team coaching in the workplace: Critical success factors for implementation. *SA Journal of Human Resource Management, 17*, a1125. https://doi.org/10.4102/sajhrm.v17i0.1125

McCann, D. (2021). *Emotional intelligence and psychological safety for teams*. ICF Team & Group Coaching Community of Practice.

McChrystal, G. S., Collins, T., Silverman, D., & Fussell, C. (2015). *Team of teams: New rules of engagement for a complex world*. Penguin Business.

McLeod, A. (2000). *Similarity and difference, in me, myself, my team*. Crown House.

McRae, M. B., & Short, E. L. (2010). *Racial and cultural dynamics in group and organizational life: Crossing boundaries*. Sage.

Michalik, N., & Schermuly, C. (2023). Online, offline, or both? The importance of coaching format for side effects in business coaching. *Journal of Managerial Psychology*. https://doi.org/10.1108/JMP-01-2023-0068

Moon, H. (2023). Dialogic orientation quadrant. In J. Passmore, M. Grieve, J. Flower, & J. Moon (Eds.), *Coaching tools* (Vol. 3). Libri.

Moral, M., & Angel, P. (2009). *Coaching: outils et pratiques*. Armand Colin.

Murphy, C. (2023). *How does team coaching contribute to team effectiveness?: An action research study* (Doctoral thesis). University of Portsmouth. Retrieved January 1, 2024, from https://research-portal.port.ac.uk/en/studentTheses/how-does-team-coaching-contribute-to-team-effectiveness

Murphy, C., & Sayer, M. (2019). Standing on the shoulders of the science of team effectiveness: Building rigour into your team coaching design. In D. Clutterbuck, J. Gannon, S. Hayes, I. Iordanou, K. Lowe, & D. MacKie (Eds.), *The practitioner's handbook of team coaching* (pp. 75–88). Routledge.

Newton, T., & Napper, R. (2007). The bigger picture: Supervision as an educational framework for all fields. *Transactional Analysis Journal, 37*(2), 150–158. https://doi.org/10.1177/036215370703700208

Norcross, J. C. (2010). The therapeutic relationship. In B. L. Duncan, S. D. Miller, B. E. Wampold, & M. A. Hubble (Eds.), *The heart and soul of change: Delivering what works in therapy* (2nd ed., pp. 133–141). American Psychological Association.

O'Connor, S., & Cavanagh, M. (2016). Group and team coaching. In T. Bachkirova, G. Spence, & D. Drake (Eds.), *The Sage handbook of coaching* (pp. 485–504). Sage.

Passmore, J. (2021). Developing an integrated approach. In J. Passmore (Ed.), *The coaches handbook* (pp. 322–330). Routledge.

Passmore, J., Day, C., Flower, J., Grieve, M., & Moon, J. J. (2021). *Coaching tools* (Vol. 1). Libri Publishing.

Passmore, J., Day, C., Flower, J., Grieve, M., & Moon, J. J. (2022). *Coaching tools* (Vol. 2). Libri Publishing.

Passmore, J., Day, C., Flower, J., Grieve, M., & Moon, J. J. (2023). *Coaching tools* (Vol. 3). Libri Publishing.

Passmore, J., & Evans-Krimme, R. (2021). The future of coaching: A conceptual framework for the coaching sector from personal craft to scientific process and the implications for practice and research. *Frontiers in Psychology, 12*, 5189. https://doi.org/10.3389/fpsyg.2021.715228

Passmore, J., & Fillery-Travis, A. (2011). A critical review of executive coaching research: A decade of progress and what's to come. *Coaching: An International Journal of Theory, Research and Practice, 4*(2), pp. 70–88.

Passmore, J., & Lai, Y. (2019). Coaching psychology: Exploring definitions and contribution to coaching research and practice? *International Coaching Psychology Review., 14*(2), 69–83.

Passmore, J., & McGoldrick, S. (2009). Super-vision, extra-vision or blind faith? A grounded theory study of the efficacy of coaching supervision. *International Coaching Psychology Review, 4*(2), 143–159.

Passmore, J., & Rehman, H. (2012). Coaching as a learning methodology – a mixed methods study in driver development using a randomised controlled trial and thematic analysis. *International Coaching Psychology Review, 7*(2), 166–184. https://doi.org/10.53841/bpsicpr.2012.7.2.166

Passmore, J., & Sinclair, T. (2021). *Becoming a coach: The Essential ICF Guide* (1st ed.). Cham: Springer.

Passmore, J., & Sinclair, T. (2024). *Becoming a coach: The essential ICF guide* (2nd ed.). Springer.

Passmore, J., & Tee, D. (2023). The library of Babel: Assessing the powers of artificial intelligence in knowledge synthesis, learning and development and coaching. *Journal of Work - Applied Management*. https://doi.org/10.1108/JWAM-06-2023-0057

Passmore, J., Tee, D., & Gold, R. (2024). Team coaching using LSP: An RCT study measuring team cohesion and psychological safety. *Journal of Work - Applied Management*. https://doi.org/10.1108/JWAM-12-2023-0137

Passmore, J., & Velez, M. J. (2012). Coaching fleet drivers – a randomized controlled trial (RCT) of 'short coaching' interventions to improve driver safety in fleet drivers. *The Coaching Psychologist, 8*(1), 20–26. https://doi.org/10.53841/bpstcp.2012.8.1.20

Personnel Today. (2006). *Team coaching: Team work.* September. Retrieved March 25, 2023, from https://www.personneltoday.com/hr/team-coaching-team-work/

Peters, J. (2015a). *High performance relationship and team assessment.* Inneractive Leadership Associates Inc. [online] Retrieved August 31, 2023, from https://app.assessmentgenerator.com/assessment/1913

Peters, J. (2015b). *High performance relationships: The heart and science behind success at work and home.* BookBaby.

Peters, J. (2019). High performance team coaching: An evidence-based system to enable team effectiveness. In D. Clutterbuck, J. Gannon, S. Hayes, I. Iordanou, K. Lowe, & D. MacKie (Eds.), *The practitioner's handbook of team coaching* (pp. 180–191). Routledge.

Peters, J. (2022). Team coaching for culture change. In D. Clutterbuck, T. Turner, & C. Murphy (Eds.), *The team coaching casebook* (pp. 122–130). McGraw-Hill.

Peters, J., & Carr, C. (2013a). Team effectiveness and team coaching literature review. *Coaching: An International Journal of Theory, Research and Practice, 6*(2), 116–136. https://doi.org/10.1080/17521882.2013.798669

Peters, J., & Carr, C. (2013b). *High performance team coaching.* FriesenPress.

Peters, J., & Carr, C. (2013c). *50 Tips for terrific teams! Proven strategies for building high performance teams.* FriesenPress.

Peters, J., & Carr, C. (2019). What does 'good' look like? An overview of the research on the effectiveness of team coaching. In D. Clutterbuck, J. Gannon, S. Hayes, et al. (Eds.), *The practitioner's handbook of team coaching* (pp. 89–120). Routledge.

Price, C., & Toye, S. (2017). *Accelerating performance: How organizations can mobilize, execute, and transform with agility.* Wiley.

Proctor, B. (2000). *Group supervision: A guide to creative practice*. Sage.

Professional Association for Social Work and Social Workers. (2016). *The autism employ-ment gap*. [online] Retrieved August 31, 2023, from https://www.basw.co.uk/resources/autism-employment-gap-too-much-information-workplace

Rafferty, R., Fairbrother, G., & Cashin, A. (2023). Maximising leadership coaching training out-comes: A randomised controlled trial. *International Journal of Evidence Based Coaching and Mentoring, 21*(2), 146–161. https://doi.org/10.24384/cwrs-bv43

Reitz, J. (2019). Question asking quadrant series. In *303 Questioning, in the ACC Pathway course*. ©FLUXIFY Limited.

Revans, R. W. (1971). *Developing effective managers*. Praeger.

Robinson, T., & Yanagi, D. (2019). Coaching for consciousness: Team coaching to support sys-tem, relational, and internal awareness. In D. Clutterbuck, J. Gannon, S. Hayes, I. Iordanou, & D. MacKie (Eds.), *The practitioner's handbook of team coaching* (pp. 163–179). Routledge.

Roche, C., & Passmore, J. (2021). *Racial justice, equity and belonging in coaching*. Henley Business School.

Rogers, C. R. (1975). Empathic: An unappreciated way of being. *The Counselling Psychologist, 5*(2), 2–10.

Rowland, H. (2010). Team coaching: Case study from NHS South East Coast. In *Harnessing the potential of coaching*. IES Research Network Conference, Royal Institute of British Architects, London, 27 April.

Sandahl, P., & Philips, A. (2019). *Teams unleashed: How to release the power and human potential of work teams*. Nicholas Brealey Publishing.

Sauer, J. R. (1999). CEO succession planning in a petroleum exploration company: A case study. *Consulting Psychology Journal: Practice and Research, 51*(4), 266–272. https://doi.org/10.1037/1061-4087.51.4.266

Scotton, N. (2020). *Neil's Wheel*. Retrieved February 5, 2024, from https://neilswheel.org

Sherman, S., & Freas, A. (2004). The Wild West of coaching. *Harvard Business Review*, November. Retrieved January 10, 2023, from https://hbr.org/2004/11/the-wild-west-of-executive-coaching

Shohet, R., & Shohet, J. (2020). *In love with supervision*. PCCS Books.

Solomon, R., & Flores, F. (2001). *Building trust in business, politics, relationships, and life*. Oxford University Press.

Sonesh, S. C., Coultas, C. W., Lacerenza, C. N., Marlow, S. L., Benishek, L. E., & Salas, E. (2015). The power of coaching: A meta-analytic investigation. *Coaching: An International Journal of Theory, Research and Practice, 8*(2), 73–95. https://doi.org/10.1080/17521882.2015.1071418

Stokes, J. (2019). The unconscious at work in groups and team: Contribution from the work of Wilfred Bion. In A. Obholzer & V. Z. Roberts (Eds.), *The unconscious at work: A Tavistock approach to making sense of organisational life* (pp. 28–36). Routledge.

The Agile Manifesto. (2001). *Twelve principles of Agile Software*. [online] Retrieved August 31, 2023, from https://agilemanifesto.org/

Theeboom, T., Beersma, B., & van Vianen, A. E. M. (2014). Does coaching work? A meta-analysis on the effects of coaching on individual level outcomes in an organizational context. *The Journal of Positive Psychology, 9*(1), 1–18. https://doi.org/10.1080/17439760.2013.837499

Thornton, C. (2010). *Group & team coaching*. Routledge.

Thornton, C. (2016). *Group and team coaching: The secret life of groups* (2nd ed.). Routledge.

Thornton, C. (2019). The making of a team coach. In D. Clutterbuck, J. Gannon, S. Hayes, I. Iordanou, K. Lowe, & D. MacKie (Eds.), *The practitioner's handbook of team coaching*. Routledge.

Tobias, L. L. (1996). Coaching executives. *Consulting Psychology Journal: Practice and Research, 48*(2), 87–95. https://doi.org/10.1037/1061-4087.48.2.87

Tomoiagă, C., & David, O. (2023). Cognitive-behavioral coaching an empirically supported approach to coaching? a meta-analysis to investigate its outcomes and moderators. *Journal of Rational-Emotive & Cognitive-Behavior Therapy, 41*, 489–510. https://doi.org/10.1007/s10942-023-00498-y

Trom, P., & Burke, J. (2022). Positive psychology intervention (PPI) coaching: An experimental application of coaching to improve the effectiveness of a gratitude intervention. *Coaching: An International Journal of Theory, Research and Practice, 15*(1), 131–142. https://doi.org/10.108 0/17521882.2021.1936585

Tuckman, B. W. (1965). Development sequence in small groups. *Psychological Bulletin, 63*(6), 384–399.

Turner, E., & Palmer, S. (2019). *The heart of coaching supervision, working with reflection and self-care*. Routledge.

Van Hoey, K. (2023). *Ethical practice case studies. In foundations of team coaching training guide*, Team Coaching Global Alliance.

Wageman, R. (2001). How leaders foster self-managing team effectiveness: Design choices versus hands-on coaching. *Organization Science, 12*(5), 559–577.

Wageman, R., Fisher, C. M., & Hackman, J. R. (2009). Leading teams when the time is right: Finding the best moments to act. *Organizational Dynamics, 38*(3), 192–203.

Wageman, R., Hackman, J. R., & Lehman, E. (2005). Team diagnostic survey: Development of an instrument. *The Journal of Applied Behavioral Science, 41*(4), 373–398.

Wageman, R., & Lowe, K. (2019). Designing, launching, and coaching teams. In D. Clutterbuck, J. Gannon, S. Hayes, I. Iordanou, K. Lowe, & D. MacKie (Eds.), *The practitioner's handbook of team coaching* (pp. 121–137). Routledge.

Wageman, R., Nunes, D. A., Burruss, J. A., & Hackman, J. R. (2008). *Senior leadership teams. What it takes to make them great*. Harvard Business School Press.

Walter, G. (2023). *Team coaching tip of the month*. Team Coaching Global Alliance.

Wang, Q., Lai, Y.-L., Xu, X., & McDowall, A. (2022). The effectiveness of workplace coaching: A meta-analysis of contemporary psychologically informed coaching approaches. *Journal of Work - Applied Management, 14*(1), 77–101. https://doi.org/10.1108/JWAM-04-2021-0030

Whitmore, J. (2009). *Coaching for performance: GROWing human potential and purpose. The principles and practice of coaching and leadership* (4th ed.). Nicholas Brealey Publishing.

Whittington, J. (2012). *Systemic coaching & constellations: An introduction to the principles, practices and applications* (1st ed.). Kogan Page.

Whittington, J. (2016). *Systemic coaching & constellations: An introduction to the principles, practices and applications* (2nd ed.). Kogan Page.

Whittington, J. (2020). *Systemic coaching & constellations: An introduction to the principles, practices and applications* (3rd ed.). Kogan Page.

Whybrow, A., Turner, E., McLean, J., & Hawkins, P. (Eds.). (2023). *Ecological and climate-conscious coaching: A companion guide to evolving coaching practice*. Routledge.

Widdowson, L. J. (2018). Understanding team leaders' and team coaches' perceptions of the effectiveness of the 'Creating the Team Edge' framework (Unpublished MSc Dissertation). Henley Business School, Henley, UK.

Widdowson, L. J., & Barbour, P. J. (2021). *Building top performing teams: A practical guide to team coaching to improve collaboration and drive organizational Success*. Kogan Page.

Widdowson, L. J., & Barbour, P. J. (2021b). Systemic team coaching. In J. Passmore (Ed.), *The coaches' handbook: The complete practitioner guide for professional coaches* (pp. 267–279). Routledge.

Widdowson, L., Rochester, L., Barbour, P. J., & Hullinger, A. M. (2020). Bridging the team coaching competency gap: A review of the literature. *International Journal of Evidence Based Coaching and Mentoring, 18*(2), 35–50. https://doi.org/10.24384/z9zb-hj74

William, J., & Lowman, R. (2018). The efficacy of executive coaching: An empirical investigation of two approaches using random assignment and a switching-replications design. *Consulting Psychology Journal, 70*(3). https://doi.org/10.1037/cpd0000115

Wilson, C. (2011). *Best practice in performance coaching*. Kogan Page.

Wilson, P. (2018). *Blob Tree*. Retrieved April 21, 2023, from https://www.pipwilson.com/p/blob-tree.html

Winum, P. C. (2005). Effectiveness of a High-Potential African American Executive: The Anatomy of a Coaching Engagement. *Consulting Psychology Journal: Practice and Research, 57*(1), 71–89. https://doi.org/10.1037/1065-9293.57.1.71

Woods, D. (2022). *The triumphant team: 40 dynamic practices to transform any team.* Teamgenie Books.

Woolley, A. W., Chabris, C. F., Pentland, A., Hashmi, N., & Malone, T. W. (2010). Evidence for a collective intelligence factor in the performance of human groups. *Science, 330*(6004), 686–688. https://doi.org/10.1126/science.1193147

Woudstra, G. (2021). *Mastering the art of team coaching: A comprehensive guide to unleashing the power, purpose and potential in any team.* SRA Books.

The manufacturer's authorised representative in the EU is Springer
Nature Customer Service Centre GmbH, Europaplatz 3, 69115 Heidelberg,
Germany. If you have any concerns regarding our products, please
contact ProductSafety@springernature.com

Printed and bound by CPI Group (UK) Ltd, Croydon, CR0 4YY

24/04/2026

02096317-0005